BACK TO THE BASICS (OF LOVE)

A Single Christian's
Guide
to Dating, Sex, and Morality
in a Secular World

Zachary Lindquist

Back to the Basics (of Love)
A Single Christian's Guide to Dating, Sex, and Morality in a Secular World

Zachary Lindquist

Published by Austin Brothers Publishing, Fort Worth, Texas
www.abpbooks.com

ISBN: 978-1-7375807-6-8

Printed in the United States of America

2022 -- First Edition

To my wife, Lauren, my biggest cheerleader,
who never let me quit
and supported me through my every frustration.

To Rohn, who was the first to read this book
and give his honest feedback and advice.

To my mother,
who raised and instilled me with the Christian
moral foundation that made this book possible.

To everybody who is tired
of living in the ways of a broken world
and who has resolved to live life God's way
(and even those who have not yet
made up their mind which way to live),
this book is for you.

Contents

Introduction

As far back as I can remember, I had a strange, almost obsessive focus on wanting to get married one day. I knew early on in my life that I was destined to be a married man. The problem was, I discovered, that I was not particularly good at being *single*. Ironically, that just made me want to get married even more, but it equally made that goal difficult.

I was not good at the single life, I was not great at feeling lonely, and I was even worse at trying to fix my dilemma of solitude. Dating did not come naturally to me. Attracting pretty girls and getting them to go out on dates with me was not a natural talent. I was shy, socially awkward, and had a persistent habit of saying stupid things in conversation, which I would only make worse by continuing to talk and say more stupid things. I did manage to go out on a handful of dates in high school, but I never managed to find my first steady girlfriend until I entered college, which did not last long.

Early on, I began seeking advice from friends of mine who, by all appearances, had it together and were significantly better at dating than me. I discovered, unfortunately, that their advice was significantly lacking in substance.

As I got older, I turned to books and programs written and created by people who claimed to be experts in the field of dating and attracting members of the opposite sex—often pseudo-famous and well-known names.

Something always stuck out to me about the advice that I was consuming from these self-described "dating experts," however. While there were a few gems in the coal mine, the dating advice always seemed to assume that readers were seeking to live as they had—as much of the world does. The advice offered was all-too-often a step-by-step manual for how to *seduce* people and live a sexually illicit lifestyle—a how-to guide for how to achieve the maximum quantity of conquests before deciding on one person you like and taking the plunge into commitment—quantity over quality.

The advice for single people that I managed to dig up was almost always lust-based dating advice, rarely relationally based. It treated people as though we were machines to be used, with levers to pull and buttons to press, rather than as individual human beings to be uniquely valued and connected with. What advice I did find that wasn't aimed at a secular, sex-crazed culture was overflowing with overly romantic language and, frankly, made no rational sense: "If you want to find your *soulmate*, you have to stop looking for them." What kind of a crock is that? And I do not just mean the term, *soulmate*, which we will discuss in a later chapter.

None of the guidance readily available for single people was right for me, or any Christian person for that matter. It was not enough, it was not morally sound, and I know that I am far from the only person who has ever felt this way. What I was learning from the culture and society was not geared toward somebody seeking a spouse to grow old with, rather than a "conquest"; someone who wanted, not to have meaningless flings, but who wanted to make a meaningful human connection with a single special person and get married. I found over and over again in my days as a single man that virtually all of the advice for dating and living life as a single person offered to young people in our society, who want to find the same thing that I did, followed the same themes: assuming that everyone will, and indeed should, be as sexually active as possible prior to marriage, preparing young people for lives of hollow relationships by giving them deep emotional and relational scars early, and leaving them woefully unequipped for lasting love and marriage. Even as an immature teen, this was a trend that I thought was dangerous and erosive to the culture.

It's no mystery how the ethics and morals of even the Christian world are becoming more and more confused when these are the kinds of messages that our young people are being saturated with in the schools and culture (entertainment, television, music, and all sorts of media). We become a product of what we consume, and virtually everything that young and single people hear about dating, relationships, and love tends to flow from questionable sources that prioritize lust over love and even seem to often conflate the two as if they are synonyms. I have seen many friends and loved ones fall down the slippery slope of giving in to anti-Christian messages constantly relayed to them. I have seen far too many Christians drawn in by the lures of secularism, materialism, and sexual sin and eventually lose their faith altogether.

I wanted to put a stop to that chain. It was not long before I met the love of my life—the wonderful Christian woman who is now my wife—that I decided to write this book. I felt called to provide an alternative to all of the bad information floating about—an alternative that advises people on forming meaningful, romantic, built-to-last relationships that take root in a biblical perspective. It does not take much study to recognize that youth are caught in a struggle, not of their own making, to separate the secular world's version of morality and love from the correct, original version that we learn from God.

In the midst of all of the information floating around about being single, dating, sex, and the ultimate pursuit of marriage, it is easy to be confused about what the right way to live is, what is acceptable, and what is questionable at best, how a wise individual makes important moral and life decisions and why these decisions matter. I understand that it can be frustrating and difficult for even reasonably intelligent people to penetrate past the heavy influx of cultural influences and determine what is moral and what an ideal Christian way of life is supposed to look like. Further, it can be challenging to convince ourselves to live according to God's standards when we don't always know what the standards are and don't understand the reasons behind the Christian ethics and rules. Of course, we cannot expect to understand everything concerning God because so much of Him is ultimately beyond our human capacity. There is, however, always a reason for the rules and guidelines God puts in place, and there is nothing wrong with seeking to understand what we can. I aim to answer some of those "why" questions in this book.

As our culture morally erodes and voices of reason seem muted, it can feel like we are drowning in a sea of confusion and turmoil. And so, I think that it is time that we come up for air and get *back to the basics*: back to the basics of human relationships, back to the basics of expectations we set for ourselves and ideals we set for our prospective significant others, back to the basics of sexual morality, and (at the risk of sounding quixotic and corny) back to the basics of love.

I have not set out to write anything groundbreaking or transmit profound, unheard-of knowledge. I am here only to remind people of important truths that have always been true, explain why they are true, and give my thoughts on such issues as have been twisted by strange ideas circulating in our culture. It is time that we unplug from what the world tells us is the right way to think about things and pause to seriously look at and think about what God says about such things.

Now, it must be said that I am not a pastor or a greatly accomplished biblical scholar. I'm simply a relatively normal man with a few of my own unique life experiences, who happens to read many books and works with his hands for a living. I just thought that my blue-collar status warranted disclosure since, in this day and age, people seem more inclined to accept the advice of "experts" in a given subject or intellectuals with a host of letters and acronyms following their name. It seems to me, though, that God has a special place in His heart for the meek among us, and He seems to have often used the least likely of individuals to spread His message and do wonders in His name. Sometimes, the common man with no renown is easier to use than the proud wise man with the best education.

Jesus Christ was born to a poor family. The Son of God, the greatest teacher of men, and the single most influential person in human history was a carpenter by trade. That sounds fairly blue-collar to me. And who did the Son of God ask to follow Him as disciples and preach His message? The greatest scholars? The most accomplished religious teachers? No, most of Christ's disciples were fishermen—including Peter, who would lead the first church. The greatest missionary in history and the author of 1/3 of the New Testament, Paul made his living as a tentmaker.

If humble beginnings or lifestyles are reasons to discredit an individual, then you can call all of Christianity into question on those grounds. You can also demean and discard the cultural contributions of the impoverished Socrates or the creations of the lower-class Leonardo da Vinci. As rumor has it, "the meek will inherit the earth."

You are also being warned, from the start, that there will be a fair amount of talk about sex and other such adult topics throughout this book. If you believe Christians should not talk so openly or bluntly about such raw subjects, you may be hesitant to read or accept this book. However, that is a childish and, frankly, dangerous outlook on the Christian worldview. The secular world has no qualms about bringing up these topics in conversation—crude as they might sometimes be in their delivery—and it's no wonder why their views on the matters in question dominate the culture when Christians have often gone mum. In our silence, we surrender ground in the moral battlefield, and the other side is more than happy to take up more territory in cultural spheres.

We cannot afford to stick exclusively to Sunday school, toddler-friendly Bible lessons for our whole lives. Child-like faith is fine, up to a point, but eventually, we have to stop drinking Gerber's baby formula and soiling diapers and graduate to eating steak and putting on big-boy pants. The world is full of real adult issues, and we need to approach and talk about them as mature adults, so take your fingers out of your ears and start listening.

Chapter 1

There is Nothing Wrong with You

Being single and dating should be fun. However, that is not to say that single life is without challenges. It can be frustrating, cause doubts, or lead to bad experiences. Searching for a romantic partner can be a grueling process. The dating scene is often vast and unforgiving, and the process can be stressful, demoralizing, and emotionally taxing. Are you excited yet?

Dating and the pursuit of companionship do not come easy to everyone. One can become discouraged, particularly if your search goes on extensively with little success. I speak from first hand experience. Some years ago, I was getting nowhere in my dating life. I had a few girlfriends but no relationships that could lead to marriage. I struggled with finding someone interested in me. Whenever I did end up in conversation with a woman, the sparks never flew—at least, not for both of us.

More than once I was interested in a girl but watched her go out on dates with other guys. I became that cliché of the guy who secretly harbored romantic feelings for his female friend. I couldn't say anything to her because of the uncertainty that she did not share the same feelings. Eventually I vomited my fondness for the girl in hopes she would miraculously reciprocate, Instead, I scared her away and lost a friendship. Later, I will discuss why you should never harbor secret feelings.

After being unsuccessful with dating, I inevitably viewed myself as the problem. I know I am not the first person to experience this state of mind, though it often felt like it. I was convinced that something was fundamentally wrong with me, which grew incrementally worse over time. Maybe you have felt that way before too. Maybe you still do, at times.

I had friends who shared the same opinion and were also convinced that I was broken somehow. Those friends never failed to share their thoughts about my problem and what needed changing or fixing. Usually, their advice was extremely misguided and would make matters worse if I followed it.

Please do not misunderstand me. We should always be looking to improve and grow. However, what I was experiencing was something entirely different. I thought I needed to become someone else entirely but, that was not and *is* not the answer. If you have friends who insist you need to become a different person, or you are under the impression that who you are is not who you ought to be to attract members of the opposite sex, I have a message for you: there is nothing wrong with you!

I am not insinuating you should not grow, mature, evolve, and improve. I am not claiming you should not strive to be a moral person. My meaning is that you, as an individual, are unique. You were made in God's image with intentionality and careful planning. While it may evolve, your personality is distinctive to you and your experiences. Your physical appearance is unique, and thank the Lord for that! *"I praise you, for I am fearfully and wonderfully made. Wonderful are your works; my soul knows very well"* (Psalm 139:14).

I am sure that you have heard this overused piece of advice a billion times: "just be yourself." That sounds simple enough. While it is certainly not bad advice, in essence, no one ever explains what the heck that means! *What does it mean to be me? Who am I, really? How do I know when I am me or someone else entirely? How do I know if I am doing it right?*

Being yourself is simple, though notice that I did not claim it is "easy." There is a distinct difference between the two. Running a marathon race is simple in that you run straight until you cross the finish line, but it is certainly not an easy task when you start running, become exhausted, and feel like vomiting. Simple does not mean easy. In fact, while being yourself is simple, it is probably one of the hardest things you will ever do. The difficulty becomes apparent if you ever told a little white lie to get someone's approval. That lie was probably something like, "You like romantic comedies? So do I!" when the truth is that you would have no problem going your whole life without seeing another one of those awful movies on your television screen. That little lie was not very genuine. That's not being yourself. And yet, it is so easy to tell a seemingly inconsequential little lie without even realizing it.

It is a simple example, being honest, and it is directly related to "just being yourself." There is no question about that. And, if you are thinking of asking me, "what if my real self is a compulsive liar?" or some silly question like that, then I would ask you to read that question again out loud until you realize how nonsensical it sounds. It is like the asker of the question is stating, "Lying to people is how I am honest with them!" That implication is completely self-defeating. If you are a liar, then you cannot possibly be genuine! It would be the equivalent of protecting the sanctity of life by murdering many people or promoting chastity by having promiscuous sex. If you are a compulsive liar, you are very good at *not* being yourself.

If you tend to tell even the tiniest of lies to gain approval, then that needs to end. You are not your sins, and thus, justifying your sins by claiming that you are "just being yourself" is a lie in and of itself. We are all born with a compulsion to do wrong, but that is not how God defines us, nor how we ought to define ourselves. You can and should hold yourself to a higher standard than that.

An honest person is genuine, and a genuine person is (by definition) being themselves. Be truthful toward others and yourself, and you may find some things out about yourself that you never knew! It is true what they say: the truth will set you free—the real you.

If somebody were to ask me, "do you like to read?" my response would probably be something along the lines of, "Yes, I do. I love to read, though I used to detest it. Of course, that was before I developed an appreciation for knowledge and wisdom and began to crave the experience of seeking after truth and understanding. I love to learn from books written by wiser or more intelligent authors than myself and grow in my perception of the world and what exists beyond it. There is always something to be gained from reading, and I wish I had read more earlier in life." That is as honest an answer as I could muster, and it tells you something about what is in my heart and mind, namely that I desire understanding and growth, but also that I was not always like that. You might say that I learn something about myself from the process of *giving* that answer.

What would you say to me if I asked you the same question? Maybe you do like to read. I mean, you are reading this book right now. On the other hand, perhaps you hate reading like I used to, but you figured that you had nothing to lose by trying your hand at this book because it seemed like something you could benefit from. Or maybe you still hate reading, and you don't have high hopes for this book, but you gave it a chance because you heard that the author was unbelievably handsome and infinitely wise! Maybe your honest answer is something beyond a simple yes or no.

But is that honest answer the one you would give if I asked you the question? Perhaps you would worry I would think less of you if you honestly told me that you are not a big fan of reading. Perhaps you would bend the truth slightly to appeal to me for some odd reason. I can tell you one thing for certain: I have a much higher opinion of an individual who tells me honestly that they do not share my enthusiasm for knowledge than I do for someone who lies about having that in common with me. Seriously, it is perfectly fine if you only started reading this book because you saw my stunningly beautiful face on the *About the Author* page! That would not offend me at all!

You cannot control how people will act toward you or whether or not someone will like the genuine you, but you *can* control how you respond and act. You can control what *you* do. There is nothing else in this world that you can control in the same way.

There is nothing wrong with you, what you look like, or who you are. Save for the fact that we should always strive to be our best selves morally, spiritually, relationally, etc. There is nothing about your individuality that requires radical change. If you understand that, then who you are might pleasantly surprise you.

Chapter 2

What is Beauty?

Throughout time, the world's various cultures have valued and appreciated the concept of beauty. Every culture ascribes to its idea of the word and what it means. Through the existence of art and poetry, we can see how the members of each culture saw beauty. Leonardo captured his image of what is beautiful in the Mona Lisa. The ancient Greeks did the same with their statues and depictions of Aphrodite. Shakespeare immortalized his thoughts through his sonnets, and King Solomon tells us about the woman of his desires in the Song of Solomon.

In like fashion, our western society relays the ideal of beauty, not so often with the use of art and gripping poetry, but by flaunting airbrushed images of men and women on magazine covers and underwear advertisements. Are we to believe that they have truly uncovered the secret of beauty? Should we be convinced that the true standard for beauty is so unattainable that it cannot be achieved without *Photoshop*?

There is always a cultural standard for what is aesthetically appealing, but how do we know which culture got it right? Who had the truest standard for beauty? How would we know if we understood beauty properly? Is there even a correct standard to be held?

Seeking to determine who is beautiful and who is not is the problem. Our criteria are superficial and not based on the true nature of beauty. My wonderful bride does not share an identical face or body with any of the models in a magazine, and I praise the Lord for that. She is uniquely beautiful in many ways, and I would not change a hair on her head. I have never fallen in love with a supermodel on a billboard.

I fell in love with the woman God made unique. Furthermore, I do not love her because she is pretty. She is beautiful because of the love I have for her.

I do not want my wife to think she is not beautiful because her reflection in the mirror does not match *Victoria's Secret* catalog image. Comparison is a strange temptation that urges us to think less of ourselves because of our uniqueness. We compare ourselves to another person who has a different talent, body, job, life, or face and focus on what they have that we do not. Yet, at the same time, we seem to ignore the blessings that we have and do not possess. That is scratching the surface of covetousness, which God dedicated a commandment against.

This is not to say men and women should not make an effort to look their best. I am all for showers, proper hygiene, nice clothes, and fashioned hair. The problem occurs when we believe that one cannot be beautiful without engaging in fashion trends, glamour, or expensive trips to the hairstylist. That is not the case. I love it when my bride puts effort into looking good for me. It makes me feel special.

In the same way, she appreciates it when I go out of my way to do romantic things for her. This keeps with the general rule that men tend to be visually stimulated, and women more relationally stimulated. My wife appreciates romantic gestures as simple as bringing her flowers. I have never understood why giving a woman flowers became a tradition. It has always seemed a strange gift to me. It feels as if I am saying, "Here, these roses are representative of my love for you! They will be dead in a matter of days! I'm sure there's no correlation." It is terrible symbolism, but my wife likes it, so I keep doing it for her.

I want to look good while trying to be romantic, and the common denominator in both the case of the man and the woman is *effort*. People who *try* to look good or *be* good are inherently attractive. Men who go through the effort of taking care of themselves, working out, eating healthy food, grooming, and wearing shirts that don't display mustard stains are generally considered appealing. Slobs, on the other hand, are less so. Apathy has never been the most desirable trait to embody.

There is nothing wrong with looking (and smelling) our best, as long as the pursuit is not our only model for beauty. My wife is among the many women who like to wear makeup on occasion. There is something about putting the extra work into her appearance that makes her feel special and pretty. I will never complain about her being intentional with her image. I think the effort is usually rewarded. I feel honored when she makes sure I can't take my eyes off her, which is often the case.

On the other hand, I would never want her or any woman to forget that makeup enhancements are just that—enhancements. The additive can never take the place of the real thing. I say this as somebody who loves black coffee.

In my opinion, the natural flavor and aroma of the coffee beans are the true essence of the coffee. Adding anything else, such as cream and sugar, dilutes and covers up the goodness of the coffee. In the same way, a woman relying on makeup masks the natural beauty God has blessed them with. The cream and sugar would be nothing without the natural coffee, and makeup would be plastic tubes full of mush without the woman's natural beauty. The enhancements a woman makes to her appearance are not what make her beautiful. Of course, just like there is nothing wrong with wanting to add a little bit of extra flavor to one's coffee, there is also nothing wrong with adding to her appearance, as long as she does not forget the natural beauty that is being covered up. Nothing we contribute to our aesthetic condition can change our inherent value.

Being beautiful does not mean everybody should be romantically attracted to a particular individual. Women are beautiful, that much is certain, but acknowledging physical beauty does not always go hand-in-hand with romantic attraction. After all, mountain ranges and landscapes are beautiful, yet some are unimpressed by them—as opposed to an artist who finds them worth the tedious painting effort. Beauty and physical attractiveness to members of the opposite sex is not completely disparate, but they are not entirely the same thing. It is possible for one man to completely lack attraction to a beautiful woman, and vice versa.

In his short book, *The Abolition of Man,* C.S. Lewis begins his three-chapter-long argument by citing a story pointing out two men's observations of a waterfall. One man calls the waterfall "pretty," and the other calls it "sublime."[1]

If someone says, about a waterfall, "that is pretty" or "that is sublime," are we to take that as a fact, or should we dismiss it as a perception? How can we know, for sure, that our perception of something is correct? Perhaps the waterfall in question is truly horrifying! Or maybe

---

1   Lewis, C. S. *The Abolition of Man*. Oxford University Press, 1943.

that is only the person's perception being swept down the river toward the drop at the end, the waterfall.

So, what is the nature of beauty or lack thereof? Is it existent only in my head and therefore irrelevant, obsolete, and subjective? Either this waterfall is truly sublime, or I perceive it to be, in which case I could be wrong. Without God's existence, it would be likely that the latter option is true.

Without God, what is beauty? Beauty assumes meaning and, without God, there could be no meaning. Beauty would be a made-up construct in our heads that we use to process the world around us, in which case beauty would not genuinely exist. Without God, nothing would be beautiful. Things would exist in a vacuum where everything is neutral and meaningless. That waterfall would be a compilation of H^2O molecules moving rapidly via gravitational pull toward a still body of H^2O molecules. Nothing would be special, just base physics and chemistry.

On the other hand, with God, nothing is neutral. He created everything with purpose and intentionality. With God, *nothing* is without meaning, and *everything* has a purpose and inherent value. God created that waterfall, and he gave me a mind that can perceive it and make judgments based on my observation. I see the water falling in a mist of white and the faint but distinctly colored rainbow that results from the water and sun. I witness the surrounding nature along with the sounds and scents. By using my God-given senses and mind, I can recognize the aesthetic wonder and extravagance of what my eyes see. I can call the waterfall what it is, sublime.

God created it this way intentionally, and its beauty is to be noticed and appreciated. Who can say differently about you, another one of His intentional creations?

And you are no mere waterfall or inanimate object. No, you were created with the breath of life—His life! He created you as such with His image in mind!

So, God made you intentionally, in His likeness, gave you life with His breath, and put you here on this beautifully designed earth where everything and everyone has purpose and meaning. If a simple waterfall is sublime, you must be something far greater!

Now, I am not personally the biggest proponent of the term, self-esteem, and I could write an entire boring separate book about why. However, setting that term aside, it is in fact important to care about yourself and see your worth. All I wish to say is that it makes a difference where you believe your esteem comes from. Does your value come from yourself, or does it come from something or someone higher?

I don't wish to improve your self-esteem, but to point out that you are already infinitely esteemed by the one who created you. Beauty and value are inherent in you, as a creation of the one who invented the very concepts of value and beauty!

All things, with God, are good and therefore are beautiful. The things that God is absent from (i.e., sin, evil deeds, etc.) lack the good and are therefore lacking in what we call beauty. Even the mundane becomes a gorgeous artwork canvas with God, and monotonous sounds become a symphony. With God, all of us, whom He created with great care and intention, are a masterpiece!

Chapter 3

The One, the Myth, the Legend

The dating pool is vast. There are billions of people in the world to choose from who have the potential for a committed relationship! But, for the sake of narrowing down your search, let us assume you plan on sticking within the confines of your nation or continent to find a loving companion—that still leaves you with potentially millions of prospects! It is overwhelming!

But you don't want just anybody. You want that special someone. Of all the billions of souls on earth, you are holding out for one person in particular. You want to find that one special individual, *soulmate*; the *one*! You will only be satisfied when you finally find that *one* person whom God made just for you!

If that is your plan, you are never going to be satisfied. I hate to burst your romantic bubble, but is it reasonable to scour the earth searching for one person out of billions, and nothing less than the *one* is acceptable? The odds of that happening are comparable to being struck by lightning multiple times. Furthermore, do you think God is going to whisper in your ear, "That's the one with the 'reserved sticker'?"

If you are under the impression that your *soulmate* is out there, waiting for you to miraculously show up and experience an immediate, shared spiritual awakening, then I ask you something: do you worship at the Temple of Zeus? I mean, if you believe in one, I must assume you believe in the other! I am not picking on you for your misguided beliefs but informing you that Zeus and *soulmates* both originate from the same place: Greek Mythology. The two coexist within the same story, the same myth, the same dead religion. I hate to be a buzzkill (most of the time) but claiming to be looking for your soulmate is one of the most pagan things you could do. The secular world has romanticized this term and fused it with their sensibilities. Where in mythology does the term, *soulmate*, originate?

In ancient Greek Mythology, Zeus, though a product of his own Titan father, Kronos, was the creator of humankind. According to myth, when Zeus created humans, they were each initially formed with four arms, four legs, and two heads. That sounds a little bit creepy. At some point, Zeus became displeased with humans and elected to punish them by splitting every one of them in two. The intended penalty caused them to spend their whole lives in torment, desperately searching for their "other half." This was the day on which romance was born. Beautiful.

The secular world took this myth out of context and attempted to make it sound romantic and normal. After the secularists did their part, some in the Christian world decided to adopt the pagan concept and *spiritualize* it. The number of Christians who unwittingly believe in a paganistic Greek mythological concept is astounding. They do not always use the same term when referencing this piece of lore. They try to make it sound more spiritual by changing the terminology or substituting the word *soulmate* for phrases like, "the *one* God made for you." The Bible does not reference anything related to "the one" or "God's creation of a human life just for your pleasure and indulgence." It is not there.

I have been asked about Adam and Eve. "Would you not say that God created Eve for Adam? Was she not his other half?" My answer is: Are you one of only two people on earth? No. In the context of billions of people inhabiting the planet, I do not think that a one-time occurrence at the beginning of humanity constitutes a pattern, much less that we should expect God to create someone from each of our ribs.

That "perfect" individual would become your idol, the sole object of your affection. Of course, holding any one person to such an absurd standard of fulfilling your every need and desire is foolhardy and unfair in any case. No human being on earth can satisfy every emotional need you have, every physical desire you crave, or every subjective standard that you construct in your mind.

This idea of your *soulmate* and the one person whom God made *just for you* is not only unbiblical, but it is a selfish and immoral idea, which caters to an "it's all about me" attitude. It has mutated into one of the driving forces of infidelity and dissatisfaction with one's existing partner.

If someone allows this narcissistic idealism to take root, they can easily be convinced that any person they have pledged their life to does not fit their criteria. A married man can be deceived when meeting a new girl. He becomes discontent and unsatisfied with the woman he originally thought was *the one*. Rather than focus on loving her and working on the relationship, he tells himself that his wife has not lived up to his expectations. He convinces himself this new girl is the one God had intended for him to marry and further thinks he is justified in sinning because God would not want him to stay with the wrong woman, right? It seems like an injustice for him to stay with his current, substandard wife and pass up the chance to be with his real *soulmate*—the one truly made for him.

Do you see the problem yet? Not only is the idea of soulmates utterly ridiculous, but it is selfish. When one begins thinking in these terms, a certain level of narcissism may result. It is the natural state of any selfish human to be ungrateful for their blessings and eventually become resentful because they didn't get what was on the other side of the fence.

Everyone else comes in second for someone who caters to this mindset. The selfish mind demands, "I must care for myself first, find myself, and do whatever it takes to make myself happy, even at the cost of hurting everybody else around me." That does not sound like a Godly concept to me. It sounds more like a self-serving and futile way to live.

You are not the center of the universe. You cannot make yourself the center, even in your personal life, no matter how hard you try. It is not how you were designed any more than how the world was meant to function. If everybody lived selfishly, humanity would eventually cease to exist. We cannot rebel against the nature of God's design without expecting a reprisal.

There is a reason that God calls upon us to esteem others before ourselves and Him above all else. Our value does not come from focusing on ourselves, selfish pursuits, putting our interest ahead of others at any cost—despite what you may have been told. Our sense of worth and meaning does not come from our "self-esteem." Attempting to assign value to ourselves in the vacuum of our little world would be the rough equivalent of trying to get rich by printing money in our own homes. No matter how hard you try, you cannot make that counterfeit money valuable by yourself. It is just paper.

Our value comes from God, our creator. Our purpose comes from pursuing Him and serving others. Esteem God, and you have value in the spiritual realm, esteem others, and find a purpose in the physical world. Then you may find that you are valuable and esteemed despite yourself.

Statistically, those with big families tend to be happier than those who live alone. That is not coincidental. A father finds purpose in providing for his family, a mother in serving her children, and both tend to value their family above themselves.

Selfishness leads to an empty life. While it is good to care about yourself, it matters from where you seek your sense of value. Always thinking of yourself first does not make you feel valuable—quite the opposite, as ironic as it seems—it leaves a void in purpose.

Instead of finding the one person who was made for you—an endeavor that would never end—focus more on finding someone you love to make smile. Love is not selfish; it is a service. It is an action that tends to provide wonderful results! It is not self-serving, and those who try will leave destruction in their wake. Turn your attention away from what you can gain from a romantic partner and toward what you can do for them.

God gives us the secret to living a joy-filled life: the secret is not to think more of ourselves; it is to think of ourselves less.

Chapter 4

Dating for the Right Reasons

When I was a 6-year-old child playing little league soccer, I was not very good—even with my mother as the coach. The problem wasn't so much that I couldn't kick the ball into the goal. It was that I could hardly manage to kick the ball itself. My feet and the soccer ball did not have the most symbiotic relationship.

One day though, it seemed I was on a roll. I kept possession of the ball without accidentally kicking it across the field and into the grasp of the opposing team, my passes to my teammates did not fly over their heads or into their faces, and I didn't miss every single pass that was sent my way. It was a good game so far!

Finally, at the game's climax, I got the ball and had a clear path to the goal. I ran, kicking the ball along with me, eager to make my first goal ever. I took my shot at the goal, and the ball went directly past the goalie and into the net. I had scored! The excitement was so euphoric that my little 6-year-old body couldn't stay on the ground.

I ran back to my mother/coach, giddy with excitement, and asked, "Did you see that? Did you see what I did? I made a goal!" It was among the happiest moments of my half-decade life.

It was then my mother gently tried to break the news that I had scored a point against my team. The goalie I had kicked the ball past was wearing the same-colored jersey as I was. In my anticipation to brag to my mom about my greatest achievements, I had unknowingly run past all of my teammates, who were upset with me for making such a silly mistake. My little peewee heart was shattered.

I was so happy that I had finally scored, but I never saw that I had been going for the wrong goal, making the achievement meaningless.

Such is often the case in today's world of single life and dating. Folks are wandering around, trying to get as much enjoyment as they can out of the single life, attempting to live it up before they finally "take the plunge," as if their life ends at the altar. The idea that suddenly one's life after commitment is a dull void of boredom is far from the truth, but it is the lie young people believe.

Single people play the field, meet people, date around, all-too-often sleep around, and try to have fun being carefree and enjoy dating. Is that the point, though? Dating is solely for its own sake? For fun? We kick the ball around the field, passing it to whoever will receive it, hoping we will finally score a point for fun?

Dating has become a game in and of itself. So many single people want to have fun and keep playing. That is the real drawback of a culture that hands out participation trophies to peewee athletes; we end up just wanting to play the game with no intention of *winning*.

Dating for fun has become fairly normalized in western society, but is that the goal we want to aim for? What is the point of that pursuit? Companionship? Entertainment? Variety? Sex? I will be honest; I never saw many benefits in dating for fun, even as a teenager. I would see my peers playing this little game, and all I could think was, "that just seems like a waste of time, energy, and emotion."

Think about it. How healthy do you think it is to attach yourself emotionally and possibly physically to somebody, just for fun, and then break up that connection resulting in heartbreak. Furthermore, how easy might it be on your mental and emotional well-being to do that to yourself (and others) over and over again, on purpose? Does that sound like a fun or productive use of your time? It sounds daunting and draining to me.

Taking this beyond energy and emotion, what about time? How much time do you have to waste? How long do these "fun" single people think they will live? If you date for fun in your teens and 20s, packing on all of that mental and emotional baggage all the while, you have wasted over a decade of your life fooling around when you could have easily made a meaningful connection to somebody and started building your lives together. That is a lot of time that you don't get back.

Then, after spending ten or more years chasing after fun, you decide in your thirties to finally get serious about settling down and getting married. It is not impossible, but it is harder now that the dating pool has thinned out. Men in their 30s may find that most women their age are either married, divorced, or have pre-started families. Not only that, but a single woman in her 30s might very well have as much baggage as him, if not more. A few men might have the option of tossing their net into the pool of younger women, but pickings are still slim, especially if the man is not as youthful, vibrant, and attractive as he used to be.

Women do not often have the same option of dating younger people as men do. I do not mean to sound pessimistic, but most men tend to like women their age or younger. I am describing how it is. You can either get mad at me for telling the truth, or date smarter.

Women also have the additional issue of a ticking clock on their physiological ability to have children. Women are born with a set number of eggs capable of fertilization, and that quantity decreases every month from the moment they hit puberty. By the age of 32, the average woman only has a small percentage of her eggs left, meaning that her chances of conceiving a child significantly decrease. The process of infertility accelerates for this age group. Compare that to a woman in her 20s, who has an average 90% chance of conceiving within a year of trying and only a 3% chance of fertility problems. If a woman wants to have children, it is far better to start young, if possible, assuming she is married. We will delve more into this in later chapters.

A woman's option for finding a marriageable partner when she hits her 30s are slimmer than they might be for a man in the same situation. A single man her age will often want to find a younger girl. Often, the best option is to date older men who may have already had a family and do not want to start a new one. Finding a suitable partner gets more difficult the older you get, whether you are a man or a woman. Is all that time wasted on dating for amusement worth it?

Another reason that I never saw the appeal of dating as a game is because it never struck me as being all that fun. Being single was stressful. Dating seemed to be a rough emotional minefield to walk through, and the prospect of blowing up has never amused me.

Those who date for entertainment are usually the folks who enjoy the pursuit of premarital sex. That is the only payoff they seem to aim for, and fornication is far from a wise recreational pursuit, as I will explain in later chapters. If you are dating in the interest of sex, may I suggest you are wasting your time, love, and fragmenting pieces of your heart? It is far too high a price to pay for a little bit of waning *fun* that will be over in minutes. You will eventually look back on such casual relationships with regret, as you consider the time and parts of yourself wasted. I have yet to meet an individual with a past of meaningless flings who lacks significant regret or damage. They don't think the "fun" was worth the price they paid.

That is the nature of a game where nobody wins but only partici- pates: a waste of time, energy, and emotion. I would much rather set my sights on a more fulfilling endgame. I don't just want to play the game; I want to win.

How does one win the game of dating? We have to score. And, when we score, we must be aiming at the right goal: marriage. That is the only way to win, and winning is a great accomplishment with the greatest of prizes.

The only legitimate goal of dating is *marriage*. That is not simply my personal view on the matter. It is *the* reason that dating exists: to find somebody to marry. If you have been single and dating for a long time, absent the singular goal of marriage, I am willing to wager that you have not had much success in that arena. How could you if you are trying to score in the wrong goal?

The minute you decide marriage is your goal, not only does your perspective on dating and relationships change, but your entire dating life will change. You will not waste chunks of your life with people who do not want or intend to marry and will clarify on the first date you are dating with the sole intention of getting married down the line. You will quickly weed out the weak from the herd when that standard is set. Anybody who is not interested in marriage will not date you, nor will you date them.

If a man is dating for sex, you will know after you make it clear he will not get any such reward until the wedding night. If he is on board with that standard, great. Suppose the information is a deal-breaker for him, great! Let him go; he was a weak link and is disqualified from the race!

If a man wants to live with you before getting married, you can dis- miss him. He is a waste of your time! If you were to give him everything he wants now, before a commitment, he would not give you what you want later. That is the nature of any man who wants the perks of mov- ing in without committing his life to you. If he can get away with not marrying you, he will take full advantage! He will live with you for years without a commitment, getting what he wants from you free of charge all the while. Eventually, you will find yourself alone again, having wast- ed years of your life if you go down this path. Better to set your sights on the right goal to begin with than make that mistake.

The kind of man that a woman wants to marry is the type who clarifies the goal he is aiming for: marriage. The kind of woman a moral man wants to marry is the type who makes it clear that the "fun" will not be had until after the wedding.

Can you have a good life before you get married? Absolutely! Can you have fun with your significant other before saying your vows? Of course! As long as you know where you aim and do not have the kind of fun reserved for the marriage bed.

Nobody wants to be the kid who kicks the ball around the field and never scores a goal. It's less likely that anybody wants to be the kid who scores the *wrong* goal. Know which direction you are running in, take your shot, and win the prize that awaits you on the winner's podium— also known as the marriage altar. The trophy comes in a convenient travel size and can be worn on your left ring finger!

Chapter 5

Insecurity

The Temporary Things

It has been said if you invest your happiness in temporary things, your happiness will be temporary. The truth is if you invest any part of yourself, emotional or physical—in things that have a shelf life, all will expire. If you rely on money or material things to make you happy, the joy will wear off quicker than it arrived. Money burns, and fancy cars rust.

I have known a few people who collect. I have no qualms with collecting as a practice or hobby. I, myself, have quite the collection of Star Wars merchandise from my childhood and a collection of items with historical significance that feed my fascination. However, there is a difference between compiling items for fun because of a nerdy historical interest versus collecting things because of some sense of purpose. If your *passion* is collecting, your happiness and security are temporary and hollow. No matter how much I like cars, buying a new one will never result in the sense of fulfillment. Do you think my friend from years past who "dedicated" his life to collecting hard copies of classic movies would be fulfilled by that endeavor?

"Laws of Materialism don't account for the human need for purpose."[2]

If you invest in temporary things, the result will be temporary. A rich man might feel secure with his fancy car and large mansion, but

---

2   Turek, Frank. "Is It a Wonderful Life?" *Stealing from God: Why Atheists Need God to Make Their Case*, NavPress, 2015.

if he goes broke and loses everything, does he have any choice other than feeling insecure and defeated? Or might he find his security
source in something less material that does not come with a price tag?
If a supermodel finds herself the survivor of a horrible car accident,
which leaves her physically scarred on her face and body, does her value as a person burn along with the car? Or does she have reason to be
thankful for being alive, choosing to live the rest of it with a purpose?
Does she have ample reason to value herself aside from what her eyes
pick up in a mirror or on a magazine cover?

It matters where we invest our hearts and extract our sense of security. It makes a difference if we choose to live for things that will not
matter 10, 20, or 50 years from now, or if we place our stock in a cause
that moves mountains.

I pursued bodybuilding for a time in college. While I made great
strides toward my goals and built a relatively impressive physique at
that time, the practice proved unhealthy for me, even though I was in
fantastic physical shape.

I eventually gave up bodybuilding and the pursuit of a career in
the fitness industry not because it wasn't a worthwhile goal or because
I have anything against an industry that promotes health and physical exercise. I gave it up is because my identity had become reliant on
my body. Most of my self-confidence depended on my physical shape
and aesthetic appearance. If I missed a workout or an opportunity to
enhance my figure, I became severely depressed. If I became sick or
injured, one might think I was convinced the apocalypse had arrived. I
felt insecure if one body part or muscle wasn't big or shapely enough
or my abs were not tight or defined.

I described a condition commonly referred to as body dysmorphia:
a mental condition that results in an individual's body image being
completely out of touch with reality. This condition is something that
often leads to eating disorders or, as was the case with me, looking
like a lunatic when I refuse to take off my shirt at the pool because my
already very muscular physique was "not yet fit to be seen by human
eyes." The same process would occur if anyone made a good-natured
joke about my appearance. Insecurity at its finest.

It was not until after I had a long stint of illness and injury, thus
a long absence from the gym, that it became apparent I had invested
my entire self-worth virtually into this temporary, fleeting facet of my
life. After getting out of shape, I realized how debilitating the singular
focus on my body was, and I became more confident and comfortable

around people. My hobby had become my obsession, my god, my misguided purpose.

I eventually disposed of most of my muscle-bound pictures because I did not want to define myself or my self-worth from my body. *For I am fearfully and wonderfully made, declares the Lord!* He gets to determine my worth, and it is *great*! He does not care about my physical appearance. No, my worth far exceeds what I could place upon myself, especially if I use such shallow criteria.

I still work out and take care of my body. I enjoy it, and it is always a good thing to be a good steward of the gifts God gives us. We are blessed with one body. But my body is no longer my idol—it is not my purpose for living.

My existence gains meaning when I choose to love God, pursue His purpose, and love my neighbor above myself. I find my security in the creator, not in what He created. That is not to say that I am ungrateful for all that He has done and made, but all of it would be meaningless without Him. Just as He is the creator of all things, He is also the meaning behind all things—the very reason that all of it exists. If we take God out of the equation, we subtract the reason for anything to exist or be done.

Our creator intentionally made us to be purpose-driven. We each need something to pursue, a reason to be here, something that gives our lives a sense of value and meaning, in which to feel secure. I find my purpose and security in God and serving other people to His ends. That is why I elected to write this book.

Some might say I could help people without paying God any mind, but what purpose would good deeds serve without the standard for what is good? What meaning would any action have if it was not for the source of meaning—if we were just random sacks of DNA that will one day decompose and feed the soil? How could I ever feel secure if I only ascribe to a material world where everything is temporary and insecure? Even Friedrich Nietzche, the famed atheist philosopher, knew that we could never have meaning without God, when he said, "I fear that we may never be free of God as long as we still believe in grammar." In other words, as long as things still matter, God is present.

If you want security in your life, God must be a factor. You need not be a missionary or a minister to make Him such a factor, but pursue Him in everything you do and thank Him for everything you have.

On the other hand, if you do not believe in God and you are reading this book because someone told you the author was a brilliant, insightful, slightly egotistical genius, let me direct this request to you. Whatever purpose you pursue, as we all crave and need one, please do not make it fleeting and worldly (i.e., collecting). Do something that is a credit to society—that serves other people and improves their lives. Beyond that, while spouse and family are wonderful and life-giving, please do not make them your sole source of security and purpose. Be good to them, provide, and enjoy them, but do not try to invest all your happiness and reason for living into them. People who apply such pressure to their loved ones usually either make their families miserable or make themselves miserable and depressed.

You and Gideon

Insecurity and I are well acquainted. We are old friends. Insecurity is a *she* because, like any woman, it has the power to make me sweat profusely and stammer through every word while worrying I've said something stupid. Now that I'm married, the only woman who makes me that nervous is my wife, and usually, it's because I *did* say something stupid.

Insecurity has gotten me fired from jobs, dumped by girlfriends, or rejected by women before a relationship was even on the horizon. In life, it has made me fearful and wary of living with purpose, pursuing my callings, or forming meaningful relationships. Fear of failure or rejection has often kept me from helping those in need, taking care of something that needs to be done, or making a decision in a time-sensitive or high-pressure situation. Insecurity still whispers its grating and deceptive lies into my ear even as I write this book. You are possibly trying to imagine the last time you came across such an impressively confident individual like myself.

When I felt called to write this book (my first one), certain voices rose and tried to dissuade me: "You have no business trying to tackle a task as tedious and challenging as writing a book; you have failed at so much, you can't possibly imagine that this will be an exception; best to give up before you even begin and save yourself the humiliation of trying and failing." With all of this negativity flowing through my mind, I imagine I felt much like Gideon of the Old Testament when he was called upon.

Gideon was a coward from the moment of his introduction. The first time the book of Judges mentions Gideon, he is hiding in a winepress (a pit in the ground) from the Midianites, who had conquered and oppressed his people. Gideon was so afraid of the Midianites that he didn't want them to see him threshing wheat, so he hid while making his bread. At that moment, an angel sent by the Lord appears before Gideon and calls him by a nickname: "Mighty Warrior."

Hold on, what? Did you just read that right? "Mighty? Warrior?" That's what he called the guy who was hiding away in a pit making lunch? The reigning champion of antisocial introverts? Yes, indeed! Nobody knows the power of affirmation quite like God does. Even in our worst, least flattering state, He sees the potential in us—He knows what we are capable of because He made the plan and assigned us to the task before creating us. Even if we do need the occasional nudge and positive reinforcement, there is no limit to our potential despite our insecurities. Of course, the angel's seemingly misplaced remark about this timid man being "mighty" was only the beginning of the interaction.

The Lord then said to Gideon (paraphrased), "I am sending you to save Israel from the hands of Midian! Go!"

Of course, Gideon was not quick to jump on board with God's plan. He flat-out told God He had made a mistake coming to him with such lofty goals. Can you imagine the amount of fear that must have gripped this man for him to view telling off God Almighty? As often happens when one is insecure, excuses began pouring out of Gideon's mouth: "Lord, I'm too this, this situation is too that, I'm not good enough, I am not capable of doing this, it cannot be done, someone else may be more qualified to handle this problem, so I will just leave it up to them to take care of it." The list could go. There is never a shortage of potential excuses for any situation. Do any of the listed excuses look familiar to you? Have they crossed your mind? Your lips?

Excuses and insecurity have a symbiotic relationship: each feeds the other, and both tend to energize one another. Excuses feed insecurity, and insecurity breeds excuses. It becomes a rather consistent and repetitive cycle of slamming ourselves and letting ourselves down, as well as anyone else who may be counting on us for whatever reason. You need to or want to do something, but you are afraid of failing or not doing well enough, so you make excuses not to do it, and thus become even more insecure because now you know you "weren't even good enough to try." As hockey Hall of Famer Wayne Gretzky said, "you miss 100% of the shots you never take."

This problem touches on the fear of rejection. Suppose a man sees a woman he is interested in, but he's too insecure to start a conversation. He might make an excuse that sounds like, "well, I'd love to say something to her, but she looks preoccupied, and I don't have time to stop and chat anyway. Maybe next time." He knows that's just an excuse, so now he is even less confident when his next opportunity rolls around, on the off chance that it does. Often, we are not that lucky. If he is fortunate enough to get a second chance, after failing to try the first time and diminishing his confidence, he sees that girl again and resolves to himself, "You know what, it's not even worth trying at this point. She wouldn't like me."

Women are not immune to insecurity. I have heard some excuses from my female friends, past and present, that make little sense. Some excuses are nonsensical, involving the color a girl is wearing or the state of the weather outside. Others are simpler yet silly and involve jumping to irrational conclusions such as, "that guy is cute, but he probably isn't into girls of my body type or hair color." They sometimes go with a cliché, "he's just not my type," which is number one in the *Excuses for the Timid* handbook (not a real book). I've come to realize "not my type," more often than not, is code for "I don't see myself attractive enough for him." If the woman making such a statement is genuinely uninterested in the man she is directing the statement to, that is fine, but that is not always the case.

A woman might see a guy she has a crush on and say to herself, "oh, he's just too good for me," which is nonsense, or alternatively, "He'd have to be an idiot to show me attention, so if he expresses interest in me, I'll know I don't want him." You might think I am exaggerating, but you would be mistaken. I have heard these excuses uttered, and they become self-fulfilling prophesies when the women saying them become convinced of their validity, imaginary as it may be.

Excuses fuel insecurity, and insecurity demands excuses. We must end the cycle! The only way to do that is by acting in opposition to our feelings and unease, which means taking action before you have time to think of an excuse not to.

I used to play a game with my friend in college to help us both get out of the habit of excusing ourselves from talking to people. We never actually had a name for the game, but here's how it worked: Whenever one of us pointed out a girl, the other had to talk to her without hesitating. If he [the challenged] hesitated for even a second, he earned a swift punch to the arm, usually at full power. My friend and I started to play this game any time we went out in public together, and the game was always in motion, so neither of us knew when we would be challenged by the other. We could be out on the town or just at the store for a grocery run, and my friend would point somebody out to start a conversation with. The goal was to work past some of our inhibitions. When we first started to play, we developed serious bruises on our arms. It wasn't until our fear of getting punched outweighed our approach anxiety that either of us became good at talking to people without thinking about it.

Of course, you do not have to resort to such a crude method to overcome your insecurities. The point of that odd game was to get us into the habit of taking action before we had time to come up with an excuse to chicken out. It's similar to why I prefer to work out in the morning before I go to work. I do not want to give myself the entire day to think of reasons why I shouldn't get a workout. If I wait until the evening to hit the weight room, I have plenty of time to convince myself that I'm too tired, too busy, or too sore from yesterday to get it done. If I go straight from my bed to exercise, my brain is still too foggy to realize what I'm doing until I'm already doing it.

The longer you hesitate to do something, the easier it is to talk yourself out of it. Granted, that can be a good thing if what you are hesitating to do is immoral, and you should *not* be doing it. By all means, take the time to talk yourself out of doing something bad. The same practice of hesitating should not be applied to things worth your time and effort. You can try to act before giving yourself time to formulate an excuse for things of that nature. Swim against the current of your insecurities and act regardless of your negative feelings.

Just today, excuses began subtly suggesting reasons why I shouldn't bother writing: "You won't write anything good anyway; your book is going to suck no matter what you do or how hard you try; nothing you write is going to be as good as you want it to be; you can always make up for it tomorrow if you do nothing today." All those thoughts went through my head today, right up to when I got home this afternoon, tired and wanting to sloth out. Yet, here I am, writing. I may not have felt like getting to work on this after a long day of labor, but those feelings matter little relative to what I know I *should* do.

I am sure any feelings of insecurity about writing pale in comparison to what Gideon must have felt when approached by God.

The Lord told Gideon he was to save his nation by meeting the Midianites in battle. It was at that time Gideon, the King of Insecurity, started explaining why he could not do what God asked him: "I am the weakest man of the weakest clan of the weakest nation! I am far too afraid, anyhow! Besides, how do I know that you are truly even God?" This man was simply masterful at finding reasons to ignore God's call. Of course, God was not having any of it. He knew what plans He had for His child.

Eventually, Gideon relented and resolved to end the cycle of excuses and insecurity through action. At God's command, he assembled an army. Gideon gathered 32,000 men in the pursuit of facing the army of 120,000 Midianites.

It is easy to imagine that Gideon was probably not relaxed about being significantly outnumbered. He probably reasoned that there was at least a chance of victory with God on their side. Then, God did something that Gideon did not expect.

God told Gideon to cut down the size of his forces twice until there were only 300 men left in his army. If Gideon was insecure with over 100 times that number, you could be sure he was reaching for his inhaler by this point! But this was God's will—His intent. God showed the power of faith and the importance of leaning on Him by presenting Gideon with this seemingly impossible task.

Low and behold, Gideon appeared before the Midianites with his measly 300 men. His foes retreated before Gideon had the chance to lose even a single man!

God used a cowardly, insecure, unqualified man to lead an army. He gave a timid man a task to perform that a rational person would call impossible. But God did not send him in with only his human strength and resolve to fall back on. God was there every step of the way, at Gideon's side. God's power shone brightly!

Through Gideon's story, we have the perfect lens to see and be sure of one thing: God will never give us a situation that we cannot handle. There is no obstacle that you cannot vault over, no temptation that you cannot resist, no task or skill you cannot master, no pretty girl or handsome guy you cannot talk to!

I do not expect anybody to be confident and secure 100% of the time. I know that I'm not. We are all human. But, even in seasons when we doubt ourselves and let insecurity open the door to excuses, we can be sure that God is ready to shoot them down, just as He did with Gideon!

When we say, "I am unworthy," God replies, "You are *most* worthy!" When we exclaim, "I am not good for anything," God corrects, "I made you for a great purpose!" When we cry, "I am too afraid," God roars, "I am with you, Mighty Warrior!"

God does not see what we see, nor does He see what other people see. The God who created us knows who we are, far better than the world knows us, or we even know ourselves! His opinion matters more than anyone else's!

Chapter 6

Rejection

Brace yourself: you probably won't believe the words you are reading. As hard as it is to believe, not everybody likes me when they first meet me, and many people still find my presence distasteful long after getting to know me.

I know! Try to contain your surprise at that unfathomable revelation. I have received many different forms of rejection throughout my lifetime, coming from many sources. This trend began when I was born from my mother—though not how you might imagine. It is more in a way that makes me laugh today.

Back in 1994, my poor mother had just gone through the grueling process of delivering a baby that weighed more than 10 pounds. There was no conceivable way for anything the size of a moderate Thanksgiving turkey to fit through a slim woman's birthing canal, so the doctors had to cut me out. My mother, thankfully, came out of the ordeal in perfect health but, as you might venture a guess, being cut open and bringing an over-sized tub of lard into the world after being in labor for tens of hours can have a slight tendency to make a woman a little bit sleepy. To the surprise of nobody, my mother fell unconscious and stayed that way for quite some time.

After no less than several hours of post-labor napping, my mother still had yet to meet her new baby. She was guided by a nurse to the viewing window of the newborn holding area and followed the nurse's finger as she pointed to the baby.

Now, here's the problem: according to how my mother tells the story, the nurse's finger pointed to the one and only baby that was doing a full push-up (yes, I was already a fitness beast fresh out of the womb), had managed to support his body weight with his arms and hold his head up and was currently looking around the room with eyes of wide-eyed amazement as if to think, "what is this new place I find myself in? This is fascinating! Much more colorful than that dark, confined prison from which I just escaped!"

Logically, my mother saw this massive child, who looked and acted like he was no less than several months old, and her mind concluded this could not possibly be her child—the one whom she delivered this very day! My mother proceeded to shout at the nurse in tears and anger, "That's not my baby! Where is *my* baby?" because she had only given birth, and *this* offspring of Jabba the Hutt could not have been born less than three months ago! I can understand her shocked reaction, as exhausted as she must have been in both body and mind, expecting a cute and plush little newborn instead of bearing witness to a morbidly obese full-grown hobbit.

Even some of the nurses were freaked out at the sight of me because they had never seen a newborn infant doing push-ups in the crib, muscling himself up like some tiny, neon-white Incredible Hulk. This is the actual story my mother tells of the day I was born, detail-to-detail. Whether or not she exaggerates is anyone's guess.

My mother was so freaked out when she saw me for the first time she wouldn't even pick me up. The first rejection of my life came right at the beginning, thus, starting a long-standing trend.

You might think that this story paints my mother unflatteringly, but let me clear the record. Like most of the rejections I have experienced in the past, this initial one from my truly remarkable mother was no cause for concern or revisiting. As it stands today, I love my mother very much, and she and I have a great relationship. My bride loves to remind me what a wonderful and loving mother I have, and not because she raised a man as *marvelous* and almost *supernaturally awesome* as me (there's that hyperbole I was talking about), but that she did so from the seeds of the devil. That joke can be aimed either at my dad or me. Seriously, I was a terrible and nightmarish child.

It is understandable why rejection seems a crippling fear for most of us. Such fear is not exclusive to the world of dating. Experiencing rejection is a primary reason many, myself included, make poor moral and life decisions. None of us is the standard for perfection. We are all human, which implies our negative emotions, which often arise from various forms of rejection, can overtake us at times. Sadness, loneliness, anger, and fear are all states of mind capable of leading us to do foolish things. I would pose this question to you: how do you deal with negative emotions?

How often do we let our hardships pull us down the wrong way—away from God? When our faith and commitment are tested, how much does it take for us to fold through trials and rejections of many kinds?

It is easy to call ourselves good, virtuous people and do the right things and say the right words when things are going well—it's effortless to praise God and worship when we are happy, and life feels like a fairytale! But what do we do when Cinderella doesn't get her slipper; Beauty doesn't transform the Beast; Snow White doesn't wake? What do we resort to then? Do we turn to God in praise, prayer, and worship or turn to vice? Do we look toward heaven or gaze upon our earthly comforts? Do we show kindness and generosity to others or focus on ourselves? Do we turn to faith or despair?

I will be honest with you: I have been the number two guy more times than I care to admit.

I believe most of our negative emotions (anger, hate, envy, bitterness, desperation, depression, etc.) are raging fires given life by the initial spark of rejection. If a person is rejected enough and lets those destructive emotions manifest long enough, the result is a wildfire that can burn away the best parts of us.

Have you ever known an extremely nice and caring individual? The kind of person always trying to make someone's day, treats people well no matter who they are or what they do, has a giving spirit, and wouldn't hurt a fly? I want you to picture such a person in your head.

Such kind-hearted and caring individuals can be a great gift to society and the world. Still, there is an unfortunate and rather unfair side-effect of being this sort an individual: they are often prone to be taken advantage of, pushed around, socially rejected, romantically rejected, and hurt. It is not uncommon for this person, during adolescence, to be bullied in school because they are "easy targets" who do not desire conflict and have nothing malicious to say from the outset. However, even the most kind-hearted person can only take so much abuse. Even the kindest person, pushed far enough, can reach an emotional or mental breaking point. They can snap. If you have ever seen this phenomenon occur, you know it is not a pretty sight. It is rather scary to witness the nicest person you know go ballistic. It is worse when you watch a good-hearted person gradually change as they become bitter, angry, and resentful as repeat offenses of mistreatment or rejection harden their hearts.

Rejection is a matter that should not be overlooked, and these bad experiences should not be internalized or ignored until they form an ulcer or result in explosive outbursts. If you are a kind and caring individual, perhaps a bit shy to boot—you have my heart. You are among my favorite kinds of people to engage with and spend time around! We should get together and exchange cheesy, borderline weird compliments toward one another! I love making people feel happy and awkward at the same time!

If rejection is the spark and negative emotions are the fire, then words and actions of love and affirmation are buckets of water to throw on that fire and put it out. Unfortunately, as the fire grows from the fuel of emotion, it takes a great many buckets to put it out. It is better not to let the fire get out of control, to begin with.

If you know somebody who suffers from rejection of any kind, offer them kind words or, better yet, loving favors. Make them feel valued and appreciated, and put some water on those flames! If you are the one starting the fires for somebody, become a fireman instead and love those people to the best of your ability. I am not suggesting you are obligated to date somebody you don't like just so they don't feel rejected, but you don't have to have a romantic relationship with somebody to make them feel valuable and loved.

If you are suffering from an excess of rejection and pain, let me suggest you do not ignore that pain. If you ignore a fire, it will spread. A fire that spreads too far will cause more damage than necessary. Internalizing your struggle seldom does any good to anybody, especially if you reach a snapping point. Speak to someone about your struggles and voice your frustrations. I know that the suggestion may seem cliché and unappealing to many. I speak as an individual with a history of not talking about his problems.

You may have heard the advice, "don't sweat the little things." I disagree. That advice only leads you to internalize and compile all of your problems until your frustration tank reaches capacity. There is no room to contain them and no place to put them. In such an event, you will tend to burst. My advice is to feel free to vent to a friend or loved one about things that may seem like minor infractions. This leaves you with enough storage in your frustration tank to endure the big challenges in life that you will come across and less inclined to break under the strain that such adversities cause.

Confiding in a trusted individual, whether a friend, family member, pastor, counselor, or therapist, you may be amazed how much lighter you will feel after listening to their affirmation and response. The most important person to talk to, however, is God. While venting to somebody in front of you is certainly a benefit, not to be discounted, nobody else can help you more than Him. Cast your frustrations on Him and feel them virtually evaporate.

You cannot control how people treat you. The only thing you have control over is yourself and how you respond. In the aftermath of rejection or heartache, you will be presented with a choice: allow the denial of affirmation to break you or let the hurt do its work and grow from it productively. You can accept the victim mentality, although that would be unproductive. It is easy to feel sorry for yourself and indulge in self-pity when you feel wronged. Still, the result would be bitterness and inward loathing with a rancorous attitude toward those around you. Alternatively, you can consciously choose to let unfortunate events mold you into a person of character—one we need more of in this world. You can choose to love those who have wronged you rather than lashing out at them; choose not to take rejection as a personal assault on your character; choose not to pity yourself but aim to better yourself, and choose to put out fires rather than start them.

The spirit of rejection can come from any number of sources and show itself in various ways, obvious or subtle. It is a force that threatens to prevent many of us, not only from finding a spouse but from living our lives to the fullest with purpose and intention. However, it only has such power over us if we allow it.

As scripture says, if God is love, then we were created *by* love. God commands us to love others above ourselves, love our spouses as Christ loved the church, love our enemies as much as our friends, and of course, to love Him. It seems evident that we were created *to* love! If we were created by love and our purpose is to love, it would only make sense that our greatest desire and number one need is *love*. That is why rejection has such destructive potential—because it represents the deprivation of what we desire above all else, what we were created to share. If love is our creator and love is our purpose, then it is not a surprise that rejection is often what most of us fear over anything else.

Because love is our greatest need and desire, its denial understandably leaves quite a scar. Whether it comes from the lack of affection from a parent to a child, being bullied in school or treated as a social outcast, being passed over for a promotion at work, being turned down when asking somebody on a date, and the list could go on, rejection takes a toll and weighs us down. Often, when that weight is on us, it prevents us from moving forward. I have been quite guilty of this myself, much to my lament.

After a lifetime of rejections from various sources, I gradually went from being an out-going, attention-loving child to quite the recluse for much of my college life. I did join a fraternity and occasionally got out of my shell, but I always felt most at home in the privacy of my bedroom, with no one around but my dog, Cinder. I suppose it was easier than feeling like an outcast among my peers and experiencing their gaze or lack-there-of as if my presence was an inconvenience to those around me. This was a fantasy I had constructed in my self-loathing head. This was not the time I was at peak mental or emotional health.

I had let past rejections speak lies so deeply into my subconscious mind that I no longer needed to be actively rejected to *feel* rejected. I could walk into a room full of people wearing a defeated face and slumped body language because I assumed everyone would hate me. Sending such negative signals with my body language would likely guarantee nobody would try to engage in conversation with me.

I gave in easily to the self-pity I mentioned earlier. I allowed myself to feel like a victim and submit to depression. I may have had some encouragement to dip my toe into that hole, but I am the one who willingly jumped in. I could have stayed away from the pit or climbed out at any time. The truth is I grew fond of playing the victim and feeling sorry for myself after all of my past tribulations. I never took responsibility for things of life that were within my control. I neglected to claim responsibility for my part. I failed to take ownership of my failings and opted to resign myself to feeling powerless. I missed many opportunities to make a positive difference in somebody else's life. Maybe a simple smile could have brightened their day.

Only when we choose to take responsibility for the part we play in our sufferings and rejections do we allow ourselves to feel like we have any power over our condition. As long as I am focused on how somebody hurt me, I cannot concentrate on what part I played in the event and fix it. We can ask: "Did that girl reject me out of some malicious intent or because she just has no taste in men?" or we can acknowledge: "perhaps I should have brushed my teeth and practiced my conversational skills."

You can feel sorry for yourself because members of the opposite sex do not seem to be interested in you, or you can put more effort into your appearance, work on your posture, practice making eye contact while talking to people, or do whatever else you need to do within reason. It is okay to ask for advice from a trusted source on what you may need to work on. We all have room to improve in one area or another and have the power to affect our circumstances. As long as you avoid facing things within your capacity to control, you will feel hopeless. That is avoidable.

We all experience rejection in our lives; it comes with existing in the world. Avoiding it is hardly a valid option. The question is not whether or not we will have to deal with it, but rather *how* we will do so. If I am brutally rejected, I have the option to either crumble under the weight of that rejection as I used to do; thus, this gives my rejector power over my heart and mind, or to grow from it and learn from the experience and possibly joke about it later. Rejection of virtually any form is a powerful weapon the devil will use to try and break us, make us lose faith, and keep us afraid of trying to live up to our potential. I would prefer not to let a broken heart keep me from living a life full of purpose and fulfillment.

The Most Rejected Man in History

Can you guess who the single most rejected person in all history was and, in fact, still is? I will give you one hint; it is not you. As far as rejection goes, you undoubtedly have nothing on this guy! That is not to undermine anything you may have been through in your life, of course, but to illustrate some perspective. The most rejected man in history is, in fact, Jesus Christ.

That statement probably does not come as much of a surprise to you but, if it does, consider how many people in today's world alone not only choose to deny Jesus Christ but are even provoked to anger by the very mention of His name! I have encountered quite a staggering number of such people. Nobody has ever been so hated for loving people, much less trying to save them.

People rejected Jesus before he was born over two thousand years ago. The book of Isaiah prophesies Jesus' rejection centuries earlier: "He grew up before him like a tender shoot, and like a root out of dry ground. He had no beauty or majesty to attract us to Him, nothing in His appearance that we should desire Him. He was despised and rejected by men, a man of sorrow, and familiar with suffering. Like one from whom men hide their faces, He was despised, and we esteemed Him not" (Isaiah 53:2-3).

Jesus' earthly father, Joseph, rejected Him when he discovered Mary, the woman he was pledged to marry, was pregnant with a child Joseph had no hand in making. I guess Joseph wasn't buying the "virgin conception" story. It wasn't until an angel appeared to him and explained the truth that Joseph began the process of acceptance.

As if the pre-birth rejection wasn't bad enough (at least my mother had the good courtesy to wait until I was out of the womb before she freaked out), King Harrod caught wind that a newborn baby was being called the "K" word by a multitude of people and tried to have baby Jesus killed. The man felt threatened by a harmless infant because he wanted to be the only king whom people recognized and revered. Talk about insecurity!

When Jesus first began His ministry, His own family publicly said Jesus was out of His mind!

When Jesus read the prophecy of Isaiah (referenced earlier) aloud in Nazareth to a large crowd and claimed that He was here to fulfill that prophesy, the crowd became enraged and not only drove Him out of town but wanted to throw Him over the edge of a cliff!

At the Feast of Dedication in Jerusalem, Jesus spoke that He was the Christ, and the Jews, His own people, tried to stone Him.

Jesus underwent severe rejection when His disciple, Judas, betrayed him, and it only got worse from that point on. He was rejected three times in a row by his most trusted friend, Peter, who repeatedly shouted to the angry mob, "I do not know the man!" Jesus was betrayed by one, denied by another, and abandoned by those who had followed Him for years. Many loved Jesus, but many also hated Him so much that they called for His crucifixion! His rejection by countless people resulted in a gruesome, excruciating, and drawn-out death. As a final blow, while Jesus hung on the cross, He was rejected by God, His father. That was the price that Jesus had to pay for our sins to be forgiven—to have God the Father forsake Him and to die alone on that cross. That is certainly no easy burden.

I don't know about you, but no rejection I have experienced in my life comes close to what Jesus endured on our behalf! Yet, here is the miraculous thing: He knew everything in His life would lead up to that conclusion. He told the disciples what was to come and even prayed to God to provide another option to Him because He feared what was to come. Jesus knew He would be rejected in the worst of ways, beaten, flogged, and despised, and knew what tree He would end up hanging from. He feared it just as any rational human would, but Jesus knew what His purpose was. He knew to be rejected by the world was the only way to save it. He knew He had to be forsaken by God the Father on that cross so that we, whom He loved so much, would never have to endure such a rejection. It was Jesus' willingness to be the most reject-ed person in history that guaranteed our heavenly father would never forsake us. He will *never* reject us as long as we do not reject Him.

Frequently, the fear of rejection causes us to avoid taking risks. Of course, life without risk is a life lacking substance. You actively risk get-ting hurt when you get close to someone and open your heart. With-out that risk, you never build meaningful relationships, show love to people, never feel a loving embrace, and seldom experience meaning and belonging. Jesus did not simply *risk* being hurt and rejected—He knew what would happen. He was scared. That was the human side of Him that we all share and can relate to. We fear rejection and pain. But Jesus did not let that feat keep Him from fulfilling His purpose on earth and living out His courageous act of love, and neither should we! God gives us clear instructions in the Bible over a hundred times, "do not fear." Somehow, I get the impression that He means it!

When the World Chimes In

"So we say with confidence, 'the Lord is my helper; I will not be afraid. What can man do to me?'" (Hebrews 13:6).

I love that verse because men can be cruel. In the United States of America alone, countless people seem to make it a personal goal to persecute and humiliate anybody who disagrees with them. Things like this make it particularly unnerving for a person of faith to come out of hiding and speak the truth of what they believe. A small percentage of Judeo-Christians are willing to speak up honestly about their faith for fear of society's rejection.

Admittedly, religious persecution in the U.S. is exponentially less severe than that which occurs in nations overseas, where many are still imprisoned or executed for having a Bible or refusing to deny the name of Jesus. While that certainly puts things in perspective, I still empa-thize with those who fear the rejection that society so often seems to threaten us with if we dare to base our values on scripture and be out-spoken about such things. If I tell certain circles that I do not believe in same-sex marriage because the Bible says it is wrong (along with other reasons that I will discuss in a later chapter), I am likely to be shouted at and hated by many, even when I make it abundantly clear that I do not have to agree with the homosexual ethic to love homosexual people. This is just one of the near-infinite potential examples.

That is the kind of rejection that Jesus dealt with every day of His life on earth, and often it was more severe than being shouted at profanely. Our Lord understands what it is to be disliked and spat on, and He assures us that, while it may be painful at times, it is not always such a bad thing. It can be a good sign, in a way.

"Zach, are you seriously suggesting that being rejected and hated can be a good thing?" you might be asking. And the answer is: No, I am not. Jesus is! I am just relaying the message! Allow me to refer your attention to a passage from the book of Luke: *"Blessed are you when men hate you, when they exclude you and insult you and reject your name as evil, because of the Son of Man"* (Luke 6:22).

The truth is that people do not always like to hear the truth. If you are an honest and upstanding individual, people will criticize and look down on you. If you live by God's standards, you will be on the receiving end of insults and ridicule, and certain peer groups will probably exclude you. The same is especially true in the dating scene. The situation arose when I was single in which I was talking to a woman who was interested in me. Still, when I told her about my moral standards, such as not having sex before marriage, etc., she would scoff, and her interest would be quickly diminished. Yes, I have been rejected on numerous occasions by multiple women for the very fact that I had every intention of standing by my moral convictions. There is no one I find less worthy of admiration than one who castigates a person for having moral standards.

This does not seem fair by any stretch of the imagination: to be the best we can be and live by God's standards, only to be rejected for it. But, fairness rarely has any place in reality. It was not fair for Jesus to have to take the punishment for our sins and die on the cross for us, and yet He did! If the world were fair, our sins would never have been forgiven, and we would all be doomed! For that reason, I could not be happier that our world is unfair!

But the passage in Luke does not stop there. Jesus went on: *"Woe to you when all men speak well of you, for that is how their fathers treated the false prophets"* (Luke 6:26).

If everyone seems to like you, speaks well of you, praises you, and agrees with you, odds are that you are not speaking the truth in many instances and are being anything but genuine. As a man who has a history of being a people-pleaser, I know this first-hand. When I was in high school, I wanted so badly for people to like me that I would end up bending my values to be agreeable, solely in the pursuit of being liked and accepted. Of course, such acceptance was short-lived because I failed to show who I was and what I believed—I gave a false impression—and the rejection was far worse than it would have been had I been honest with and about myself from the start.

When Jesus mentions false prophets, He is essentially saying that the only individuals who are not hated by a multitude of people are those who feed those people lies and fantasies. It's like a politician who promises his constituents and voters a bunch of free stuff and a utopian society to get the vote. However, the reality is that said politician can never follow through with such promises. All that matters to him is getting votes and power. To get them to like him, he tells them what they like to hear, rather than being genuine with them.

People are drawn to what is convenient and easy to hear rather than what is true. That was the big appeal of movements like the Sexual Revolution in the 1960s. The truth is that having sex with anyone you want at any time is ultimately damaging in so many ways (for each person involved). The idea that marriage should not confine us to one person is erosive to the whole of society in, again, many ways (we will dive into this in later chapters). However, it was a convenient thing for folks to hear! Young people were all over the idea that sex doesn't *mean anything and* doesn't have to come with commitment. It may have been a lie, but it was an attractive lie because it was more convenient for young people to follow their immediate desires and impulses than to concern themselves with what is true and right.

Now, when I talk about sex being intended exclusively for marriage, it tends to rub people the wrong way. Such truths are not convenient, and they imply that one should exercise a little bit of self-control, rather than following their heart and feelings, which can be so much easier in the short term!

All of that was simply me trying to say easy is rarely what is right—a recurring theme in the real world. It would seem far easier to live a life in which rejection was never an issue, and all you had to do was "go with the flow" of society rather than standing for your principles and what is right and true. Of course, to live a life of ease, with nothing to stand for, with no risks or difficulty, without obligation, is to live a life devoid of purpose. Honestly, it is impossible to achieve a life entirely free of difficulty or rejection at some level, so you may as well not even try very hard to avoid it.

The more you attempt to avoid the unnerving phenomenon of rejection, the more it will affect you when it happens. Note that I did not say *"if* it happens." I am not trying to be cynical or induce discouragement in anybody, but I must be honest about this. If you expect rejection never to happen to you and you go to great lengths to avoid it, it will still find you, and you will be all the more resentful. Studies have shown it to be true that those rejected by their peers, from whom they try too hard to gain acceptance, often grow to be some of the angriest people in the world.

A study done by Leary, Kowalski, Smith, and Phillips, published in 2003, delved into the worrisome topic of school shootings and what could push a person to some extreme and gruesome acts. It was not surprising to those performing the study that rejection was a common theme in these unfortunate events. "Various forms of rejection cause anger and may lead to aggression."[3] As rejection becomes more frequent or severe, the same becomes true of chances of aggressive or defensive behavior. The cause of these horrible events goes deeper than just being teased or bullied, but the fact remains that it is a consistent pattern.

Consistent and significant rejection can most certainly bring out people's worst emotions and actions. This certainly does not mean that being rejected is doomed to damage us or cause us to lash out, and I would strongly emphasize that it is no excuse! The news is much better than that! The key is not in avoiding rejection but in dealing with it the right way! The ball is in our court; hence, we get to choose what direction to hit it in!

Dealing With It

You may never be one to deal with rejection and negative emotions with flawless ease and grace. I know that I am not. If even Jesus Christ feared His impending painful rejection upon the cross when He asked God in the garden if there was some other way (all while sweating blood), I don't think any of us will reach a point in which fear and

3   Leary, Mark R., et al. "Teasing, Rejection, and Violence: Case Studies of the School Shootings." *Aggressive Behavior*, vol. 29, no. 3, 2003, pp. 202–214., doi:10.1002/ab.10061.

rejection don't phase us. For this reason, it is probably not wise to pretend that it doesn't. A wound left untreated is the most likely to fester.

Putting on a brave face may seem like the proper response when we are in pain, but holding everything in and pretending that everything is fine only discourages us from putting our negative emotions to rest while allowing our pain and frustrations to build up gradually. Remember when I talked about the frustration tank? You do not want to allow your problems to build up until that tank is filled and erupts in a fiery explosion of emotional outrage. If you are hurting, angry, depressed, or worried, the last thing you want to do is lash out at people and drive them away.

Sweat the little things. When small inconveniences happen, feel free to make light-hearted complaints about them. When slightly larger problems occur, don't be afraid to vent your frustrations to somebody. I am not suggesting you vomit your feelings all over your friends or become an endless stream of negativity. There is a great divide between being a relentless whiner and cracking jokes about little things that bother you (a sense of humor is always a benefit). Nobody would blame you for occasionally emptying your frustration tank by confiding in a friend or loved one about a rejection you recently suffered. You can be as honest and open as necessary in a private confession.

You should not ignore emotions that arise from rejection and emotional trauma any more than you should ignore broken bones or profuse bleeding from a serious injury. The result in either scenario is that you do not heal properly and, in extreme cases, do not heal at all.

Arguably just as bad as ignoring your problems is setting unrealistic expectations for how things *should* be. It seems that most people like to imagine an ideal world in which life is fair, and people get what they *deserve*. From that imaginary world, they formulate their expectations of how they decide things ought to be, and some concept of fairness usually graces the top of that list of expectations. It seems like a nice idea, but the reality is not often kind enough to cater to our delusions. What is *fair* seldom makes an appearance in the real world. If your life expectations are based on what is deserved, fair, or should be, the most likely result is frustration and bitterness. Nothing else comes from impossible goals.

It is perfectly acceptable to have expectations for your life but keeping them realistic and reasonable is paramount. If you are a 35-year-old with a degree in fine arts, but you set a goal for yourself to play football in the NFL, even though you've never played football in your life and weigh 140 pounds, you are setting yourself up to be miserable. You are unlikely to achieve that unreasonable goal detached from reality, and you will kick yourself upon reaching the first obstacle. In like fashion, if you expect to ask out a lot of women and never hear the word "no," you are going to be disappointed. The most handsome man in the world would not be immune to rejection. If you expect everybody you meet to like you and desire to be your friend, you may find yourself fighting a losing battle against depression.

Conversely, you could expect nobody to like you at all and for nobody to want to date you, to begin with, and just skip straight ahead to the depression without going through the rejection, save for those you imagine in your head preemptively. Setting aside the fact that that was my strategy at one point, I must agree that it is not the most appealing option either.

So, if we do not want to set up unrealistic expectations of never experiencing rejection and we do not want to resign ourselves to loneliness by avoiding the risk, we are left with the less extreme middle-ground. You can accept that not everybody will like you and you can get on with your life. Since the total avoidance of rejection is not possible when dealing with human beings, the choice is simple: You can be loved by some and despised by many, or you can be ignored by all.

You have the option to let various rejections of many kinds take you down, or you can decide that they mean relatively little when you know full well that God has never rejected you and never will. Yes, rejection hurts, but you can rest easy knowing that there is always a place for you in God's arms. He's a hugger.

If you don't want to take my word for it (which is a mistake because I'm kind of a genius, but it's your prerogative), maybe you will believe Leah. You can find her story in the 29th and 30th chapters of Genesis, and I recommend you read it for yourself, but let me give you the abridgment:

To set the scene, Jacob, the son of Isaac, had just fled from his brother Esau in fear for his life and sought sanctuary with his uncle, Laban. Laban had two daughters: Rachel, the young and lively one, and Leah, the older one. Jacob met Rachel upon arrival at Laban's land and immediately fell in love. When he asked her father for her hand in marriage, Laban said that he would only grant his blessing for Jacob to marry Rachel if he worked for Laban for seven years. I don't know about you, but I have never been quite that patient. I couldn't even wait more than three and a half *months* before giving the love of my life an engagement ring. But Jacob agreed to the 7-year arrangement, so I guess he's a better man than me.

After the seven years had elapsed and Jacob had fulfilled his end of the bargain, Laban kept his word that he would give Jacob his daughter in marriage. The catch of the story is that he gave Jacob the *wrong* daughter. Laban sent his older daughter, Leah, into Jacob's tent in Rachel's place to consummate the marriage on the wedding night. Jacob did not realize the deception until the following morning when he saw Leah's face lying next to him. I would have hated to witness Leah's reaction when she saw her new husband's disappointment when he laid eyes upon her that morning.

Laban's excuse for tricking Jacob was that, by custom, he could not give away his younger daughter without first marrying off his oldest. After agreeing to an additional seven years of labor, Jacob married the daughter he wanted.

Think about that. Jacob was married to two women—sisters, no less—and he only loved one of them. From the text, we can gather that his feelings, or lack thereof, for Leah were no secret.

That was Leah's lot in life. She was to share her husband with her little sister and live knowing that her little sister was the only one he truly wanted. That certainly seems a terrible way to live. So, as you can imagine, Leah is far from a stranger to rejection. She lived with that sensation every day of her life, from the moment her husband laid eyes on her the morning following her wedding. After Leah's earthly father put her into this life-long situation, it was her heavenly father who went to work in her life after that.

God saw that Leah was not loved by her husband and saw fit to show His love to her by making her fertile and Rachel temporarily barren so that Jacob would see Leah as his best chance to have children. Leah conceived and gave birth to a son exclaiming, "The Lord has seen my misery. Surely my husband will love me now." She named her son Reuben. And no, he was not named after a delicious sandwich.

Then Leah gave birth to another son, again crying, "it is because the Lord has seen that I am not loved." After having each of her first two sons, Leah desperately clung to the hope that her husband would finally stop rejecting her and depriving her of the love and affection that she craved, now that she had blessed him with children. Since she kept trying to earn his favor, we can probably assume that it did not happen like that.

Leah again conceived and gave birth to a third child. This time, however, she merely hoped that her husband would at least become "attached" to her, that he would concede to having a bond with her even if love was not the word to describe it. Leah still felt his shoulder cold to her touch.

At last, Leah gave birth to her fourth son, this time looking to God and saying, "this time, I will praise the Lord." Though cast into an unfair situation beyond her choice and control, Leah was now far less concerned with the feeling that her husband expressed toward her or did not express as the case may have been. She understood that God had never overlooked her the way Jacob had and that He would never allow her to be truly alone. Where Jacob had rejected Leah, God embraced her and, in addition, gave her many children to love and to be loved by. While she could not choose to make Jacob love her the way she wanted, she could certainly choose to love her children and find joy in the blessings that God *had* given to her.

Even under the worst of circumstances, God shines a light into our lives. I have come to observe that He shines it the brightest when times are hard. Taking terrible circumstances and turning them into something good is what He does.

In 2017, I could only have described myself as miserable. Two hours into the year (2 am on New Years Day), somebody tried to kill me. As the year progressed, I was dumped and rejected fairly consistently by women and people in general; After a heart-wrenching experience, I left college in the interest of pursuing a new career, only to be tossed aside by my employer after just under five weeks; I then went into a job that I couldn't stand to get by on very little pay; friends of mine, including a man I called "brother," died; I got my heart torn to shreds by a woman I had been head-over-heels for since freshman year of high school; I went completely broke; my little brother, who had been living with me, was taken to rehab; and the year just trekked on.

In the end, everything that happened in what could only be described as the longest year of my life led me to move in 2018 to the small town that I currently reside in. I started working in a job that I enjoy; I attend a wonderful church, wonderful people surround me, and I met Lauren—the most wonderful woman of God—and asked for her hand in marriage.

I have found that it's often true that the night is darkest just before dawn. It is pretty incredible. God took the worst year of my life, during which the people who knew me best had been known to question how

I kept going and keep a smile on my face for much of the time, and He used it as an Exodus to where I am now, and where I am going from here.

It doesn't matter what you have endured, what rejections you've received, what troubles and tribulations have brought you where you are. God can and will bring you out of it, and He will use the bad for purposes of good. You can be sure of that. The Bible tells us to count it as a blessing when we face trials of many kinds, for it will "produce steadfastness, that we will be complete, lacking in nothing" (see James 1:2-4). The best thing we can do is smile and keep our sense of humor and joy alive while keeping faith in Him and praising Him in good times and bad.

Chapter 7

Loneliness

You probably know what it feels like to be alone? Like nobody gets you? Like no one wants you around? Like you do not receive enough attention? As if no one is ever going to show you the love and affection that you crave? If so, then you are in good company, my friend! It is not exactly an exclusive club.

To feel lonely can make you feel isolated, as if you are the only one on the island, enduring emotions, and misgivings, but the truth could not be more contrary! Loneliness may have a voice of its own that tries to convince you that you are the only one but that feeling in the pit of your stomach is not exclusive to you.

The most common emotion that people report regularly experiencing in western culture is "loneliness!" Feeling alone and isolated is *normal*! In other words, everybody feels alone, and everybody thinks they're the only one. In a world of 7 billion people, and with the modern technological capabilities to communicate with anyone, one would think that "lonely" would be the last term to describe the average American. But, alas, people never cease to feel isolated.

The dangerous thing about being in a consistently negative state of mind is that we seldom make good and wise decisions. If a powerful emotional state takes hold of our thoughts and dominates our decision-making, clear and rational thought are impossible. We often lash out, do things impulsively, seek any thrill or gratification that can produce in us a feeling that differs from what our brain is producing by itself at that moment—anything that might potentially feel like an improvement even if it is a short-lived release.

Lonely people will often seek embrace from any source they can find. A woman might leave her boyfriend for any number of valid reasons: he's unreasonably immature, he cheats on her, he's abusive, or he's just a regular jerk. Once she starts feeling alone, getting back together with him seems like an appealing idea, no matter how little logical sense it makes. A man can be committed to chaste living until he gets married, but make him feel lonely enough to begin to despair, and he might begin to loosen his grip on moral principles and take the easy path.

As I said before, in chapter 6, love is what we humans were designed to do. God is love, God created us in His likeness, and thus we were created by love itself. If love is the source of our creation and our likeness, then it seems that love is an inescapable part of our very being. Our greatest desire and need is love. When we do not have that desire met, it understandably feels like a fundamental part of our being is starving. When we are lonely, our greatest craving is not being met, or it is in a deficit at the very least.

Single people are in danger of experiencing loneliness—especially those who want more than anything to find a spouse and get married. It is not unnatural to feel alone when without companionship, but all the same, it is a dangerous road to walk. As I pointed out, a lonely mind is poor at decision-making. Often, when waiting or searching for something we want, we have to trust God and His timing to find it. This is especially true of the Christian man and woman's search for a spouse. One must be patient and trust in God, and a significant part of that trust lies in following His rules and doing things the right way. In our patience, we are expected to limit our search parameters to fellow believers; we are expected to follow Biblical standards of sexual morality; we are obligated to keep our eyes clean and our hands to ourselves and above our belts.

When the deceptive voice of loneliness whispers its lies, it can be easy for a man to grow tired of waiting on God's timing and rules and seek to follow his own to try and speed up the process. There are definitely easier paths to walk, rightly outside the boundaries of God's instructions, and quicker options for seeking sexual gratification or intimacy that require no marriage and probably less patience. This is a precarious line of thinking and, if we are not careful, we run the risk of making a similar mistake as that of Abraham in Genesis when he grew tired of waiting on God's timing.

God promised Abraham that, in due time, his wife, Sarah, would become pregnant and his descendants would be as numerous as the stars in the sky! Abraham had God's promise that he would have an heir and a legacy. However, after some time had passed, Abraham got tired of waiting, and he resolved to get what he wanted in his way and of his power. In essence, Abraham intended to take control of his circumstances from God. Abraham made a significant moral blunder in his misguided attempt to outperform God and do things his own way—the quick and easy way.

The result of Abraham's impatience was the pregnancy of one of his servants, Hagar, and the subsequent birth of Ishmael. This whole affair ended with little more than pain for the rebellious Abraham, his betrayed wife, his heartbroken and mistreated servant, and his illegitimate son. God wanted to bless Abraham and his wife with children and a legacy, but Abraham lost patience and trust in God and caused unnecessary pain in the process.

The moment we turn our backs on God to take things into our own hands is the moment we start our journey down the ever-frequent repetition of history and cause far more damage than solutions.

To my shame, I have been guilty of going down that road myself. I allowed my loneliness to turn to despair, and my despair turned my trust away from God. I turned to very un-Godly methods in my pursuit of what I wanted.

I, like most people, went through seasons in my singlehood of feeling utterly alone. In the later stages of my college years, I went through many rough times and emotional salvos. At some point in my compromised state, it seemed that all I could get myself to think about was how badly I wanted to meet a girl, fall in love, and start a life with someone. In my mind, I was waiting patiently. I had been trying to do things God's way, abstaining from premarital sex, trying to meet a good Christian woman with good values, but I had come up empty on my search, and my loneliness was beginning to outweigh my patience. I met some decent women but getting rejected is something I was becoming more and more proficient at.

Out of certain desperation (another emotion that I do not recommend leaning on or making decisions under the influence of), my search for companionship expanded from Christian women to *every* woman. My dating standards had dropped, and I would be kidding myself if I claimed that my moral standards were not in constant danger of compromise along with them. If I am willing to date non-Christian girls, then I will be open to doing non-Christian things. I had let my loneliness dominate my conscious thoughts and decision-making. Does anyone else smell smoke?

We will discuss dating nonbelievers in a later chapter, but not just understand that loneliness can turn quickly to desperation, which may lead you to lower your standards, pursue people you would not otherwise date, and make decisions that you will come to regret.

Like most people, I desire happiness, sexual gratification, companionship, and love. Many of us grow impatient, lonely, and eventually desperate to fulfill those desires and resort to the wrong means to achieve them. In doing so, we ditch our trust in God and His great plans for us in favor of quick gratification. You know that the quick and easy way seldom produces the best results if you've been paying attention. Anybody who has ever grown a garden knows that the process cannot be rushed. If you try to fast-track your crops with too much water or sunlight, the result is not a healthy plant. Patience has always been a vital virtue for a reason. The fable of the tortoise and the hare has not changed; the tortoise wins every time you read it.

It is not as though there is a lack of alternatives to doing things the right way: pornography, fornication, etc. However, these quick fixes to human urges always cause more damage than they are worth. As with Abraham, when you try to do things your way instead of the right way, whether out of impatience, loneliness, or otherwise, destructive results will follow the action, whether you foresee them or not.

I understand what it is to feel lonely at times, all too well. There have been times when I have felt utterly alone and unloved; times I have thought my efforts at caring for others have gone unappreciated; times loved ones and strangers alike have seemed to stay distant from me; times when I have felt insignificant, as though nobody much cared about me, as though I were a waste of life. If any of that sounds familiar to you, please let me assure you that you are far from the only person to experience such thoughts. I am inclined to believe that everybody experiences those feelings at one point or another.

I love how Mitch Albom said it in *The Five People We Meet in Heaven*, "No life is a waste... the only time we waste is the time we spend *thinking* we're alone."[4] You can never truly *be* alone—it is simply not

_____

4   Albom, Mitch. *The Five People You Meet in Heaven*. Hachette Books, 2003.

possible. No matter how lonely you may feel, no matter what you think or believe, no matter what you have suffered and endured in your life, you have never been alone, and you will never be alone. You can try as hard as you like, drive to the highest mountain top in the most remote point of the world, climb into a cellar, lock it from the inside, try your best to hide in the pitch blackness, and you will still be unable to find yourself alone. God has never left your side. He is there at any time, should you choose to acknowledge Him, talk to Him, or go to Him for comfort.

God has never allowed you to be truly alone, and He never will. If you feel alone in the fact that you are as of yet unmarried or can't seem to get a date, do not despair. Trust me; despair is the absolute last helmsman you want steering your decision-making. You can and should trust in God's timing. As long as you do not give up on searching or doing things His way, He will lead you in the right direction. In the meantime, follow His rules, don't do anything that a happy and content you wouldn't do, and definitely do not date anybody a happy and content you wouldn't date.

Chapter 8

Should Men Make the First Move?

I have a question for my female readers (and don't you men take this as an excuse to nod off or skip ahead): have you ever received a piece of advice from anyone that sounds like, "always wait for the man you are interested in to pursue you; it's his job to make the first move; you should *always* play hard to get?" This piece of advice tells women that, in any situation in which they see a man they may be interested in, it is the man's responsibility to muster the courage to approach her, make a move, or ask her out.

If you have ever received advice such as this, or do in the future, I have one suggestion! Cover your ears and run!

You could go with the second option of choosing to ignore the advice—perhaps politely disagree with it. If you have no intention of running, I recommend you settle for option number two and disregard the bad advice.

Yes, I called it bad advice.

You can look behind door number three and choose to follow said bad advice. You can place all responsibility upon the man's shoulders and expect him to begin the interaction. You can make him do all of the chasing and rely on the judgment of men to determine whether you get a chance at a date with the guy you like. If you go down that route and rely solely on men to initiate a romantic interaction or commitment with you, the odds are high you will still be single when you are 112 years old! Pickings are slim at that point.

I am not trying to be mean-spirited or insult anybody who believes it is a man's chivalric duty to initiate romantic interactions or shoulder the pressure of approaching a girl and risking rejection by asking the woman out. I have no problem with men summoning the courage to do all of that. Nonetheless, I challenge the advice that says a woman should not be involved in the initiation process. There is no purpose in telling a woman she must wait for the men to come to her. Such instructions are culturally imposed and counterproductive.

Speaking from personal experience, approaching a beautiful woman can be terrifying! It seldom matters what the setting is—whether on the street, a store, bar, club, or even at church. The average man is petrified when he gets the chance to speak to a pretty girl whom he would like to get to know and, perhaps, ask out. It is so scary that most men will not even try to talk to the girl. He may love the idea of dating the girl he is looking at at that moment, but she may as well be Medusa. The second she looks him in the eye, he seems to turn to stone. The average man often turns to stone at the first conversation with a woman. Most such chances are never seized upon.

Anxiety is a real and frustrating thing when trying to initiate a social interaction or conversation with a member of the opposite sex. It stems from a fragile male ego, regardless of what acts of bravado they may express on the surface. I am trying to be honest about the state of men. Getting rejected successive times by women can shatter a man's confidence to the point equal to running a marathon wearing ankle weights. This is no excuse for men to resign themselves to loneliness and self-pity, but it does present a challenge for men trying to find love. This roadblock becomes apparent if the woman is playing "hard to get" before interacting with her.

Many ladies seem to be under the impression that "playing hard to get" means acting like they are not interested in any man because "men can't resist what they can't have." Ladies, I assure you that while many women may play the game that way, that is not how the game is played to win. That is not the correct order. If you are making it hard on the men *before* they have made an effort to speak to you, you are flirting wrong. A man with any sense of self-preservation is unlikely to try to talk to you if you seem disinterested.

When a woman is not in the mood for conversation or has no interest in the man, she tends to put up her defenses. Some women exhibit a mean face; others turn their backs and act like they don't notice the person or avoid eye contact. If you are genuinely disinterested in any conversation, in that case, there is nothing wrong with putting up shields or with letting them down should you pursue the interaction.

On the other hand, if you are interested in having a conversation with a member of the opposite sex but have your "hard to get" defenses, I suggest you lower the deflector shield.

I don't care how often you have heard the cliché "men want what they can't have" line; it simply does not apply in every context. Signaling that you are unavailable will certainly not get a nice man to ask you out. If you have your shields up, that nice man will not break those defenses or get anywhere near you. It is possible that if you give him the slightest eye contact while you are acting disinterested that you *might* give him hope for starting a conversation with you. Then again, this is not a James Bond movie. He will not think of anything good to say, and he may shoot himself down before you get the chance to do it for him. If that is what you want, then mission accomplished. You shall now be awarded your license to kill morale.

To put the point more plainly, most decent men—men with moral standards and a sense of respect—are shy.

By now, I can hear some of the female readers saying, "Well, if the man doesn't have the confidence to make the first move, then he's not the kind of man that I want!" Are you 100% confident with that assertion? While I can understand the tendency to think that way, with cultural influences being what they are, I challenge you to keep an open mind as I put that line of thinking to the test.

Does the confidence level make the man? I grant that confidence is a highly attractive trait, but think about what *kind* of confidence you would like a potential spouse to have.

Yes, there are different kinds of confidence. More specifically, there are different ways in which to be confident. Different men are confident in different areas of their lives and expertise. Some men are confident at their jobs, some are confident public speakers, some are confident in a classroom setting, and some are confident in any social framework.

For virtually every man, the circumstances will dictate their confidence level. A professional athlete who makes $10 million a year playing football in the NFL can look confident on the field, in front of the press and cameras, or at an autograph signing. If you put that same athlete in a college philosophy class where nobody knows his name, he is no longer the most beaming man in the room. On the other hand, the professor is in his element and radiates confidence. It's cool to be an athlete in a stadium or a professor in a lecture hall, but put either of those people in the other's place like some *Freaky Friday* switch, and they might crumble.

The context of our surrounding environment can dictate our level of confidence. I have yet to meet someone who is secure in every situation they find themselves in. Of course, an individual who may have been timid in certain circumstances can become secure and competent over time through practice and exposure—like overcoming a fear of public speaking by talking in front of groups of people. Confidence is a by-product of proficiency, and proficiency is gained through practice and repetition. Consider a man who seems confident when approaching women. Where do suppose such confidence comes from? Practice, perhaps?

I have known several military men in my life. Besides growing up in a military family, many of my friends are either active duty or veterans. I used to see these men as relatively powerful figures who commanded respect and admiration anywhere they went. My patriotism as a child ran deep, and I naturally viewed veterans as heroes, larger than life, and, for a long time, I wanted nothing more than to join their ranks. While I never did join the military, I will always have respect and appreciation for those who did.

Years ago, when I was still single, I talked to a military man who was home on leave. He was single too, and our conversation turned towards the topic of women and dating. I made the mistake of assuming out loud that it must be easy for him to get a girl because of his uniform. I went even further by presuming he must have confidence that borders on the supernatural. After I voiced this opinion, the soldier showed me the error of my preconceptions by telling me something that caught me off guard but got me thinking. In the middle of this casual conversation, he stated, "It's not as easy as you might think, brother. I don't think I have an easier time walking up to and talking to a girl than you or the next guy would. Now that I think about it, it would be easier for me to be in the Middle East, breaching a building full of hostiles, than to walk up to that cutie over there and start talking." That confession genuinely floored me.

At first, I thought this guy was speaking hyperbolically. I mean, this tough guy has been shot at! Not to mention he could have killed me with the damp napkin lying on the bar in front of us. There was no way this guy was truly afraid of talking to pretty girls—a minor action by comparison—right? Then, I gave it some serious thought.

Soldiers go through extensive and rigorous training before entering any combat situation. They repeatedly undergo combat drills and simulations hundreds of times until the action can be performed by muscle memory. By the time a soldier enters a real-life combat scenario such as breaching an enemy building, he has been conditioned so well that his body goes through the process automatically. Practice and repetition.

My soldier friend felt reasonably comfortable doing something as dangerous as entering a firefight because he had been extensively trained to do such things. He was prepared because he had had countless hours of practice keeping his focus and performing complex tasks in precarious scenarios. However, he had had no such practice at approaching and talking to women. Do you know who *does* have that kind of practice when it comes to approaching pretty women? Players.

To be sure, not every man who summons the courage to spark a conversation with a stranger falls under the category of a *player*—which I would define as the kind of man who is primarily interested in sex and is likely to move on to another girl as soon as he gets what he wants from the first one. I have known my fair share of scoundrels like this and, while they are scummy, successful ones make up a very small percentage of the male population.

These players generally radiate confidence in social situations, especially when talking to the opposite sex. Approaching women and getting phone numbers is like an art form to them. They are in the minority and appear to have no problem initiating contact, especially when a girl has her "hard to get" shield up. Players often like a challenge and enjoy the opportunity to pursue what they can't have. The forbidden fruit is the sweetest to a man with no moral backbone.

It's a mistake for a woman to follow the advice of those who tell her, "always make the man make the first move. If he doesn't have the confidence to make a move on you, he's not a real man." Most of the men these women meet will be the kind that meets another one 10 minutes later. I have seen this happen too often to remain silent on this topic. A confident man is not always a good man. Self-assurance can be a great quality in the right context, but it is not synonymous with virtue.

If a player is not the kind of man you are hoping to catch, you may wish to change the bait you are throwing into the pool. It's time to consider the possibility that the woman can and sometimes *should* make first contact.

Ladies, if a man catches your attention, make an effort to make eye contact with him. You don't have to say a word; give him a reason to come to you. 80% of communication is expressed via body language, so use some non-verbal cues! Give the guy a coy smile, flash your eyebrows, wink, gaze, blink at him in Morse Code if you have to! There is nothing wrong with being flirtatious. Flirting is part of the fun, even if some of us are not so great at it (ask my wife). Put yourself out there!

If you like a guy, give him some positive attention, then you can play a little "hard-to-get" to see if he chases. Don't start pulling away before the chase gets started.

Despite what you may have heard, the one thing to take away from this is the man you want may need you to give him the green light before he begins his move. Hopefully, he's nothing like me with his bad jokes and wasted time recovering from stupid comments.

For clarification, I am not proposing that anyone go out of their way to get the attention of every member of the opposite sex! I do not want anybody to act desperate, and I most certainly am not suggesting anybody be promiscuous! Know your worth and have self-respect. Be conservative, but do not be afraid to make the first move if you are interested in someone. I would argue that the willingness to put yourself out there shows that you know you're a quality catch.

Most married couples that I know first got together due to initiation by the woman! I do not think that this is a coincidence. This seems to be the natural order of things if you ask me. A man often has a hard time settling down and making a commitment. Even the men who desire a marital union can be clueless or oblivious when a woman expresses interest in him. A woman who knows she is worth a life-long covenant will pick the man she wants, convince him that he should marry her, and make him earn her with a ring and life-long vows.

Have you ever read the book of Ruth? Now there is a book of the Bible that is dedicated to a woman who made the first move! Then, when the first move didn't do the trick, she made the second move! Ruth *pursued* the man that she wanted!

Ruth worked in the field, and she met a rich and handsome single man named Boaz. He was nice to her (an important detail), she liked him and went after him! While she did not get aggressive or start stalking the boy, Ruth went so far as to cover herself in nice clothes and scented oils, sneak up to him while he was sleeping, uncover his feet and lie down. This whole ordeal was a cultural and symbolic action that meant she was interested in the protection of marriage to Boaz.

So, not only did Ruth pursue the man she desired, but she went so far as to propose to the guy! She met the man who interested her, and she, knowing that he wasn't just going to walk up and put a ring on her, made sure he noticed her and gave him the green light to "make his move!"

There is no need to take my word for it when it comes to the story of Ruth. Don't just listen to what I and others have to say about what's in the Bible. Go and read it for yourself so you can become an all-knowing genius like me! If you'd ever met me, you'd know that it was impossible to finish that last sentence without chuckling just a little bit.

Even in the Old Testament, thousands of years ago, some women knew that men have a general obliviousness when it comes to women being interested in them. Women knew that to get a man to acknowledge or pursue them, they would have to take action, whether subtly or clearly, depending on what the particular situation demanded.

I will let you in on a little secret: I was not the one to initiate first contact when I first met my bride. Sure, I saw her at the opposite side of the club from me, hanging out with her friends and enjoying a night of two-stepping, but I did not move a muscle. I stood frozen in place. She noticed me and observed I hadn't made a move in her direction. She wanted to meet me, so instead of standing around and waiting for me to do something I might not do, she walked right up to me and introduced herself. Like Ruth, she took the initiative and made the first move when I didn't. *She* approached *me*. I have to say; I am overjoyed that this incredible woman was willing to go after what she wanted. Had she not, she would not have had a diamond ring on her finger months later, and I would have missed out on knowing the most wonderful woman—far beyond my previous expectations for who I imagined myself marrying.

Ladies, I am not suggesting you do all of the work, but you might benefit from helping the men out by making at least a small gesture of interest. You can initiate a conversation or smile in his direction to signal you want *him* to initiate, make eye contact, or be a little flirtatious. It certainly beats the alternative of waiting for a shy man to do something totally out of the ordinary for him by pursuing you because while you are just waiting around, he is probably mentally convincing himself that there's no way you wouldn't reject him. Often the kind of men you want are not proficient at hitting on women, so consider helping him out and get the ball rolling to see what happens! Green light!

Chapter 9

Beyond Happy

Have you ever heard the phrase, "I just want to be happy?" More importantly, at least in my opinion, have you ever observed and noticed that the individuals who seem to spend the most time and energy trying to make themselves happy tend to be some of the most miserable people you know?

I was in the midst of a group conversation with several of my coworkers not so long ago that happened to land on the topic of *happiness*. All of us in the group talked about goals, aspirations, dreams, and ambitions. I talked about my writing this book and the possibility of attending seminary, and the others shared what they ultimately wanted to do with their lives.

Then, after most of us had taken a turn to talk, one of the men in this discussion let loose from his mouth what may be the most hollowed-out answer to a question about life goals. He said, "Look, I don't want to be dragged down by worry or stress, and I'm definitely not out to get rich. The more successful you are, the more problems you're going to have. All I want to do is just be happy."

Now, I can understand why the idea of happiness is appealing to virtually everyone. Here is the problem. Not only is that an unspecific and ultimately meaningless life goal, but I will give you one guess as to what emotion never seemed to cross this guy's face the entire time I worked with him: happiness.

I decided to probe my coworker a little bit: "So, how does one reach that goal? When he's reached a certain quantity or dollar amount of happiness and cashes in?"

He replied, unamused, "I just do it. I focus on things that make me happy. I don't have much, but I have a job, a wife, and a kid, and I avoid stress as much as I can."

Of course, his "just do it" approach did not seem that successful, as he always appeared more bitter than gleeful.

Now, do not get me wrong. It is great to be content with what you have. The contention I had was his logic that his only goal should be doing his best to be happy. He had no dream, no objective, sought no further purpose other than his emotional state, and, beyond that, he seemed to think that the avoidance of stress was the secret to his happiness. It is an unavoidable fact of life that we will experience stress. Some of the most fulfilling parts of our lives come at the end of stressful situations. There is stress involved in most things that I find worth doing, but I find happiness after such tasks that I could never have had without the hardships I endured along the way. There is stress in marriage and definitely in raising kids. If my workmate viewed the concept of anxiety only as a joy-sucking vampire, he would not experience the best parts of fatherhood. But I digress.

I continued my pseudo-interrogation, "and because of those things (job, wife, and child), you are always happy?"

"Of course not!" he replied indignantly.

"No one is. It doesn't seem to work that way. In fact, the more you focus on being happy, the more you will notice when you do not feel happy, and the less happy you will ultimately be."

"And just how would you know that? How do you measure happiness?"

How, indeed. He did not realize it yet, but he had just supported my point beautifully. If happiness is the goal, how do you know when you have reached that goal? What quantity of happiness must you achieve? How long must you hold onto that quantity? How do you maintain that quantity? The easy answer to all of those questions is that you can't. And, if you can't measure it, then how do you know if or when you have reached your goal? If you never know, then you spend all of your time reaching with no success—trapped in a revolving door of disappointment.

Let us say, hypothetically, that you *could* measure your level of happiness. Let's say you fill the measuring cup to your goal quantity. Now what? How do you maintain that goal? Do you make sure that only good things happen around you or to you for the rest of your life?

Do you have the power to guarantee that the measuring cup won't spill or shatter due to some force that you can't predict or control?

Happiness is great, but it *is* an emotion. Emotions are not exactly known for sustainability. Certain things in this world make me happy, and some make me unhappy. Sometimes, those things come from the same source! Take my lovely bride, for example. In general, I am a happier person for having her in my life. When we are together, doing something fun, watching a movie on the couch, going on a romantic date, I'm happy!

Conversely, when she gets sick, or she gets upset about something, or gets mad at me (and it's definitely justified), I am not very happy! I love this woman like crazy, but that does not mean that happiness is the only emotion that she brings to the table of my life. I can't have the good without the bad.

Sometimes, we even do things that promise happiness in the moment but have the potential to make us miserable in the long term. This brings us to the "follow your heart" myth. Emotions are not a good life compass. If I *feel* like drinking a lot of alcohol tonight will make me *feel* good, I can pursue that temporary dopamine rush. Then again, when I am hungover in the morning with a headache and nonstop vomiting, I will be convinced that it was not such a good idea for me to listen to those feelings. That quick pursuit of happy feelings would not bring me sustainable happiness but make me feel utterly contemptible in the end.

If you just do what makes you feel happy all the time, your life will end up a complete disaster. I often feel like staying home from work would make me happy in the moment, but I would feel less happy if I acted on that feeling, skipped work, and ended up unemployed as a result; I may have felt like playing videogames when I got home from work today would have made me happy in the moment, but then I would not have had the satisfaction of writing and finishing this chapter; A man may feel like an adulterous affair with a pretty stranger will make him feel great, but that is only until he sees the disastrous results of his broken marriage and his wife's shattered heart. Chasing that happiness doesn't seem to always result in happiness.

More than just being unreliable as a decision-making method, our emotions are not very resilient through hard times either. Let us say that you win $250 million in the lottery. That would lift your spirits. But what if your mother or another loved one were to die on the same day?

Would you still be happy? I sincerely doubt it, and you would be right not to be happy in that instance.

Emotions are fickle and fleeting things. One emotion can be replaced by another in a fraction of a second, and you will hardly be able to stop it. Just ask my wife, who can be cheerful and giddy all day right up to the millisecond that she sees the truck driving in front of her on the road changing lanes without his turn signal on.

Happiness, like any emotion, is a dependent factor. It depends on external factors—things outside of your control, the world around you, and what does or does not happen.

If your primary goal in life is to "just be happy," then you are unwittingly setting yourself up for countless disappointments. It's a goal that you can't reach because the end of the line does not exist. Even if you reach maximal levels of happiness today, the feeling will drift away. A particular emotion is an unattainable goal because it's always just out of your reach and, the moment you touch it, it rolls away again. The more you focus on achieving a positive emotion, the less you feel it—though you may feel other emotions in its place, such as frustration and discouragement, which will gladly sit on the pedestal you thought you had on reserve for happiness.

If your life is a dinner plate, emotion makes a great seasoning. It adds flavor to our lives. It makes the mundane interesting. It makes us enjoy the once bland meal more. But no one makes the spices the *focus* of the meal! I can assure you that you will never catch me chowing down on a great big bowl of paprika!

Happiness is a fantastic seasoning, but it makes for a terrible meal by itself.

The truth is that no dependent factor should sit on the throne of your heart—not a feeling, not a possession, not an earthly desire. God calls us all to put Him as the main attraction of our hearts, to make Him the priority, to put Him on that throne. To hold something else clenched to our chest in His place is called "idolatry," which is a commandment we don't want to break.

Counting on Someone Else for your Happiness

It seems that every time I watch a romantic movie or television episode that contains a wedding, I inevitably hear one of the characters give a list of reasons why they love their significant other. On that list, without fail, that character says something to the effect of, "I love you because you make me happy." Really? That's why you are marrying this person? You love him because he gives you butterflies and good vibes? Well then, I have some unfortunate news for you: you will not be married for very long.

If your love for somebody hinges on them supplying you with happiness and glee, your love is made from wet tissue paper. It's going to fall apart the moment the tears start to fall and soak into the two-ply fabric, and I promise you, the tears will come eventually. There has never been a marriage free of arguments and the occasional exchanging of negative emotions.

Marriage is a wonderful thing! However, it is not a selfish endeavor. Many marriages fail because one or both spouses got selfish at some point along the way. It is a common denominator of every marriage that ends in divorce—they all have selfishness in common. Of course, human beings are all selfish to some degree, are they not? So, what chance do any of us have at making it through marriage if narcissism is the big relationship killer? Rest easy. It is entirely possible to set aside such a human flaw, even if we cannot completely eradicate it. God and every successful marriage assure us that overcoming is possible and probable.

Time to Digress: The more we allow western culture to focus on and preach to our children the priority of *self-esteem*—the implication that we should always focus on ourselves first, above all others, to be happy and fulfilled—the more obvious it becomes that we are collectively becoming more selfish (and more miserable, by extension) as individuals.

Roger Scruton was the first I heard point out that, if you want to know and understand how selfish individuals in our society are becoming, observe how they dance today compared to many decades ago. Consider what dancing looked like in the 1940s when ballroom dancing was commonplace. A man would politely ask a lady for a dance and respectfully offer his hand to her; if she accepted his hand, the man and woman would step out onto the dance floor together; the couple would then proceed to engage in a partnership that required cooperation and skill to achieve graceful and aesthetically pleasing maneuvers. This method of dancing, such as ballroom or even swing dancing, necessitated mutual connection, respect, and trust and often resulted in genuine appreciation of the individual one was partnering with in the dance. There was a beauty to this—elegance. Over the decades since, dancing devolved to require less human partnership and connection. Folks on the dance floor began to grow apart gradually.

If you were to find yourself in a dance club in 2020, there is absolutely nothing graceful about how people dance. Men do not respectfully ask women to dance anymore but just walk up behind a girl on the dance floor and press their bodies against the girl's behind. The girl, for her part, begins rubbing her behind against the man's private area. This is not a genuine human connection. This is public sexual assault.

There is no looking into one another's eyes, no graceful motion, no partnership, no mutual respect. There is only the display of narcissistic men interested solely in fulfilling their sexual appetite and making it clear by rubbing against a girl they've never met without saying a word. When my friends dragged me to one such dancing establishment years ago, I walked out feeling dirty and violated after mere seconds on the dance floor.

Dance has devolved into a debasing and dehumanizing act that serves only to rob women of dignity and makes everyone involved look like mindless animals, pursuing their base desires. It is no longer about cooperation and human connection but selfish lust.

Marital relationships are a wonderful gift, but boy are they an act of sacrifice! That is one of the gifts that God intends for us within marriage. I understand that the suggestion may seem strange that "sacrifice" is a gift, but it does make us all better people in the long run. Human beings always grow more from pain than pleasure, and sacrifice can bring a certain level of discomfort. Through marriage, we learn to love *sacrificially*, put another individual's needs and desires ahead of our own, and give our everything to somebody other than ourselves!

God said in Genesis that it is not good for a man to be alone (see Genesis 2:18). This is, in part, because it is through a fully committed partnership that a man becomes all that he can be—reaches his fullest potential. He loves more deeply, thinks less of himself and more for another, and seeks to serve and give willingly, and of course, he fathers children, which makes his previous capacity for love seem like a joke. It is good for a man to have a partner to help him be the best he can be.

Lauren guides me to such ends every day, inspiring me to be constantly growing and improving, to give all I can in everything I do (especially in our relationship), whether I particularly like it or not. Lauren is a factor that I cannot understate in why I never gave up on writing this book, even as it felt challenging and frustrating.

So many people, especially under the influence of television and movies, pursue courtship, dating, relationships, and marriage as a means of making themselves happy—for purely self-serving reasons. A healthy, life-long marital commitment is anything but self-serving. Granted, everybody wants *something* out of marriage, or nobody would ever do it. On the other hand, if you make a relationship *all* about you, what *you* can get out of it, how your partner can make *you* happy, you are ironically going to end up very far from a "happy ending."

Doing anything to make ourselves happy, including relationships, will not supply us with sustained joy. As I once heard Mike Rowe say in an interview with Ben Shapiro, "Happiness is a great side effect, but it is a horrible goal."

There is not a single person on this planet who was designed to make you happy! There is no relationship you can form that will result in pure euphoria. Marriage was *never* designed to fill you with bliss. Please do not count on another person to *make* you happy! I am pleading with you: do not put that kind of lifelong pressure on any mortal human being with human limitations! That would be cruel!

Paul writes in the New Testament, "He who marries will have trouble in this life, and I want to spare you this" (see 1 Corinthians 7:28). In Paul's estimation, while marriage is a blessing, singleness is just as much of a blessing in its own right. There are advantages and disadvantages to both. Paul argues fervently that sex is the single greatest motivator for getting married and that anybody who feels sexual urges should find a spouse as soon as possible. Conversely, he clarifies that any man who does not feel a highly motivating sexual drive should remain single. Why would he advise anybody not to get married? The first reason is that single life leaves a man or woman free to pursue God's purpose for him or her without any other obligations, such as with Paul and his unrestricted freedom to be a far-reaching missionary. The second reason is that marriage is *hard!* Marriage is hard as any other thing worth doing. Paul never questions the beauty or value of marriage, but he also never ascribes the term "happiness" to marriage either.

If you are among the many people who blame their singleness for their unhappiness, I must suggest to you that you are blaming the wrong thing. You may not be overly happy with the fact that you don't have a boyfriend, girlfriend, or spouse, but none of those things is going to cure you of depression. If you are not happy single, you will not be happy in a relationship and most certainly not in marriage! To quote the evangelist, and one of my biggest sources of inspiration growing up, Nick Vujicic: "If there is one thing worse than being single and alone, it is being married and alone."

Believe me (and anybody who has ever been married), romantic entanglements are not an effective antidepressant. If romantic relationships were considered a medical prescription for depression, the list of common side effects would include "worsening depression."

You may have heard that famous and overused expression, "two negatives equal a positive." That statement implies that two sad, lonely, miserable people can get hitched and magically make one another happy as a result. There are a lot of expressions that become clichés for good reason because they speak to a valuable truth, but "two negatives equal a positive" does not fall under that category.

Just ponder that claim for a moment. If both of the people in a romantic relationship are miserable and depressed, how does being around another sad downer for life bring about joy? It's expecting light to be created by adding extra sadness to an empty black void of despair; it's expecting a five-star meal to be prepared with sour ingredients; it's trying to climb out of a deep hole in the ground by digging the hole even deeper; it's trying to start a fire underwater.

"Two negatives equal a positive" is a statement that only applies to the multiplication table. It does not have universal application, nor does it work when you *add* two things (or people) together. $(-1)+(-1)=(-2)$. If you add two negatives together, you only succeed in getting farther into the negative. If that doesn't explain it well enough, I have an alternative mathematical equation for you that has some applicable truth to it:

$$X + X = 2X$$

Do not let the appearance of algebra put you off if you are not a fan of math. I'm not a devout fan myself. What this equation means is quite simple, so allow me to explain.

See, the variable (X) in this equation represents a sad, lonely, miserable individual (X=sad person). If you add two of the same variable together, thus putting two miserable people together, the variable does not change. It is still X, and X is still a sad person. You just have two of them in the same place now. One miserable person added to another miserable person equals two miserable people being miserable together.

What if we were to change the equation? What if we replaced one variable with another? Let's say that X still equals a miserable person (X=downer) and that Y represents a happy and content person (Y=upper). Now, let's make a new equation:

X + Y = XY

If we stick to the same mathematical rules, the variables *still* do not change. If you add two different variables together, the variables themselves stay the same; they are just side-by-side now. That is the only difference. The joyful person (Y) did not transform the miserable person (X) into another joyful person (Y), even for another variable (person). People can and have changed in these categories from sad and lonely people to happy and content people, but adding a marriage or a boyfriend/girlfriend to the mix is not how it happens. I know this both from first-hand experience and from basic observation.

If you are the joyful person in the equation above, you will not fix the miserable person or make them happy by your presence. On the contrary, being with you might have the opposite effect of making them even more depressed because of how intimidating your positivity is or how insecure they become for not sharing in your infectious joy. Smiles *are* infectious in a general social sense, but that domino effect does not work the same way in a romantic relationship dynamic. More than that, you may find that miserable people do not generally enjoy being told or having it implied that they need to be "fixed." Take it from a man with a notorious hero complex. I have a history of always wanting to be the guy to "save" the girl, whether it was from a bad situation, poor relationships, decisions, or depression by itself. The result has never been what I had hoped for. Only Jesus saves. I could not give any of those girls what they needed. I could not "save" them from their flaws and brokenness because I am very flawed and broken. We should always show love to those who need it, but that does not mean that what they need is romantic love.

If you are a downer, a happy boyfriend or girlfriend will not make you happy, and neither will another downer! If you are not happy single, you will not be happy in a relationship. Talk to anybody who has ever been married and see if I'm wrong. Ask a happily married individual if being married is what makes them so happy—they will laugh in your face.

Paul writes in Philippians 4:11-13, "...I have learned to be content whatever the circumstances. I know what it is to be in need, and I know what it is to have plenty. I have learned the secret of being content in every situation, whether well fed or hungry, whether living in plenty or in want. I can do all things through Him who gives me strength." And, so that you know, Paul wrote this while he was in prison.

I have learned to be content whether in a relationship or single and alone. It was not always so, but toward the end of my single life, I found joy in pursuing purpose through church and ministry and service—in something beyond myself—and you can find it in whatever purpose you choose to pursue. The kicker is that I was more fulfilled when my focus was not centered entirely on my personal, often selfish, desires. I was content and happy without a wife or a girlfriend. Of course, I still wanted to get married and have a family, but God had some lessons to teach me first.

"Being human always points and is directed to something or some-one other than one's self, be it a meaning to fulfill or another human being to encounter. The more one forgets himself by giving himself to a cause to serve or another person to love, the more human he is and the more he actualizes himself... self-actualization is only possible as a side-effect of self-transcendence."[5]

Only after I learned a certain level of contentment as a single man did God open the door for me to get a wife. I am not saying that He brought a spouse to my door or revealed my "soulmate." I was search-ing for a wife throughout the whole journey. I just had to trust in His timing. I only found her when my pursuit of a spouse wasn't consuming my life and thoughts. Because I wasn't miserable and desperate to find love, I came across as a lot more appealing to the right kind of woman than I would have before—when getting the girl was practically all I ever thought about. It was then that I met Lauren.

Before I could have plenty, I had to learn to be content in the want of singleness.

---

5   Frankel, Viktor. *Man's Search for Meaning.* Pocket Books, 1997.

Chapter 10

God's Fruit vs. Satan's Fruit

In the beginning, God created the heavens and the earth. He created light and dark, land and sea, plants and living creatures. Then, to oversee His creation, God created man from the dust of the earth and breathed His own life into him, a man in His own image, and from man, He created woman. God gave them dominion over the land and allowed them to live in His paradise. God had one rule for His children: do not eat the fruit from the Tree of the Knowledge of Good and Evil.

Then, the devil approached them in the form of a serpent and told them that the fruit from the forbidden tree was superior to the rest—that eating from the tree would make them like God. Ungrateful for the blessings that the Lord had already given them, and wanting more, they ate the forbidden fruit, thinking that it was worth the price of defying God. And so it was that sin and death made their entrance into the world.

In the beginning, man and woman chose Satan's fruit over God's fruit, thinking that it would make their lives better. They didn't want to miss out. Today, we are still making the same mistake.

The world has convinced people that sex is a thing to be enjoyed under any circumstances, with as many people as we like and that it should not be restricted to one partner within marriage. Contrary to God's intent, people believe the more they engage in meaningless sexual encounters and pursue pleasure with no commitment, the better their lives will be. It is not difficult to open our eyes to reality and see just how wrong they are—how destructive to oneself and those they interact with that such behavior can have. God's fruit has *always* been sweeter than Satan's fruit.

Satan's fruit, sexual conduct outside of marriage, is like that bowl of fake plastic fruit that people put on their coffee tables for decoration in the living room. It often looks real, looks good and appealing, but bite into it, and you can tell that something about it is different from the real thing. It doesn't satisfy, and it is not as sweet as the real thing, but instead has a rather hollow and bitter taste. Not to mention, the stuff is not very good for you!

Sir Roger Scruton, one of the great philosophers of our day, said, "Sexual desire presents us with a choice: Adoration or appetite; love or lust. Lust is about taking, but love is about giving."[6] Many cultures throughout history have often chosen to prioritize the latter option of lust. That has never ended well from a cultural standpoint, as history and anthropology demonstrate. History eventually repeated itself in western culture in the 1960s.

In his book, *The Right Side of History,* "[After World War II] there remained a hole in the center of Western civilization; a meaning-shaped hole. That hole has grown larger and larger in the decades since—cancer eating away at our heart. We tried to fill it with the will to action; we tried to fill it with science and world-changing political activism. None of it provided the meaning we seek." Shapiro is entirely correct in his assertion here. Our creator designed us with a need for purpose— the purpose we were intended to find in Him and living out His ways. Instead, the secular world rejects God and encourages us to seek (or invent) purpose elsewhere.

One of those "political actions" that western civilization took up in the search for purpose was the Sexual Revolution in the 1960s—seeking fulfillment through physical pleasure and the normalization of loveless promiscuity. An entire generation prioritized appetite over adoration and lust over love. An entire movement was specifically designed to value *taking* above *giving*.

As the heirs to that generation, is it any wonder that modern women complain so often that men are "self-serving, sex-obsessed pigs?" Ladies, listen to me closely here: if a man is interested in and pursues premarital sex, it is safe to say that his motivation is driven by *lust*—by an interest in *taking*!

Of course, trying to fill the void in our hearts with such goals as pleasure and promiscuity ultimately leads to people feeling more than

---

6   Shapiro, Ben. *The Right Side of History: How Reason and Moral Purpose Made the West Great.* Broadside Books, 2019.

empty. If all you desire is to take—to clench your fist tightly around something that you want—your hand is not free either to give or to receive. You cannot give love or receive it if your hand is wrapped securely around lustful pursuits.

The central claim of the "free love" of the Sexual Revolution ("free love" itself being an oxymoron) is that pleasing ourselves and doing whatever feels good at the moment is the truest and quickest way to happiness. I could not be less convinced that that is true. As the playwright, George Bernard Shaw, said, "Hell is the place where you've got nothing to do but amuse yourself." Now that seems more in keeping with the truth of human nature. Humans are purpose-driven beings, after all. We need something more significant than pleasure for its own sake to feel fulfilled.

Time to Digress: In his book, *Man's Search for Meaning*—a book that I think absolutely everybody ought to read at least once—Viktor Frankl vividly describes his experiences in Nazi concentration camps, as well as his interactions and observations of fellow prisoners. Among his observations, Frankl came to liken the seeking of immediate pleasure or gratification to a lost will to live. He writes that those in the concentration camp who sought some form of purpose amid their suffering, who recognized that there were jobs to do and menial tasks to fulfill, who saw reasons to keep on living and committed their focus to that goal were most apt to survive.

On the other hand, the prisoners who began seeking forms of pleasure, immediate gratification, or temporary release from their suffering were found to have a short life expectancy. Specifically, when Frankl noticed one of his fellow prisoners smoking a cigarette (one of the few options accessible to prisoners for physical pleasure), he knew the man had given up on living and would consequently be dead within 48 hours. When a man's focus in those horrible conditions was not on survival but on whatever physical release he could find, it was akin to deciding that there was no point in trying to live anymore. Consistent with Frankl's theory, every time he saw a man wave the white flag by smoking a cigarette, that man died inside of two days.

One who lives for pleasure and the indulgence of appetites denies one's life of genuine meaning and thus can feel a lack of reason for living. Clearly, not all pursuits are created equal.

Under the lasting influence of movements like the Sexual Revolution, many in Western culture have fallen into the easy temptation of believing that duty and obligation are unpleasant—that they are leeches of joy. Activists parroted a message that claimed, "if we could only be free of the responsibilities demanded of us by society and the obligations of a family—if we were free to do whatever we want whenever we want to do it—we would all be so much happier and enjoy our lives so much more!" That sentiment proves to be absolute nonsense. Imagine, if you will, a world in which nobody goes to work or does their job because they do not feel like being productive. Farmers and ranchers would not produce food for us to eat, businesses would not provide the products that we take for granted every day, the world would fall into chaos. Imagine, as well, a world in which most parents neglect to take care of and provide for their families. It is a disturbing thing to imagine.

Not only does individual obligation provide our world with structure and sustainability, but purpose and direction in our lives are what bring us fulfillment. We gain those things by being responsible for more than just ourselves. A narcissist has no such attachments and is thus left to wallow in misery. We gain purpose and direction through obligation, which we gain, in part, from our spouses and families. Without such things, fulfillment feels near impossible to achieve, and life ceases to feel worth living.

Sex is great, it's wonderful, it's beautiful! We *should* have a desire for it! Those natural desires are from God and are meant to be pursued with gusto! However, they must be pursued and used correctly and within proper parameters. It is like the concept of *liberty* in that sense. I know it seems strange for me to draw a comparison between sex and liberty, but allow me to explain before you conclude that I am talking crazy.

We, in the United States of America, *love* liberty! It was the very core of our nation's founding. We celebrate the idea of freedom and independence with enthusiasm, as we should. Liberty is a wonderful and beautiful thing but, if it is to survive, we *must* have certain rules in place and submit to the moral law to maintain it! Freedom cannot survive in the moral vacuum of anarchy. The Founding Fathers said that this nation could not stand or remain free without a moral and just people, guided by Biblical principles. Liberty demands rules for its value to be preserved.

The same is entirely true for sex; we love it, and we wish to pursue it but, if we make it free and without rules or moral order, it loses its value. If we do not maintain the moral law surrounding sex, it eventually fails to be a beautiful, loving act.

For example, the crime of rape goes very much against the moral law surrounding sex. It is not based on love in any way and is, in fact, among the ugliest and most detestable acts in the world. There is absolutely nothing valuable about the act of sex in this context.

The same can be said about adultery or extramarital sex (though I am certainly not claiming that it is equally as evil as the previous example): it falls outside of the confines of the moral law, and humans inherently understand that it is wrong to break the chains of trust and commitment in such a betrayal. A person may gain some short-lived rush of pleasure from experiencing sex in an adulterous affair, but nothing is fulfilling about it. It is not an act born of love, but of lust; not of giving, but of taking. As such, there is no beauty or value in the sexual act of adultery, nor any other sad imitation of the real deal.

Every single time, throughout all of known history, that culture has rebelled against the Judeo-Christian standard of morality surrounding sex, it has ended badly. Anthropology tells us that marriage is the single most vital stabilizing agent of society. Those who take a "liberated" anti-marriage approach to sex ultimately erode from the inside and collapse.[7] This happens both on an individual level and a cultural level.

Since the Sexual Revolution, divorce rates in our civilization have skyrocketed, the percentage of single parents and children born out of wedlock per capita has gone up exponentially, the number of abortions per year has reached record highs, depression affects more people than ever, and loneliness is the prevailing emotion that the average person describes feeling more than anything. We, as a culture, are not getting better at this stuff. The "sexual liberation" movement is destroying us. We would be fools to believe that there is no correlation between it and all of these problems plaguing our culture since its inception.

God designed sex with a purpose in mind, to be pursued in His way. When we stray from His intentions, destruction ensues. As Scruton put it, we have a choice: Love or lust; adoration or appetite. We can choose to *give* in a marital relationship or *take* or be taken from in an extramarital relationship. We can do things God's way or the world's way. We can eat God's delicious fruit or taste Satan's rotten cast-off fruit.

---

7   Unwin, Joseph Daniel. Sex and Culture. London: Oxford University Press, H. Milford, 1934.

Chapter 11

People are Not Cars

The general mentality regarding sex and dating in the secular culture today is that you *should* have sex with a person before you marry them because you want to make sure you are "physically compatible," whatever the heck that means. People, men and women alike, tend to use premarital sex as some *audition* for commitment. "Try before you buy," as they say so commonly—the phrase being derived from common car salesman lingo. Oh, what a civilization of poets and hopeless romantics we have become.

I can't help but ask, "Seriously?" Is our culture so licentious that we are reduced to depriving human beings of basic human dignity by equating them with machines to be driven? "Try before you buy?" We are talking about human beings here, not cars! You don't "test drive" a person! I wish that were obvious enough that I did not have to say it, but alas, such truth seems lost on the masses. Fine. If the conflation that they want to make is that dating and sex is the same as shopping for a car, then a car analogy I shall use to illustrate the ridiculousness of this "try before you buy" mentality and dating strategy:

A car salesman has a sales quota to meet and money to make. A customer comes to the salesman and expresses interest in the brand new, beautiful car on the lot. The salesman tells him, "Go ahead and take it for a test drive." The customer asks in return, "when should I return it?" The salesman replies, "whenever you are ready to buy it!"

The customer takes the salesman up on his offer and drives the car off the lot. He keeps the car for a long time, free of charge, and then returns it to the salesman years later after his "test drive," which seems to have lasted for 150,000 miles. He says to the car salesman, "here's your car back. I don't want to buy it." The salesman is shocked and of-fended that the man would use his car for so long to refuse to buy the car! He cannot imagine why or how anybody would not buy the car af-ter he let them drive it free of commitment, indefinitely! Now the car is older, has more miles on the odometer, has wear and tear, it's covered in dents and scratches, and only a broke loser would buy it now! Mean-while, that noncommittal customer is now shopping around among the newer models.

Suppose the car salesman makes it his strategy to let people drive cars off of the lot without paying and just hope that they decide to buy the car at some point. Would it be surprising that he never sells the car—that nobody is willing to pay the price when there is no obligation or incentive to do so? And yet, it is considered normal for women to do the same thing with themselves and their bodies. They date men and become sexually active with them for indefinite amounts of time spanning from a day to a decade, only to find themselves back on the lot with no commitment but packing extra miles.

I will say it again: People are *not* cars! They are not designed to be subjected to something as dehumanizing as a "test drive," especially not the indefinite version that seems so common today. If you become sexually active with somebody or, worse yet, move in with them before they marry you, do not be surprised when you find yourself several years older and being returned to the lot.

I don't want that to happen. I want you and everyone else to have more respect for yourself than to open the door to be so callously treat-ed. I want people to refuse to be dehumanized or used, see the value and humanity in others, and refuse to be a user themselves. There are many reasons that God warns us not to be sexually active outside of marriage, but the simplest reason is this: we are not designed for it.

The Human Response to Sex

The true joy of sex goes so far beyond temporary, fleeting physical pleasure—provided it is pursued the right way. It matters more than most people realize what context sex takes place in, whether inside of marriage or outside. There are reasons that God has rules surround-ing sex. The creator of matter, the inventor of our bodies and designer of how they function in every capacity, might just happen to know a thing or two about matters of sex and intimacy. Our bodies yield to His design, and we cannot dictate how they operate. We are dependent upon factors far beyond our control regarding our biology.

What do you think the Bible means when it says, "the two will become one flesh?" What did Paul mean when he wrote, "he who unites himself to a prostitute is one with her in body?" This is very specific and intentional language, and I can assure you that it is not meant to be poetic. It speaks to the actual, literal bond formed between a man and a woman when they become intimate with one another.

Modern science and psychology have *finally* caught up with the Bible on this topic! For centuries, we have read in scripture about this joining of souls due to sexual intercourse and taught that sex binds people together. Many have scoffed at this "religious jargon," dismissing those who believed such things as puritanical party poopers trying to restrict our fun. Now, as it turns out, scientific studies have finally confirmed what God and the Bible have been telling us from the start: sex binds two people together inseparably. The scientific community has nicknamed this phenomenon "sex glue."

This glue-like bond that forms during sexual intercourse manifests itself differently for men and women, respectively. Both processes involve a release of chemicals throughout the body, and both men and women feel the effects of this bond both physically and psychologically.

This bond of God's design is achieved primarily through hormone secretions throughout the body for women. The pleasure hormone dopamine makes a grand entrance to make the experience extra enjoyable. However, the designated hitter when developing a woman's bond to a man during sex is *oxytocin*. This hormone, in particular, has received many nicknames, including "the love hormone" and the apt "bonding chemical." This hormone stimulates strong emotional and mental attachment every time it is released in mass quantities throughout the body.

Oxytocin is the same hormone released throughout a woman's body during childbirth to stimulate contractions and allow the natural process of birthing a child to go more smoothly. It also plays a beautifully beneficial role in bonding a mother to her child from the very moment of birth! Oxytocin continues its role of bonding a woman to her child by being released throughout a woman's body when she breastfeeds, helping to solidify this powerful, emotional, maternal bond. Clearly, this hormone is very versatile, as it plays a wide range of roles in a woman's life wherever love is involved. Yes, God knew what He was doing when He designed women.

However, long before giving birth to a child, oxytocin plays its initial role in the triangle of love during sexual intercourse—bonding her to the prospective father of the child who may be conceived! This is a truly beautiful thing, particularly if done between bride and groom when they have committed to being together for life. When a woman is sexually engaged with a man, the bonding hormone is released in massive quantities, increasing the pleasure of the experience and bonding her physically and emotionally to her partner. Once this bond is formed, it cannot be severed—the moment never taken back. As you can probably imagine, there can be some dire repercussions when this bond is formed outside of a committed, marital relationship.

This unbreakable bond can be rather damaging when a woman moves from man to man, for example, creating unavoidable sexual bonds as she goes. Binding oneself to somebody and then severing that relationship can be damaging enough when done once. When that relationship is broken, the woman leaves a broken-off piece of herself with the man she is no longer with. Remember, sex does not just attach two people together at the hip; it joins two people together *as one body*. There is no way to gently, surgically remove oneself from one's own body. If there is a separation, something is going to break. A woman who moves from sexual partner to sexual partner leaves a part of herself with each man she becomes intimate with, creating a bond of oneness time and time again, with man after man. There is no way to do this without becoming diminished and feeling dehumanized.

The toll on a woman who creates and breaks multiple sexual bonds is not simply emotional or psychological but can also be observed physically in her body. For every man with whom a woman bonds sexually, her body begins to secrete less and less oxytocin. Every time she bonds with a new man, the bonding chemical is released throughout her body in smaller amounts. As a result, she experiences less pleasure and bonds to a lesser and weaker degree with each new partner. Picture the consequences of a weakened ability to form emotional attachments, if you will. Often, this leads to some women seeking out more intense sexual experiences as a subconscious way of trying to achieve the same chemical buzz that they once experienced with their early partners—a buzz that is now unattainable and becoming more so the more they try to achieve it. Some women become rather desperate to achieve that feeling of attachment and will give themselves to virtually anyone willing for a chance of experiencing just a tiny nibble of the real thing. That doesn't sound very liberating to me. Just the opposite. God was intentional in His design of this physiological process and, as I said, knew what He was doing by giving an incentive for life-long unions.

Women's bodies secrete less and less of the love hormone during sex for every new partner for a reason: it is their bodies' natural attempt to protect them. Oxytocin is meant to facilitate the bond between a wife and her husband, to create it, and then maintain that bond for a lifetime. Her body is smart enough to know when she is with a different sexual partner from the last one and, thus, secretes less of the chemical that would bind her to him every time a different partner comes along, thus decreasing the strength of the bond and consequently giving her less of a physical buzz from sex. This is a woman's natural and unconscious defense mechanism against self-destruction. Her designer built the body to understand that giving too much of herself to multiple men will inevitably leave her feeling empty and destroy her from the inside out. So, to compensate for this, the body lessens the strength of the bond, and the woman gives less of herself to each man.

As one can guess, this weakened bonding capability does result in a price being paid for a woman and her spouse when she finally does marry. Sex is, as previously mentioned, a form of adhesive that sticks holds a man and woman together. This intimate connection is meant to bind a husband and wife together in body and spirit—to help them stay as one over a lifetime of commitment. If a wife's ability to physically bond to her husband is compromised, it can make a lifelong marriage more difficult, as the natural bond does not hold on as strong. It is like applying a strip of packing tape to the top of a cardboard box to close it, taking it off, and then trying to apply the same strip to another box. It will not hold as well because the adhesive (holding power) is weaker, and there are remnants of the previous box inseparably attached to the tape.

Of course, a long, happy, healthy marriage is still entirely possible for everyone! All is not lost because one or both spouses have a less than ideal history. It is just not as easy without that full natural connection through sex. This connection is a part of the "sex makes you stupid" affair.

It is common knowledge that sex fogs a person's brain and makes us relatively stupid. This may seem like a negative consequence at first thought, but it is actually by design! Sex has an effect on people's brains during the bonding process that essentially numbs us to seemingly minor flaws and rather stupid habits of our partner, making a spouse more bearable over time and easier to live with. Basically, when a woman is intimate with her husband, some of the flaws in his character get shifted to her peripheral vision, making them less noticeable. Plain and simple, this numbing effect makes it easier for a couple to stick together through rough patches and difficult times. Inside of marriage, this is an ingenious addition to the function and benefits of sex! Outside of marriage, on the other hand, it can be dangerous and detrimental.

Have you ever wondered why a woman you know stays in a long-term relationship with a man who you know to be bad news? Maybe he's just a jerk, maybe he's a deadbeat, or maybe he abuses her, and all you can wonder is why any woman would stay with a man like that! I would give you 9/10 odds that she is sexually active with the man. That is sex glue at work, showing you the destructive capabilities that sex can have if used and abused outside of its proper context.

If you want to make smart, rational, or just not terrible dating decisions and end up with a decent spouse, then the best thing you can do is avoid becoming sexually active before marriage and keep your mind clear! This goes for both men and women, of course, though the bonding process does occur in men a bit differently than it does in women.

Yes, men do secrete oxytocin throughout their bodies as well, but not nearly in as substantial quantities as women do, and certainly not in all of the same circumstances (unless you know a man who can breastfeed an infant). As it seems, a man's bond to a woman during sex appears to be slightly more psychological than physical, at least relative to women. However, there are physiological factors as well, such as the role that the hormone vasopressin plays in the bonding process and promoting a protective instinct towards his partner.

When men have sex, the brain's pleasure centers light up like a Christmas tree at midnight due to a radical release of endorphins. When such high levels of pleasure occur within a man's body, it triggers his brain to begin to save those feelings to memory and file them under the images that he is taking in; thus, the emotions and sexual experience are saved to the same file in his brain's hard drive. His mind documents every detail of the experience and commits it to memory in connection to a sensation.

At the climax of sexual intercourse, when a man orgasms—has a release or ejaculation—whatever the man is looking at or focused on at that moment is what his mind imprints on the most. The dopamine rush in a man is so intense in that instance that the neurons start firing, and synapses form in the brain, linking that immense pleasure with whatever his eyes are lasered on at that moment. This detail of the "sex glue" bonding experience is why psychologists today now recommend that, when you orgasm, you ought to try to make sure you are looking at your partner's face if not directly into their eyes, as opposed to focusing on any other part of her body or something in the surrounding environment.[8]

If a man's attention during the climax of an early sexual experience is on his surrounding environment, then his brain will link the pleasure of that moment to wherever he is, such as a hotel room or even in the back seat of a car, and his mind will be reprogramed to seek out pleasure in those places. It would also behoove a man not to focus on his partner's body parts, breasts, etc. Other women have those parts, but only one has that face and those eyes. The ideal goal is to imprint upon the individual girl rather than on a body, which is a more generic image and can urge him to seek variety rather than exclusivity. He becomes especially likely to crave variety over exclusivity the more women he bonds with. Synapses are formed in the brain throughout the entire sexual experience, cataloging every detail. Still, that final moment during the climax causes the biggest rush of dopamine and, thus, the most influential imprint.

The problem with a man doing this outside of marriage and forming these bonds lies in the fact that his mind and body become trained to what his brain stores in its databanks under "pleasure, emotions, and experiences." His early experiences often dictate what his appetites will later be. Outside of the context of a lifelong commitment, a man's mind during sex is not necessarily bonding to the girl but to the experience itself: the physical stimulus, the excitement, the forbidden nature of the encounter, the arousing images, and the setting and location. The connections in his brain imprint on all of the wrong things, excluding the particular girl and linking the pleasure to the backseat of his car, to the *exhilarating* fact, that he knows what he's doing is wrong, to the excitement he feels in that moment, to the pleasure for its own sake. Furthermore, when a man becomes sexually promiscuous—pursuing a multitude of sexual partners over any period of time—he further trains himself to desire pleasure over the woman and multitude and variety over the individual woman. He learns to crave variety by

8   Wongsomboon, Val, et al. "Women's Orgasm and Sexual Satisfaction in Committed Sex and Casual Sex: Relationship Between Sociosexuality and Sexual Outcomes in Different Sexual Contexts." The Journal of Sex Research, vol. 57, no. 3, 2019, pp. 285–295., doi:10.1080/00224499.2019.1672036.

bonding to multiple different women. The logical conclusion is that the man has a hard time forming meaningful and lasting relationships, and committing exclusivity to one woman becomes a challenge.

When a man's mind creates a sexual link to an experience—rather than to a person—he will always be subconsciously trying to go back and relive that initial pleasurable experience. The crevices of his mind will always be attempting to capture that same thrill, relive that taboo moment, and take in those same sights. Of course, this is not the pursuit of a worthwhile or even achievable goal, which is largely why so many men end up getting involved in weird, creepy sexual practices—trying to enhance the experience to no avail because they have so overstimulated themselves that the most pleasurable experiences now seem dull and unexciting. No good comes from overstimulating oneself with sex.

When a man has had such variety in his sex life before marriage, creating all of these pleasure synapses and developing this drive to enhance the experience, it can be very difficult for him to remain committed to a spouse. To the overstimulated man, exclusivity begins to feel boring or unfulfilling. He begins to crave alternative experiences and taboo ideas such as cheating on his wife and experiencing an exciting affair starts to look very appealing. The man who does not fornicate before he gets married virtually never experiences the same struggles to this degree, though every man will encounter temptation eventually.

In addition, a man who has his first sexual experience with his wife has nothing to compare the experience to. Conversely, a man who has had extensive sexual experience before settling down with his wife may find his mind reverting to past experiences, grading the experiences and comparing them to what he has with his wife. Comparison is the death of contentment. A 2004 study conducted at Brigham Young University delved into this very issue, and their findings were illuminating: Premarital sexual promiscuity not only invites different commitment expectations than marriage,[9] it also changes the comparison levels for expectations and alternatives. The more partners an individual has, the higher their comparison levels of expectations, which originate from

---

9   Hyde, Janet Shibley, and John D. DeLamater. *Understanding Human Sexuality*. McGraw-Hill Education, 2000.

what an individual feels they deserve based on their prior experience and what is understood of others' experiences.[10] (Sprecher, et al., 1991).

In other words, having had more experience, their expectations of what they believe sex should be like changes, and when a partner or sexual encounter with a partner doesn't measure up, expectations are not met. Additionally, the more partners an individual has previously had, the more their comparison levels for alternatives increase. That is, the more sexual experiences they have had with others, the more comparing to other partners occurs, which often decreases the attractiveness of the current choice as expectations for another relationship have yet to be explored and therefore are often exaggerated."[11]

None of what I am saying is intended to deter people from marriage who have made mistakes in the past. Virtually everybody can have a successful marriage, assuming that they are willing and able to do marriage right. For those who have been sexually active outside of marriage and experienced the kinds of bonds that I discuss, it is still entirely possible to have a happy and healthy marriage by God's grace, albeit a bit more difficult. It will generally be harder for those with an extensive premarital sexual history than those without. Better not to do this stuff to begin with, but all hope is not lost by any means, particularly for those who are born again with Jesus Christ. You cannot unscramble an egg, but you can still make a delicious omelet.

Time to Digress: It is, unfortunately, a common practice today for a single man or a woman to try to make themselves feel better with the use of sex. All too often, men have tried to get over a bad breakup with a girlfriend by sleeping with other women; women have sought to feel love or affection by simply giving themselves away to some guy; people have tried on many occasions to fill an emotional hole in their hearts with immoral and detached fornication.

Most of the time, those who try to use sexual sin as medicine (or any sin for that matter) for heartache or loneliness find out too late

10   Sprecher, Susan, et al. "The Effect of Current Sexual Behavior on Friendship, Dating, and Marriage Desirability." *Journal of Sex Research*, vol. 28, no. 3, 1991, pp. 387–408.

11   Christensen, Sherie. "The Effects of Premarital Sexual Promiscuity on Subsequent Marital Sexual Satisfaction ." *Brigham Young University Scholars Archive*, 25 June 2004, p. 41.

that they only end up feeling worse for taking such actions—that they feel hollowed out and far from satisfied.

You cannot mend a chipped glass vase by dropping it, you cannot fix a dented car by crashing it, and you cannot fix yourself by breaking yourself more.

When a man makes love to a woman for the first time on their wedding night, something different seems to happen. The couple has a ceremony before God and their loved ones, celebrating their union; the man has just committed the whole rest of his life to this one woman; after the wedding, the man and woman now cement their union by consummation, giving themselves to one another entirely for the first time. Included with sex in this context, there is love, there is trust, there is God's approval, there is a life-long commitment, there is exclusivity, there is only this other person. When the man engages with the woman, the neurons are still firing, the dopamine is still secreting, the synapses are still connecting, but this time, he is not imprinting on the experience. This time, he is bonding exclusively with the woman.

Context makes all the difference. When the bond is formed inside of marriage, the mind does not create a link between intense pleasure and the situation or visual stimuli. The man creates a link within marriage directly and exclusively to the woman. This man will not always try to recreate a scenario, explore a fantasy, or go back to some cheap rush. When the man links sex to the girl, he will always try to go back to the girl. This kind of intimate bond cannot be formed outside of marriage. It is a major and vital part of what keeps married couples together for life.

When the two grow old, and their bodies change, and their hair goes gray, the glue keeps the man firmly attached to his lady. He's not chasing some temporary pleasure or fleeting experience. He's 72, and he is still chasing the girl.

God designed us this way for a reason. He invented sex with a purpose and added pleasure as a gift to allow us to join with our spouse and deeply enjoy loving our spouse. If we abuse His gift and use it contrary to His intention, then the pleasure in its most temporary form is all we'll get out of it, and it's all we'll chase after. If we do it right, then we get the real deal, and we'll always be chasing after the girl.

For Further Study:

Insel, Thomas R., et al. "Oxytocin, Vasopressin, and the Neuroendocrine Basis of Pair Bond Formation." *Advances in Experimental Medicine and Biology*, 1998, pp. 215–224., doi:10.1007/978-1-4615-4871-3_28.

Keroack, Eric J., and John R. Diggs. "Abstinence Statistics and Studies: Bonding Imperative." *Abstinence Clearinghouse*, 30 Apr. 2001.

Chapter 12

The Purpose of the Honeymoon

God knew exactly what He was doing when He designed us. He *definitely* knew what He was doing when He invented sex! You can be absolutely sure He knew what He was doing when He provided us with rules and guidelines outlining how His invention is best to be put into practice.

God knew that waiting until marriage to have sex would develop character, patience, trust, and a deep appreciation of His invention—as well as of the person we choose to share the joyful experience with. Anyone can casually pursue sex outside of marriage and give in to their every desire. Those who brag about their casual sexual conquests are boasting about doing the most damaging thing a person can do: give in to temptation and desires of the flesh. It takes little effort to pursue every amoral sexual urge. Still, such pursuits dilute the experience of something that is supposed to be wonderful, making it seem meaningless and even dirty. Sex without trust, commitment, love, patience—but built purely on a foundation of lust—is hollow, like anything else that comes unearned.

The greatest pleasures in life come only in the aftermath of the pain and hardship required to earn them! Ask an Olympic gold medalist how much immediate gratification they felt while training for hours without end, seven days a week, year after year, in preparation for the Olympic games! They'll tell you that the gratification wasn't there yet, just the long-term pursuit of it. But, it was pure euphoria when that same athlete finally crossed the finish line after working so hard for so long, delaying gratification to reach their desired endgame! The pleasure of that achievement was without match because they had earned what few ever will by putting forth an effort that most will not! Those who achieve the highest joy and pleasure are ironically masters at delaying joy and gratification!

Compare that gold medalist to a person who pursues nothing *but* pleasure. They don't work endlessly for what they want; they resign themselves to doing whatever feels good at the moment. They don't aim for some great achievement; they may play video games all day, drink *Dr. Pepper*, eat any food that sounds fattening, and possibly develop a fondness for recreational drugs. Whatever appeals to them at the moment. If this person ever *does* have a job, his only goal is to make it to the end of the shift and go back to the lazy activities that give him his fix of immediate gratification. Those who *always* act on their desires and pursue the quick and convenient pleasures end up being a disaster and wasting their life.

When it comes to my writing, the process can be downright painful. I often become frustrated, exhausted, anguished. I have trouble thinking of something to put on paper, maintaining focus, writing pages of material only to realize they don't work and have to be discarded, realizing I need to do more research on a particular topic. Writing a book is occasionally grueling, tedious, and migraine-inducing, particularly for the less experienced writers. Then, I finish a chapter and bask in the attainment of a milestone! I feel immense pleasure at its completion because it was *hard,* and hard is good. I could have done something more instantly gratifying with my time, such as turning on a television sitcom or playing a game. Still, I would have been ungratified because I realized that I did not accomplish anything by the end of the day. I wasted several hours of my life that I could have put to better use.

The best things in life cannot be gained immediately or effortlessly. Joy and fulfillment tend to follow patience and effort exclusively. The greatest achievable pleasures are earned through grit and determination. This way, when you finally receive your prize, not only is it supremely enjoyable but there is often profound meaning behind it! If we are talking about sex, then the best thing about it comes from waiting as well! The supreme enjoyment and profound meaning come from patience and manifest themselves during this thing called a *honeymoon*—the time after a wedding, usually no less than a week, when the bride and groom finally come together and enjoy one another.

The honeymoon is not just some vacation that people take after their wedding to get out of work! It is a tradition that stretches back to the beginning of recorded history, not to be cheapened or taken lightly. After the wedding ceremony, the bride and groom consummate the marriage by giving themselves to one another in body and spirit. This is the last step of a marriage that officially makes a couple "married"— one flesh. In the times of Genesis, after a wedding, the bride and groom would remain in the marriage tent for seven days and nights—enjoying one another, learning how to please one another, growing their bond of love and trust by giving the gift of themselves. This honeymoon experience is an absolutely beautiful and incredibly meaningful thing if done right.

The Song of Solomon, in very poetic form, paints a fine picture of what this phenomenon of joining together on the wedding night is supposed to look like. As a bonus feature, the entire book is proof that God is not a prude and that it is perfectly alright, if not encouraged, for us to talk about sex. In the early chapters, this romantic book of the Bible describes the man's courtship of his love from both the perspective of the man and that of the woman. It is obvious from the language used that the two were passionate and had the near-overwhelming desire for sexual intercourse! Of course, there was no grotesque language, cat-calling, degrading treatment, or disrespectful banter being exchanged here. This man knew how to speak to a lady and treat her properly. To his great challenge, treating her respectfully also implied refraining from touching her sexually before he has ceremoniously committed to being by her side for life. The passion between the two lovers is clear, but these two, while hit hard with natural desires, practiced patience and self-control, saving all of that passion and allowing it to build up for the wedding night. They knew it would be worth the wait!

Chapter 3 of Song of Solomon briefly describes their wedding day. Solomon shows up being escorted by sixty impressive warriors in a fancy carriage made of imported wood, silver, and gold, being pulled by great stallions, and radiating myrrh and incense. Men, you had better have at least a limousine or some other peasant luxury to compete with this guy! The wedding takes place, and then we read the poetic interpretation of the only honeymoon recorded in detail in the Bible. You cannot read it without seeing how remarkably special this night is for the writer!

In chapter 4, Solomon describes his wedding night from his point of view. Mostly, he describes his bride and what he sees through his own eyes:

"How beautiful you are, my love, how beautiful! Your eyes are doves behind your veil!" You do not have to be poetically inclined to appreciate how the man describes his lady. She is the most beautiful woman in the world to him and, when he looks into her eyes, he sees her purity like that of a white dove.

"Your hair is like a flock of goats leaping down the slopes of Gilead." Alright, so perhaps that is not the compliment that I would personally give my bride—comparing her to a bunch of smelly farm animals. However, his meaning can probably be taken far better than his literal words. Solomon essentially points out that her hair is being let down and flowing freely. Letting one's hair hang naturally and loose was not customary at this time, so this private extravaganza is the first time he gets to see this beauty's gorgeous hair fall and wave. It is an intimate sight to him—something no other man ever gets to see—and clearly, he loves it.

"Your teeth are like a flock of shorn sheep coming up from washing, all of which bear twins, not one among them is missing." So, she had great, shiny, pearly white teeth! And she has them all, nice and straight! And this is before the existence of *Crest*, *Listerine*, and toothbrushes, I might add! Not to mention, I doubt that she had access to a quality orthodontist. With all that in mind, such great teeth are a pretty impressive feat for a lady to the writer. Remember to brush your teeth, kids! No romance has ever been worse off for involving quality dental hygiene! I have yet to meet a woman who looks better with no teeth or a man who can make brown or black ones attractive. So, don't forget to floss, and make sure your breath is always minty fresh! It's good insurance against dying alone.

"Your lips are like a scarlet thread, and your mouth is lovely. Your cheeks are like halves of a pomegranate behind your veil." The man loves how soft his lady's lips are. She has a great mouth, probably due to that great dental hygiene. Her cheeks are round, full, and colorful, making her look extra sweet. Sorry, I couldn't resist a bad fruit joke.

"Your neck is like the tower of David, built in rows of stone; on it hangs a thousand shields, all of them shields of warriors." Even the woman's neck does not escape the man's notice. One can probably assume that it is round, slender, smooth, strong, and upright. That must be one heck of a neck! I don't know about you, but I have never found a neck so fascinating I felt compelled to write a poem about it!

"Your two breasts are like two fawns, twins of a gazelle, that graze among the lilies." I don't know if you have ever been deer hunting, but I, myself, am quite fond of it. Anyone who has ever been hunting for deer knows how skittish they can be. To get the jump on a deer, the hunter must move quietly, slowly, and cautiously, lest the deer be alerted to the tiniest sound or scent and dart away. Gazelles are much the same way. They are cautious, easily startled, and hard to catch for any hunter who doesn't have a long-range rifle. Hunting them is a very delicate operation. Any predator must take great care to get anywhere close. Solomon is saying, "handle with care." He is approaching his bride delicately and respectfully. Her body, which is a part of something precious, is not to be roughly handled but treated as gracefully and tactfully as someone would handle a priceless artifact because "priceless" doesn't begin to cover her value to him and Him.

"Until the day breathes and the shadows flee, I will go away to the mountain of myrrh and the hill of frankincense." If Solomon's descriptions of his lady love, and the parts of her body that he enjoys start from the top of her head and descend downward from there, and he ends up at a fragrance-rich mountain, I will give you one guess as to what the "hills" are a metaphor of. He is talking about his wedding night, after all! And this is where he wants to be "until the day breathes, and the shadows flee." Translation: "I'm gonna love you **all night long**!" This couple waited until their wedding night to make love, and now they intend to enjoy one another as best and as long as they can.

"You are altogether beautiful, my love; there is no flaw in you." He loved and enjoyed every bit of this girl, all the more so because he had to wait for her—had to earn her. He paid with the commitment of the rest of his life to have her—a very high price—and so, he realizes her value.

Solomon later describes his new bride as a private garden and a water source that only he gets to drink from and be satisfied. He has the honor of being the only one to be joined to this woman and enjoy her high-hanging fruits. He takes great joy from the knowledge that she chose him exclusively. We can easily get the impression that the lady gets the same joy when she says, "let my beloved come to his garden, and eat its choicest fruits."

God's fruit is sweet, indeed.

Solomon, of course, was not a perfect man. Throughout his lifetime, he did many sinful things, including things along these same lines of lady love and marriage. He married hundreds of women, which we would rightly call into question today, and many of the women he desired and married were pagan and ungodly women who distracted his attention from his God. Solomon was not oblivious to the wrongs he had done and wrote about them and laments them at length in Ecclesiastes. However, what he did right before falling off the moral wagon is still worth writing about and celebrating, even imitating—so long as we only imitate the good things.

Safety in Marriage

You need not take my word for it that sex is best enjoyed within the proper context of marriage. Studies have been performed, and it has been scientifically proven that sex inside a committed marital relationship is far more pleasurable and fulfilling (i.e., better)! Yes, science has once again finally begun to catch up with the Bible! Studies on sexual satisfaction have shown that single women who engage in premarital sex seldom have a climactic experience physically. That is to say nothing of the emotional side of the equation. Further study indicates that Christian *married* couples have better and more fulfilling sex lives than any other demographic! Single college students do not even come close.

Sex in its intended form takes place within the safety and trust of a life-long commitment. If you do not yet believe me when I say that, let's at least agree that to achieve the best version of sex, both partners need to be fully engaged and turned on. Is it fair to start from that premise? Both the man and the woman in the room need to be willing and *eager* participants to achieve the best possible results.

Now, with that basic standard in mind, let me pose a question to the ladies: If you do not feel safe with the man you are with; if you do not fully trust him; if you suspect that he's not thinking of you during an intimate moment or that he was intimate with another girl within the last week; and if you have sincere doubts that he genuinely loves you and values your well-being, how turned on and romantic would you feel in that moment? Answer honestly. If you are honest, you most likely didn't hesitate to say that you wouldn't be excited or eager at all if you did not feel safety, trust, exclusivity, security, or affection. A healthy woman needs to feel all of those things to be aroused and romantically motivated!

Proponents of premarital sex have a problem! I have heard it argued fervently that the "excitement" of casual or taboo sex maximizes the pleasure of the experience, but casual and premarital sex lacks the key ingredients to turn a woman on in all the right ways: safety, trust, exclusivity, security, and affection! So, if both partners have to be maximally eager to get the best results in the area of intercourse, but a woman cannot reach the ideal level of arousal in this context, then extramarital sex cannot possibly be the best form of sex! I do not deny that people can find it pleasurable and exciting, but only marriage can provide the necessary ingredients for the best possible sexual experience.

That is what a wedding ceremony does: it expresses the ultimate level of trust in one another by stating, "I trust you with the rest of my life"; both partners express that they feel safe in one another's arms; bride and groom make one another feel secure in their mutual promise to honor one another; the new married couple vows exclusivity when they promise, "I will love you and only you until the day that I die."

Via the wedding ceremony, all essential ingredients for the best version of sex are in play. It is then, and only then that the two can enjoy each other to the fullest. That is not to say either partner will be great in bed that very first time on that first night together! No one ever is! But, if that first time is within the trusting and safe confines of a new marriage, it doesn't matter, and there is absolutely no reason to feel insecure about it. Just the contrary! Exploring this new experience together, learning together, and quite possibly laughing through it together is all part of the wonderful fun!

Chapter 13

Cohabitation

My wife, Lauren, talked to me recently about a discussion topic in her college psychology class. The professor brought up the subject of marriage compared to the national rate of divorce. She asked the class what factors might contribute to a lasting marriage and to preventing divorce. One of the first to speak up and answer the professor's query, "The length of time that the couple lived together *before* they got married!" This answer was reportedly followed by several classmates' affirmations and nods of agreement.

The professor of this psychology class, to her credit, answered this student honestly and straightforwardly, "Actually, studies have shown that people who live together before getting married have a far greater chance of divorce, relative to those who did not. More still, the longer a couple lives together out of wedlock, the higher their statistical chance of divorce becomes."

I was not personally present in this class. Still, my reliable eyewitness claims that there was a mass gasp of disbelief and murmurs of indignation throughout the lecture hall in response to the professor's clarification of the truth. It seems that nearly everyone was taken aback and, indeed, offended by that little nugget of truth. The professor then answered their dismay with, "I know, I was surprised to learn that too!"

Cohabitation—the term for living with a significant other without being married—is a strategy composed by people who are afraid of committing to another person but who still want all of the perks that come along with marriage: shared income, companionship, someone to share the load of chores, and of course sex, among other things.

A man will often agree to live with his girlfriend because he knows it means that he gets to sleep with her consistently, but he does not have to make a life-long commitment to her. He can still keep one foot in the back door if he ever wants to make an exit and move on to another girl.

A woman might agree to move in with her boyfriend because she sees it as a step in the right direction (though the reality is that she is taking a giant leap in the wrong direction). She wants him to stay with her, commit to her, have a family with her, and she thinks that, as long as she gives him what he wants and keeps him happy in their now shared bedroom, that will eventually happen. Surely if he sees how great it is sharing his life with her, he'll eventually have a miraculous revelation and decide to make the arrangement permanent by giving her a diamond ring and reciting a list of vows!

The problem with that woman's line of thinking is that, by agreeing to this cohabitation arrangement, she has already given him pretty much everything he is after! If the man wants affection and sex, and she gives it to him in spades by moving in with him, he has managed to con her into fulfilling his intended desires without his having to make a serious commitment! She has now eradicated his incentive to give himself to her entirely! She has fully become the car salesman from chapter 11.

I have known far too many women who wasted *years* (even decades in some cases) of their lives with men in these living situations, only to walk away with broken hearts eventually. They waste precious years with a man, hoping that he'll eventually marry her, but he doesn't feel the need to commit to her since he's already gotten everything he wants without the involvement of a ring. Then, one day when he's bored or frustrated, he leaves her behind, devastating her. Setting aside the terrible mental and emotional damage and anguish that this song and dance inflicts upon a woman, if she does this long enough, she eventually hits her expiration date (so to speak). Believe it or not, none of us will live forever, and our youth and vigor have a shelf life.

If a woman intends to get married and have a family, it is best to do it young—as young as possible within reason. By the age of 27, the average woman has only 12% of her eggs remaining; some have more, some may have less. Unlike men who can theoretically make kids when they're 80, there comes a time when she can no longer physically conceive and bear children. Not to mention that, on a medical level, when a woman has her kids by the age of 25, her chances of living to 100 practically double, relative to those who have kids later! It's healthier for both her and for the children she has. Women were not designed to wait until their 30's to start thinking about having kids.

With that being said, if a 23-year-old woman spends six years of her life with a guy and he doesn't marry her, she is now 29 and still single. If she spends another eight years with another guy, now she is 37, still single and childless. And now, only men in their 50's seem interested in dating her, but they don't want to have kids at that age even if she could still conceive against all odds. You may not think that that seems fair, but that's how it is.

If my mother had agreed to move in with my father, out of wedlock, when he tried to convince her to do so all those years ago, I guarantee that I would not exist. Nor would any of my biological siblings. He would have lived with her for a couple of years, had his fun, and moved on to the next girl leaving my mother abandoned and heartbroken. Lucky for me and three other people who share my genetics, my mother was not so naïve as to give in to the pressure and allow my father to take an indefinite test drive without buying the car.

Men who live with women outside of wedlock are users. I am sorry if that seems too harsh or blunt for your liking. That is the absolute truth of the matter. They don't want to marry the girl. They want a sex partner whom they can use for an extended period while promising that "we're slowly moving in the right direction," and then move on. These men like having the freedom to leave and move on at their leisure. Ladies, that is not the kind of man you can expect to commit the rest of his life to you. I question why you would even *want* to marry a man like that.

Of course, cohabitation may not mean every time that you won't have kids. However, those kids deserve far more than to be born into a pre-broken home. With marriage comes stability. With cohabitation, you are playing Jenga with your partner every day, with the whole relational structure ready to collapse at the slightest misstep.

I know a girl personally who got caught up in this cohabitation scheme. I have known this individual for many years and given her advice on many occasions, which she usually ignored. I fervently advised her against moving in with her boyfriend, but people rarely listen to reason when it conflicts with something they want badly to do. This girl moved in with her boyfriend against my advice.

She lived with her boyfriend for years, but they never got married. Then, she got pregnant. When she found out about her pregnancy, she feared that her boyfriend would not take it very well. She was pleasantly surprised and overjoyed when he didn't freak out or choose to abandon her when she told him about the pregnancy (although the fact that she reasonably thought that he would leave should have raised many red flags early on in the relationship)! The two of them had the baby, and it seemed to her like she was getting everything she wanted. She had her own little family, but she and her boyfriend never married. She may have thought at the moment that she was living her dream life, but she just saw the view from the top of the Jenga tower, completely ignorant to the fact that most of the base pieces were already missing. The tower was ready to topple if she made another move.

A year later, she got pregnant again. This time, her boyfriend did freak out as she feared the first time around. He packed his belongings, leaving her and her infant child behind, with a second child on the way. She couldn't afford to live in the apartment on her own, and all of the money was in *his* bank account, so she lost her home, and she and her child were homeless and broke, again with a third mouth to feed on the way. She was at least lucky enough to have a family member who was willing to let her move into their home temporarily.

Because my friend and her boyfriend never got married and chose to live together, he had no legal obligation to stay and virtually no consequences for leaving her behind. He felt no marital bond with the girl and thus had no problem walking away from her. I agree only a scummy and depraved individual would do such a thing. Still, it happens in most instances when two people "start a family" before setting the family's foundation with marriage. There was no safety net for the girl without marriage, no divorce decree saying that half of all the man's assets went to the family he abandoned, no child support, no anything.

This girl unwisely shared her life and home with a man who had only ever proved that he was not willing to commit to her. He would not marry her, and yet she surrendered her body to him; he would not marry her, and yet she lived with him; he would not marry her, and yet she thought he would step up and be there for her and her children for a lifetime. She gave him what he wanted and, in return, as soon as he didn't want to be with her anymore, as soon as she was no longer convenient, he left her alone with no money and two kids.

Forcing the marriage issue could have saved this woman (and her children) a world of heartache if he had responded positively to the issue and taken the honorable route of marrying her. If he went the other direction and left her because she would not give him what he wanted unless he committed his life to her, then great, she won't waste any more time on a man who proves himself a poor investment of said time.

If a person, man or woman, doesn't want to marry but wants to live with you, dump that person and move on! If an individual finds it to be a deal-breaker that you won't sleep with them or move in with them until after they marry you, then you know you've made the right decision by leaving them! That is not an individual of character. You will be much better off finding someone who will put marriage first.

Cohabitation Myths

Couples living together out of wedlock are unfortunately very common today, especially among millennials. Many who engage in this behavior see it as a step towards marriage. Others find marriage meaningless and would rather conveniently avoid the institution altogether. Many myths surround the increasingly common practice of cohabitation that warrant busting. If you are not yet convinced that cohabiting with a partner outside of marriage is a bad idea, I hope that exposure to a few documented facts about the practice gives you cause to avoid it at all costs.

Myth #1: Living together while dating is good practice for marriage and will help us decide if we are compatible.

Truth: People who live together before marriage are significantly more likely to end their relationship in divorce if they marry at all. As David Gudgel laid out in *Before You Live Together*, "Of eight couples that live together before marriage, four of them will split up, and they will not marry. Of the four that marry, three of them will divorce." This has been a well-documented fact in the field of family science for decades, and sources such as the *Journal of Marriage and Family* assure us that the facts have not changed.

Living together prior to marriage as a strategy to determine whether or not to get married only teaches you to have an escape plan. You don't want to commit, so you ease yourself into the room while always keeping one foot out the door. You are not thinking sacrificially or in terms of what you can do for your partner, but rather you are training yourself to look out for your interests alone. Eventually, this lone wolf escape plan mentality changes one's attitude towards marriage, and escape is cemented in your brain as an eternally viable option.

Living under the same roof as a boyfriend or girlfriend also makes breaking off a bad relationship significantly more complicated. When you share your home with somebody, breaking up is not as simple as saying goodbye at the end of the day and walking in opposite directions. A cohabiting couple shares more than just an address. They share in the living expenses, the Netflix accounts, each of their belongings are together and intermingled, their entire lives become interwoven one way or another. Breaking up would be a messy and complicated affair at that point, so even if it is necessary to terminate the relationship for any number of reasons, one or both of the partners postpone the break-up or neglect to do it all together because it's easier not to. Those two people have no business continuing the relationship, much less getting married. Still, these relationships often lead to marriage and then a messy divorce—significantly harder than just breaking up.

Cohabitation does not make for good practice at being married. Rather, it is great practice for developing warm feelings towards emergency exits and bailout parachutes.

Myth #2: Living with my boyfriend or girlfriend will help us out financially, allowing us to pool our finances and become more financially stable before taking the extra step towards marriage, lowering our chances of divorce.

Truth: Let me point out that having money does not make for a successful marriage. Money is a great tool, but if you make it your focus over your partner because you think it will make your lives easier, I feel inclined to inform you that there are many divorced, rich people in the world. Entire books have been written informing people that having a lot of money when you get married does not have a correlating effect on your chances at a lasting marriage, although your view of money might.

More to the point, studies have shown that couples who live together before marriage have a lower average accumulation of wealth than couples who married without living together first. There is a direct correlation between marriage and higher net worth.

Evidence suggests that cohabiting couples are less inclined toward long-term planning, particularly in the financial arena, because their futures are undefined. They have not determined to share their life with their roommate, and so the future is less of a point of focus. The couple does not plan for a future together because they may not have one together. And, since cohabiting has a marked effect on a person's outlook on marriage and divorce, as pointed out, those financial habits are not guaranteed to wear off even after a formerly cohabiting couple marries. Compare that to married couples who have already determined that they will be together for life and thus plan for the future they fully expect to share.

Not only do married couples generally have a higher propensity for long-term planning and wealth accumulation, but there are financial benefits to marriage that extend beyond their habits. *Consumer Reports* assures us that married couples enjoy lower insurance premiums, more tax benefits, social security, and retirement fund options, and all of that coexists with the combination of incomes.

A married couple can fully combine their incomes and manage their finances as a team. The uncertainty that accompanies cohabitation makes the arrangement between boyfriend and girlfriend less than plausible. Financially, marriage has every advantage over cohabitation, and even couples who do eventually marry after living together first are hard-pressed to reap the full benefits.

Myth #3: Cohabitating couples can raise children just as well as married couples.

Truth: As couples living together has become more normative, so has the stigma of having children out of wedlock begun to dissipate. In 1970, barely more than 10% of children in the U.S. were born to unmarried parents. By 2018, that percentage had been quadrupled—40% of children were born out of wedlock. Some call this liberating. I see it as corrosive for many reasons, including but not limited to the gradual collapse of the family, the structural erosion of society, and of course, the instability that becomes unavoidable in the child's life as a result.

Marriage offers an essential structural foundation to society, and it provides security for the mating couple. Still, more to the point, it provides security and structure both for the children of those parents. Children develop better and lead far better and healthier lives when they grow up with familial stability. There is no reality in which cohabitation can provide the same safety and structure as marriage.

When a child is born to an unmarried couple, he is significantly more likely to end up in a single-parent home, experience abuse or neglect, develop severe depression and anxiety, experiment with substance abuse and sex, less likely to succeed in school and career, and more likely to spend time in prison. It is almost unheard of for unmarried parents to stay together in a relationship throughout the child's life, and so the child ends up in an unstable situation through no fault of his own.

I have heard some geniuses say that parents splitting up doesn't affect their children all that much as long as the parents stay on decent terms with one another and both see the children. Just think about that claim for a minute. A child needs security and consistency, and said child is supposed to find that in his family. When a child is young, his parents are his whole world. He relies on them for everything. They provide him with the love and safety he needs. They make up his sense of reality—whatever he sees his parents do, the child thinks, "That is life. That is how the world works." If the parents are that child's whole world, then having the parents split up is like Grand Moff Tarkin taking a Death Star to the kid's home planet. The safety, consistency, and security have all been blown up along with the rest of the child's world. If you destroy a kid's world, they inevitably experience what feels like abandonment and something that the kid can't identify but feels entirely contrary to love.

Raising kids and having a family as a cohabiting couple is not the same as doing so within the confines and commitment of marriage. Cohabiting couples seldom see the raising of children together. The whole situation gets very messy and disorganized quickly the second that the living situation starts to fall apart. When the couple splits, the children pay the price. Children born to unmarried parents are put at a lifetime disadvantage right out of the gate. I would think that a loving parent would want to give their child the best chance at a possible great life. If you want to do that, get married before having sex and starting a family.

Better to Marry

When I started dating Lauren, we both knew that there would be no sex before marriage, as I was not a user, and she had no intention of ever being used. She would never have agreed to sleep with me—much less live with me—until I had committed the rest of my life to her and her alone. 1 Corinthians 7:9 says, "...it is better to marry than to burn with passion." Well, after just over three months of dating this woman, my clothes were at risk of catching fire. I was burning up so bad! So, I proposed to her as soon as possible and we planned our wedding.

Some would say that I moved too fast toward marriage, but I wholeheartedly disagree. I knew I would spend my life with her, and I knew that I had a burning passion for her, so I had to commit to her to fulfill that passion. You might say that I was a man with *incentive*. That's what a man has when the girl doesn't give her body to him on the first date or let him have her any time by moving in with him.

When they find out that Lauren and I did not live together before we got married, most people are taken aback. They are genuinely astonished! They insinuate, "that's rare; that is just not the way people do it these days; it is not normal for young people to do things that way today!" Sadly, they are right—it is far from normal in western culture today for two people to get married *before* they live together and have a sexual relationship. It is completely out of the norm to do things correctly and live life right. Thankfully, Lauren and I did not want to be *normal* by today's standards. *Normal* is living in sin, normal today is divorce, normal is relational dissatisfaction, normal is bringing baggage of all kinds (predominately sexual) into a marriage, normal is broken homes and kids growing up without both parents. So, yes, my bride and I are quite happy to venture outside of the current status quo and to live life a better way.

Living with a person out of wedlock is not a "trial period" or a "test drive" to see if two people can make the real thing work. That is the mindset of someone who always considers leaving to be a valid option—of someone who thinks, "this person is good enough to use for now, but I do not think I can justify loving and cherishing them." The reason that people who cohabit *before* marriage have such a high divorce rate relative to people who don't is that they are, all the while, training themselves to worry about divorce and to constantly think about leaving, thus cementing the idea in their mind that it is going to happen, making them suspect that it is the inevitable conclusion. At that point, the prophesy becomes self-fulfilling. They will leave. It just becomes a matter of how long they choose to stick it out.

When people commit their lives to one another through marriage, absent of that preemptive nonsense, they are exclaiming that leaving is not even in the cards. They are shouting for all the world to hear, "No matter what, baby, I am going to be by your side until the day I die."

For Further Study:

Akerlof, George A., and Janet L. Yellen. "An Analysis of out-of-Wed-lock Births in the United States." *Brookings*, The Brookings Institution, 25 Jan. 2018, www.brookings.edu/research/an-analysis-of-out-of-wed-lock-births-in-the-united-states/

Braverman, Beth. "The Financial Benefits of Marriage." *Consumer Reports*, 8 Feb. 2018, www.consumerreports.org/marriage/financial-benefits-of-marriage/

Gudgel, David R. *Before You Live Together*. Regal, 2003.

Martin JA, Hamilton BE, Osterman MJK, Driscoll AK. Births: Final data for 2018. National Vital Statistics Reports; vol 68, no 13. Hyattsville, MD: National Center for Health Statistics. 2019. https://www.cdc.gov/nchs/data/nvsr/nvsr68/nvsr68_13-508.pdf.

Rosenfeld, Michael J., and Katharina Roesler. "Cohabitation Experience and Cohabitation's Association With Marital Dissolution." *Journal of Marriage and Family*, vol. 81, no. 1, 2018, pp. 42–58., doi:10.1111/jomf.12530.

https://www.dropbox.com/s/4gug34svvt4hk5q/WFM-2017-Essay-Embargo.pdf?dl=0

Chapter 14

The Toxicity of Porn and Fantasy

I confess I did not hang out with the best, most admirable crowd in high school. My parents could not stand some of the friends I kept company with, often for a good reason. My parents thought I was rather impressionable and that my friends were a bad influence. They were right, of course, though that did not stop me from pretending otherwise—the dumb kid that I was.

I was hanging out at my buddy Landon's house when I was about 17 years old and living in suburban Texas. His parents were not home, and only the three of us were at his house, Landon, Greg, and me. We were all just wasting time, hanging out, and playing video games.

My friends decided things were getting rather dull, and the night wasn't fun enough. Suddenly, in a fit of brilliance, Greg decided we should all go swimming in the public pool in Landon's neighborhood. Here's the catch: it was past 1:30 in the morning, and the pool, behind a locked gate, had been closed many hours. Evidently, to my friend's logic, that was the exact reason it was such a good idea—because the pool was closed, there was nobody else there, and we would experience the fun of having to break in. You know, the kind of thing people get arrested for.

Looking back, a smart person, upon hearing Greg's superb and magnificent plan for us to break into a place to go swimming illegally, would have immediately responded, "uh... no?" My dilemma? I was not a smart person. How did I respond to my friend making this suggestion? I believe it went something like this: "Trespassing? Crime?

Pointless? Not worth the risk of getting into legal trouble? That sounds like the best idea I have ever heard!"

So, all three of us Nobel-worthy geniuses put on a pair of athletic shorts as makeshift swimsuits, left Landon's house, and walked a couple of blocks down the road in the middle of the night to the neighborhood's public pool. As expected, the whole place was locked up. The only light on the inside of the fence was shining up from below the pool water. The fence, partially covered in foliage, was not overly difficult to scale. The three of us made it over the fence and onto the illegal side just fine. Once we were all on the side of the pool fence, we jumped in one by one.

The three of us spent somewhere between 30 and 45 minutes hanging out in that pool, swimming, dunking one another's heads under the water, talking about teenage guy stuff such as who was into what girl at school, along with other locker room-type conversations.

After a while in the pool, we heard voices on the other side of the fence. It was dark, and the fence was covered in vegetation in places with no hedge so that we couldn't see anybody, but it was easy to tell at least two people were standing outside the pool area by the parking lot. Neither my friends nor I knew whose voices we were hearing, but none of us were particularly keen on finding out, largely because we had no desire to be caught doing something illegal. When Greg quietly whispered his suggestion to us that we all get out of the pool, jump back over the fence, and book it back to Landon's house before anybody caught us, Landon nor I voiced a protest (mind you, this is the same fellow who suggested that we break the law in the first place, so his history of plan-making is not to be held in high regard at this point).

All three of us moved from the middle of the pool to the edge and tried to rise from the water as quietly as possible. Greg and I climbed over the fence simultaneously, with Landon coming right behind us. To my dismay, as soon as my feet hit the ground, a bright light shined in the peripheral vision of my right eye. I looked toward the source of the light and saw the silhouette of a person coming around the corner of the pool fence with a flashlight fixed on Greg and me. Landon still only had one leg over the fence behind us when I heard a strange voice say, "Hold it right there!"

The neighborhood watch? Seriously? I felt a brief moment of embarrassment at the realization that we were such lame criminals that it only took a couple of soccer moms with an evening hobby to catch us (a thought that makes me laugh today). The police were still a couple

Zachary Lindquist

of minutes out, but they were already on their way to meet the three criminal masterminds whom these women had just caught red-handed.

When the squad car showed up, my friends and I were already lined up on the sidewalk bordering the pool parking lot. Two police officers got out of the car. They proceeded to interview the three pathetic supervillains who would have gotten away with trespassing if it wasn't for those meddling middle-aged women.

While one of the officers was still questioning us, one of the women interjected by posing a question to us, "Do y'all know why this pool was closed today?" Slightly taken aback by her silly question, I replied, "It's closed because it's the middle of the night," as if it wasn't obvious that the pool would be closed around 2:00 am.

What the woman said next taught me a lesson far more effectively than being caught by the police ever could. She explained to us, "No, this pool was closed all afternoon today. Somebody took a massive poop in the water that turned a good portion of the water yellowish-brown, and the pool is closed awaiting a chemical cleaning!" She then proceeded to let out a howling laugh remarkably similar to that of the Wicked Witch of the West.

Greg and Landon's faces both changed colors, as I'm sure mine did, at the realization we had all spent the last 45 minutes or more stewing in a giant toilet bowl filled with fresh fecal bacteria! I thought what any rational human would think at that moment: *I had my head under that water! Oh, no, did I have my mouth open in that water? That stuff was in my mouth! And my eyes were open under the water, too. Oh, heaven, I will wake up with pink eye tomorrow!*

The police officer seemed to almost feel sorry for us at that point. He gave us a quick lecture and then allowed us to go free with a written warning.

I figured you might see the humorous side of that story, but here's the serious side: My moronic friends and I thought we knew what the risks were when we went and did something illegal. We were wrong. We had no idea the consequences would be what we were! If we had known, I guarantee we would never have gone anywhere near that nasty pool! The short-lived fun was not worth the cost, nor a case of pink eye.

The truth is we often convince ourselves, as does the world—that when we go against God and do wrong— we either know the potential consequences of our actions and the risks are clear or that what we are

Page 117

doing wrong is no big deal as long as we do not perceive it as hurting anybody. But we are always wrong. We never know the full extent of the ripple effect that our actions will cause, the impact, who will be affected, or to what extent. We never know the whole picture.

On the other hand, God knows everything that we do not. That is why He makes the rules and sets them in place—that we might be spared the consequences of our sin whether we foresee them or not.

There are answers to questions surrounding why we should not engage in sexually immoral acts and why we should guard our eyes, minds, and hearts against pornography. I will present some of the answers as best and concisely as possible. I want to clarify upfront that just because we do not know the answers to certain questions and do not realize the consequences of our potential actions does not mean they are not there. Just the same, there are also right answers and wrong answers to those questions. In my lifetime, I have heard the wrong ones being passed around all-too-frequently to people, young and old. I think it is about time the correct answers came up for a breath of fresh air. I would like to expose you to the right answers just once, to the best of my ability.

Porn and the Human Mind

I am going to be frank with you: I have wrapped my head around this problem from every angle, and I have concluded that there is just no way to talk about the issue of pornography and masturbation in a strictly PG-rated way. I have little doubt that that is why you seldom hear it discussed in a church setting. Pastors do not want to offend their congregation by discussing "dirty" topics, and many of them all too often sidestep this issue and stick their heads in the sand. Well, it is a good thing that I'm no pastor!

The neglect within the church to deal with the issues surrounding porn and masturbation has profound consequences. Edmund Burke said, "The only thing necessary for evil to triumph is for good men to do nothing." Well, evil is certainly having its day. We now live in the age of pornography and self-love. In our Internet age, it is unfortunately *rare* for a 12-year-old to never have been exposed to images that he cannot forget and for a teenager not to have made porn viewing and masturbation a regular practice. Thanks to the ease of access to the Internet, among other things, young people are having their innocence leeched from them by images they can't forget as early as eight years old. Good men have done little to stop it, and now evil runs rampant.

The church is not exclusively at fault for this, but issues that are hard or *taboo* to talk about are often the most important ones to address. That is what I intend to do. Just be forewarned that I will not handle this subject matter wearing kid gloves. You may find some of what you read uncomfortable or borderline vulgar if you are sensitive. It is not my intention to be obscene or offensive but, try as I might, it is impossible to effectively engage in touchy topics like porn and masturbation *and* keep the conversation entirely clean and "family-friendly." I will do my best to handle this discussion sensitively,

I did not have an over-abundance of moral guidance in pornography when I was young. I wish I had. I wish somebody had been willing to risk offending a few people by speaking honestly about something that is not easy to talk about. I wish someone had warned me about the existence, the lure, and the dangers of such things. I wish somebody had taken the time to seek the answers to the question, "what's so wrong about porn and masturbation? It's not like it's real fornication, right?" I wish that, if they had had the answers, they would have relayed them to me.

The truth is the problem with porn and masturbation is easy to understand, but it is increasingly challenging for the average individual to accept. We live in a culture that prioritizes lust over love—pleasure over affection—and thus, people are resistant to the facts that stand in the way of their achieving the fulfillment of their appetites. The facts are there, and they are virtually impossible to refute if one is intellectually honest, but emotions get in the way at times, as they do with many issues of fact vs. feelings.

If we desire something to be true, then a lie becomes easy to accept. If we want to satisfy our sexual urges, blandly and oddly, we will search for justification in doing so. That very thing has happened on a massive scale in western culture. The way society has justified the satisfaction of our urges is subtle, brilliant, and sneaky: they classified sexual release as a *need*.

Before we go on, I would like to dispel this myth once and for all. A *need* is classified as something that your body requires to survive. You *need* to breathe air, or you will suffocate and die; you *need* to drink water, or you will die of thirst; you *need* to eat food, or you will die of starvation; you *need* to sleep, or after approximately 11 days, your body will shut down from exhaustion, and you will probably die. You may *want* a sexual release as badly as you want a glass of cold water after 24 hours in a scorching hot desert, but if you do not get that sexual release, you will not die. The epitaph on your tombstone will never read, "Cause of death: sexual frustration." Nobody in the entire history of humanity has died from a lack of sexual release! You will not be the first! You are safe! And, no part of your body will turn blue either.

Western culture has so accepted the fiction that sex is a necessity of survival that hardly anybody even questions the premise anymore. They accept that one *must* experience ejaculation as a means of life or death. So they have their justification for turning to pornography and masturbation as a means of doing so out of "necessity."

That is the core of the great lie surrounding pornography. Self-proclaimed "experts" have many of us convinced that porn is not only morally neutral but *healthy*. Of course, these "experts" have no legible evidence to support their claims because none exists. They simply make a claim and tell you to accept it as fact because *they* are the "experts." T*hey* know better than all of us because they have a degree in psychology from an educational system in which you can become a lawyer without ever having read the Constitution of the United States or an English Literature professor without ever having been exposed to the work of William Shakespeare.

If somebody tells you that viewing pornography and touching yourself are not wrong but are good for you and society, there are two possibilities: they are misguided, or they are lying to you. There is no third option, quite frankly.

The same experts who defend pornography and its accompanying practices are the ones who also go on television programs and claim that men are all toxic, self-serving, narcissistic pigs. What a coincidence! That is one of my chief complaints about the effects of the whole porn epidemic! I find it truly fascinating that people who hold their intellect in such high regard fail to see the connection. The sad truth is that so many men today are more lovers of pleasure and themselves than they are lovers of women or people in general, and pornography is a driving force of such obsessive isolation.

When I talk to young men about sexual issues and inevitably come to the topic of pornography, I generally start with the question: "Do you want to get married someday?" The answer tends to be yes. Marriage is a natural desire and a noble, selfless pursuit if done right. Then I make a point that I will paraphrase: "When you are married to your beautiful, wonderful, one-of-a-kind wife, it will be your job to make her feel safe, valued, desired, and loved. I would imagine that you would like to do nothing less for somebody you care about." How does that statement relate to pornography? My next query answers that very question: "If your goal is, indeed, to make your woman feel safe, valued, desired, and loved, then why would you want to subject yourself to something that by its very nature teaches you to view women as objects to be used as tools for your gratification, rather than as infinitely valuable human beings who should be loved, cherished, and respected?"

That is one of the many things pornography does to the mind: it teaches men to seek self-gratification first because that is what they see happen on the computer screen and what they are doing themselves by engaging in the accompanying activity. They are teaching themselves, subconsciously, that women are to be used for pleasure and then discarded at the turn of a page. They are teaching themselves to fantasize wildly and become aroused by very perverse forms of sexual activity that can never be mistaken for loving acts. They are conditioning their minds to detach sex from love, making the two seem mutually exclusive. They are associating the act of intercourse only with lust and the taboo while detaching it from affection and care.

When a man's mind becomes encumbered by such things, it is difficult—dare I say impossible—to make his wife feel safe, valued, desired, and loved. All of his thoughts about sex and intimacy are in the context of lust and fantasy. They are exclusively self-interested because he has been trained to function by viewing pornographic depictions of dehumanizing acts and pleasing himself physically. The inevitable result is that all future sexual acts he engages in have nothing to do with being a lover to his one woman but center on how he can please himself.

Through a man's use of porn and masturbation, the neurons (brain cells) in his brain will inevitably form synapses (interconnections) that link sexual acts to the self and link the image of a woman to nothing more than his pleasure. If he does this repeatedly, viewing a plethora of pornographic images and a sea of different women, another synapse forms which links women with the words "disposable" or "replaceable." His mind no longer allows him to view a woman as a uniquely beautiful human being with her own thoughts, desires, aspirations, and experiences. Now, the only message that his retinas send to his brain at the sight of her is: "another toy to play with." Harrowing, to say the least.

Some people may be dumbfounded by how much I despise pornography and the industry that peddles it and makes it available to our children, but it is because I was once one of the men whom I just described. I discovered the stuff at a young age and later fell for the lies sold to all of us, and I developed a long-term, horrendous habit. You can call me a hypocrite if it pleases you, but the fact is I know, first-hand, what this stuff does to people, and I do not wish to see it happen to *anybody*, much less see how the effects infect our society on a grand scale. I found it hard to write about what porn does to a man because it is exactly the kind of person it turned me into. I do not like to think about it, much less admit it, but much of my insight comes from my own experience. I still see the handiwork of pornography in men and women, young and old, all over the place, and it is painful to witness.

Women are not immune to the psychological effects of pornography any more than men are. A woman who gets into the habit of porn use will undergo many of the same consequences as men, though there is often a slight difference in *how* the effects manifest in women in general as opposed to men.

It has been observed that women who get hooked on pornography use tend not only to begin viewing members of the opposite sex with a less humanizing lens, but women begin to view *themselves* as less valuable. They see how women are portrayed in pornography—as mere bodies—and begin to associate themselves with the same portrayal. Not only does porn teach young women to see sex as an essentially meaningless and demoralizing act (which is a destructive mindset in and of itself), but they begin on some small level to see their selves as mere vessels of pleasure rather than inherently valuable human beings.

If, in a woman's mind, sex is only a means of pleasing oneself, she begins to view her body as a tool for such things. She mentally separates the body from the self, and if she devalues her body, she devalues herself by extension—though she may not realize it. The two are inseparable, so if she sees one as meaningless, she will devalue the other as well. The end result is inevitably a loss of personal identity, a waning sense of dignity, and a surge in depression. I have seen how depression of this sort compels people toward destructive behaviors.

A woman who dehumanizes herself may begin to feel more isolated and lonely, in which case she may seek comfort and value through acts of physical human contact. She may find herself looking for affection in all the wrong places. And, if she places little value in herself or her body, you can probably guess where that might lead.

Porn is inherently degrading, but it becomes more violent and taboo every day. The more young people, male and female, are exposed to it, the more they begin to associate sex (which is supposed to be a loving act between life-long spouses) with demeaning and harmful practices. Such an association leads to more men pressuring women into weird and uncomfortable situations and more women allowing themselves to be used in horrible ways because it is what they come to expect and accept as the norm.

The effects of pornography and self-love on the human mind that we have already covered *should* be enough to convince you of its evil and deter you from it, but we have not even scratched the surface yet of what it can do.

Self-Love and the Body

The horrors of pornography and masturbation do not stop with the mental and emotional devastation. The physical symptoms that result from such self-abuse can be just as harrowing. There are repercussions to virtually every decision we make and action we take, good or bad, and this topic is certainly far from being an exception. The problem is that so few people are aware of the ramifications, so they pretend that there are none. We have all heard the popular phrase, "ignorance is bliss." Should you choose to remain ignorant on important issues, the result is anything but blissful.

The more consumed the culture becomes with pornography and the act of self-indulgence, the harder it becomes to pretend that consequences do not exist. With the modern advancements in technology that result in Internet-capable devices in every hand, indiscriminate of age and maturity, children are being exposed to pornography for the first time at younger and younger ages. Those same kids are experiencing puberty and approaching adulthood while hiding long-term bad habits and addictions that form from such early exposure. As these young people develop and eventually get married and become sexually active, they discover, to their horror, that something is very wrong. Not only are their minds full of unhealthy views of sex and debasing practices, but their bodies are adding up the cost of porn and masturbation habits that have been fed for a multitude of years. That cost is no menial sum.

Consider this: I have been a health and fitness fanatic for most of my life. I was so immersed in health, physical fitness, and sports sciences as a teenager that I majored in exercise physiology in college—seeking to pursue a career in the fitness industry. One of the first terms and concepts that one learns in this field of study is *muscle memory*. You may already be familiar with this fairly common term. To summarize the concept, it is when your body performs a certain physical task or exercise over and over again through practice and repeated exposure (something as simple as a bicep curl or as complicated as a play at football practice). Your muscles begin to catch on to what you are doing and learn to adjust to what you do regularly. The body becomes more accustomed to performing bicep curls, and the muscles grow to compensate for the repeated stress placed upon them. The muscles of the legs begin to learn the same plays that the football player does, and they become prepared to perform certain maneuvers, ideally to the point the mind no longer has to think about performing the action.

Our bodies learn from what we do with them. They have their own form of memory, and they learn to respond to the things that we teach them to respond to. If this is true of physical exercise, weightlifting, and motor skills, both simple and complicated, are we naïve enough to believe our bodies will not learn to respond the way we teach them when it comes to something like masturbation?

When a man stimulates his sexual organs by using his hand, his body learns to respond to that particular form of stimulation. His body commits what he teaches to memory and learns to adjust its planned response to compensate for an act that it was not designed for. He teaches his penis to become sexually stimulated by his hand.

If a man teaches himself to respond in this way through the practice of porn and masturbation, how do you suppose his body will respond when he eventually tries to be intimate with a woman? The answer: it likely won't respond at all. That is not what he taught his body to do! He spent years teaching it to do something that contradicted its intended design! It would be like a track athlete training for years to run the 100-meter dash and then expecting to excel at pole vaulting! He trained his body a certain way—the wrong way—and his body will respond accordingly.

Sadly, this is not a hypothetical scenario. There are young men worldwide (though more concentrated in the west) who physically cannot be sexually intimate with a woman because they have so trained themselves and accustomed their bodies to the use of their hands. Men as young as 18 years old are experiencing erectile dysfunction in droves! That is a medical condition that used to only affect senior citizens whose bodies are shutting down (with rare exceptions related to other underlying health problems).

I have had conversations with many men who have little problem admitting they would rather masturbate than make love to a real woman. Not only are they often unable to respond properly and normally during sexual intercourse, but they have become accustomed to the immediate gratification that porn offers. They would rather avoid going through the effort of making a real connection to a living human being and instead lock themselves in their dark bedroom alone. Women are being replaced with fantasy, magazine pages, computer screens, and five fingers in many of these men's lives. I cannot think of any way to suck the substance out of one's own life more effectively and completely.

Another physiological pitfall to self-love is evident in its effect on hormone levels. Studies have provided evidence that there is a direct link between masturbation and low testosterone levels, the primary male sex hormone. Masturbation has been shown to decrease androgen receptors in the brain, which testosterone binds to to be used throughout the body. Fewer receptors mean less demand for testosterone production, and since supply only meets the demand, less testosterone is produced. When androgen receptors sleep on the job, estrogen (primary sex hormone in women) receptors try desperately to compensate for the loss, which causes a whole host of further problems.

A man with low testosterone can experience many negative symptoms: low or easily depleted energy, depression, low bone density, muscular deterioration and increased body fat, premature hair loss, anemia, mood swings, a low sex drive, and other sexual dysfunctions. As if this wasn't bad enough, excessive estrogen levels in men tend to exaggerate each of these symptoms further. Testosterone is among the most vital hormones in the body, and you would be hard-pressed to find a faster way to deplete its supply and production than to masturbate.

I am picking on the men a lot in this chapter, mostly because pornography and masturbation are predominately more of a problem for them. Still, women are not exempt from these physical side effects of such practices any more than the average man is. Women do, indeed, have the same muscle memory phenomenon and parallel hormone imbalances if they become immersed in the same habits. Women do not get a free pass on this side of things.

There are a lot of men *and* women who, as I have pointed out, get so hooked on pornography and pleasing themselves that they end up preferring the base habit to the real thing (sex). Many such people believe that they have an easier time getting pleasure and achieving orgasm if they simply do it themselves. Not only is it a depressing thought that they would willingly deprive themselves in such a way, but the claim itself is demonstrably false!

It is physically impossible to achieve the height of sexual experience by oneself. A person can have a physical response, but it is far from the real deal.

Scientific study has shown, beyond a reasonable doubt, that masturbation is a pale imitation of the orgasmic experience that occurs during sexual intercourse. It has been proven that real, traditional, penile-vaginal sex releases over 400%.[12] of the endorphins throughout the body that any other so-termed "sexual act" possibly could! Nothing else even comes slightly close: not masturbation, oral sex, anal sex, or any weird act that you could conceive of! The only thing that masturbation or anything other than normal sex could achieve is ejaculation, and almost certainly a feeling akin to shame. Remember the bowl of plastic fruit from chapter 10? Yes, that also applies here.

Anybody honest about how they feel after a self-achieved sexual release will confess that they feel dirty, compromised, and dissatisfied. The act and frequency of masturbation have been respectively associated with high levels of depression in various studies.[13] There is simply no way to experience both that *and* euphoria simultaneously. Hence, anything outside of the bounds of a true, marital, sexual experience is little more than a hollow counterfeit.

You Can't Hyde from Inevitable Results

There are few more effective lies the devil tries to deceive us with than trying to convince us, "You can indulge your sinful appetites *just a little bit*. It won't matter in the grand scheme of things, right?" That subtle trick of the enemy can make for an effective ploy. Of course, the truth is that when we give in to our temptations "just this one time," that one time turns into just one more, and one more is never enough.

---

12   Brody, Stuart. "The Relative Health Benefits of Different Sexual Activities." *The Journal of Sexual Medicine*, vol. 7, no. 4, 2010, pp. 1336–1361.

13   Ibid.

The slope of indulgence is steep, and we can easily slide into a situation that we never intended nor foresaw.

This point is symbolized brilliantly in Robert Louis Stephenson's classic, *The Strange Case of Dr. Jekyll and Mr. Hyde*, one of my all-time favorite works of fiction. It is ultimately the story of an upstanding doctor of exceptional character named Dr. Jekyll, who is well-known amongst his peers to have lived a good and virtuous life—fleeing from lustful pursuits, refusing to overindulge with alcohol or other substances, treating perfect strangers as if they were his beloved kin.

The story is common and famous enough, so I hope I am not spoiling the plot for anybody who is not familiar with it, but Dr. Jekyll, through the use of his exceptional mind, develops a sort of potion that transforms him into another person entirely, both in physical appearance and in personhood. When Jekyll drinks his concoction, he becomes the disheveled, short, and unsettling Mr. Hyde who, as it turns out, is pure evil—Dr. Jekyll's dark side, as it were, whose appearance is so undesirable and small in stature because Jekyll spent his life denying his base desires and sinful urges for the most part.

After Dr. Jekyll spends a fair amount of time as his evil alter-ego, he morphs back into his original form as if Hyde never existed. Dr. Jekyll sees this as his chance to pursue all of the sinful desires that he has denied himself over his lifetime: he can turn himself into Mr. Hyde, do anything that his morally unincumbered self wants to do, and then transform back into Jekyll, thus living two separate lives and doing whatever he wishes without consequences. At least, that is what he initially theorized.

As it turns out, the more Jekyll indulged his dark side, the more it became who he was. The more time he spent as his evil counterpart, the more control his evil counterpart gained over Jekyll. As time went on, Jekyll found that Hyde was taking over his body, first subtly, then suddenly as Jekyll discovered he was no longer using his potion to become Mr. Hyde, but rather drinking it in a desperate attempt to remain himself. In the end, Dr. Jekyll's moral and upright self ceased to exist and was replaced by the purely sinister Hyde.

Indulgence feeds and grows appetite. The more we pander to our sinful nature, the more nature attempts to control us. There is no stopping Mr. Hyde from getting stronger within us as long as we allow him to feast on his unsavory appetites. Even in the shadow of secrecy, what we do has real and often profound consequences, even if we do not see them coming or deny that they are there. If we are not careful, we may meet a similar fate to the fabled good Dr.

Our choices and actions become habits, and our habits become a central part of our being. Convenient or not, the things we choose to do become a part of who we are, whether openly or in private. If I have stolen anything in my life, that makes me a thief. If I had lied to my mother once as a child, I would have made myself a liar. If I fantasize about a woman other than my wife, I am an adulterer. Your heart follows your actions, which become habits, which become you.

I have heard it said, time and time again, "I won't keep viewing porn and masturbating forever; it's just something that I need to do until I am married and can have sex." As you may guess, based upon all of the information we have already covered, there is no validity to that claim. The consequences to those habits are real, whether one recognizes them or not. Setting aside, however, all of the reasons we have covered why this mindset is wrong, I have a few additional points that I would like to touch on, specifically about this, "I have to do it until I can have sex," way of thinking.

First of all, you do not *have* to do anything! You are not a slave to your own body, nor your desires! One of the fruits of the spirit is self-control. You can, indeed, control yourself. You can say "no" to certain urges and desires in the same way a thief can say "no" to his impulse to steal. If we would hold a bandit responsible for his immoral actions by sending him to jail, you can be assured that you will be held responsible for your decisions as well.

As I said, nobody has ever died from a lack of sexual release. Our bodies are well-designed by our creator, and they handle our lack of sex for us. Nothing in a man's body will be backed up, nor will it turn blue. The Bible talks about *nocturnal emissions*, which some weirdo nicknamed "wet dreams" to make this natural process sound somehow dirty. It is not, however. Nocturnal emission is simply the male body's unconscious process of expelling excess semen from the body in one's sleep. It is not weird or creepy; it simply means that nobody will explode from a lack of masturbation or sexual release.

Give yourself a little bit of credit. You can, and should, keep from destructive habits such as masturbation and pornography use. That level of self-control is entirely within your power! There is no temptation on this earth that you cannot resist (*see 1 Corinthians 10:13*).

To my second point, if you are among those who think that you can skate by on porn and self-pleasure only until such a time as you get married and then immediately quit with no fallout, I have some very disappointing news for you: the poison will follow you into your marriage and infect everything it touches.

If you are knee-deep in porn and masturbation habits before you get married, that habit and its side effects will not simply disappear with the exchanging of vows. Addictions seldom die in a single moment, and there is little that is more deadly to any relationship than pornography use.

I have known my share of married men who struggle with pornography habits and some who do not even consider it a *struggle* so much as a "necessary evil." How any man could think of this stuff as "necessary," I have no idea. It is a terrible problem to have, indeed. No woman should have to compete for her man's affection with a computer screen and five fingers.

How do you think it makes a wife feel when she knows that her husband was looking at other women naked and fantasizing about them before making love to her? How loved might she feel if she suspects he is picturing the naked girl on his computer while he is supposed to be being intimate with his bride? Some men cannot physically perform, sexually, with their flesh and blood wives unless they have pornographic material within visual range to stimulate them. I do not even dare to imagine how that man's wife might feel, knowing that he has less desire for her than he does for his fantasies and pornography.

It is very hard for any woman to feel love and passion for her man when she does not feel like the focus of his heart. If your heart is possessed by pornography or any other vice, that evil will not make room for your loved one. You cannot pursue love and lust simultaneously; it is simply not humanly possible! You may try to fool yourself into believing that you can do it, as Dr. Jekyll might have, but you will never fool your body or your heart. You will be forced to choose between your vice and your love for "where your treasure is, there your heart will be also..." (Matthew 6:21). If your "treasure" is porn or any other vice, your heart will be pulled from your wife (not to mention from God) with great ferocity. One cannot simultaneously face the north *and* the south; his back must be turned to one.

Immediate gratification is all the rage in the modern world that we inhabit. Temptation is always just a few clicks away on the Internet, and the Internet is always in our pockets. I understand the struggle as much as the next person. It can be very hard not to give in and allow ourselves the temporary release on demand. In such difficult times, we must ask if hollow pleasure is worth the price we will pay.

Giving in to temptation is the easy part. Dealing with the cost is what is hard, and the cost of pornography and self-pleasure is too high. Such things will destroy your mind, poison your heart, consume your spirit, damage your body, and infect your every relationship. None of that by itself is worth the temporary release, much less all of it combined. The cost is far too high.

Letting Bad Habits Die

The pornography industry, vast and wealthy as it has grown in recent decades, ruthlessly targets our children and us. This powerful force markets their products worldwide, and their material is constantly within reach for anybody with Internet access (in western society, it is virtually everybody). So, how are we to stem the tide, fight back, and keep our eyes and hearts clean of such things, as well as those of our loved ones? Some have suggested anti-pornography legislation by the government.

I do not imagine that the government is the solution to this problem. Anti-porn legislation is not the answer to healing our hearts and transforming the moral fabric of our society on a massive scale. That responsibility belongs to each of us as individuals. Only we can consistently control what our eyes see and what our hearts absorb; only we can be responsible for the values we pass along to our children; only we can take responsibility for our personal choices and resolve to be better. No law can change our hearts. Only God can do that, with some cooperation on our part.

I want to see the pornography industry die. First, however, I do not mind seeing it suffer. In my lifetime, I hope to see people turn away from pornography in large swaths; I hope to see young people choose love and reality over lust and fantasy; I hope to witness world-shaking transformations of a culture's moral fabric; I long to watch the creation of a lack of demand for pornographic material as the supply of consumers diminishes and dries up. I pray that I will witness a generation of people who refuse to be trapped by a wicked vice and who willingly allow a predatory industry to breathe its final breath.

Many struggle with pornography and masturbation, and many wish to quit and leave such habits behind. You may be one such person. You may have tried to quit before and failed. You may have tried and failed to quit a great number of times. I assure you it is entirely possible to do so. Often, it is only a matter of understanding that you have the option to say "no" to even the harshest of temptations. Yes, you can simply resolve to refuse your every desire.

Of course, it never hurts to put systems in place to help you steer clear of temptation so that you do not have to rely on willpower alone. If you wish to stop a stubborn habit or free yourself from an unwelcome addition, it is necessary to take precautions against relapsing. There are some rather practical ways of protecting yourself, though they may not be a cure-all solution.

Beware the evening. Temptation of the most persistent sort seldom attacks in the morning when we are fresh and alert. We are far more vulnerable when the hour is late, when we are tired and sapped of strength, when the weight of the day is on our shoulders, and we want to escape from our burdens. We need things to occupy our thoughts and attention in those late hours—things that pull us away from access to pornography. Those occupations do not include accessing the Internet or scrolling on our smartphones. It should be productive and does not place us within seconds of accessing our addictive substance.

That brings us to the second point to be aware of; boredom. There is arguably no more effective temptation trigger for a pornography addict than a sense of boredom. When you are desperate for an activity to fill your time, that unhealthy old friend begins to look like appealing company. If there is one thing that addicts and recovering addicts of any kind are the worst at doing, it is doing nothing. It is essential to occupy your time productively with a hobby or activity. Read more books, learn a language, build something, practice with a musical instrument or a sport, work on a project, develop a talent, fill your spare time with something worth doing.

Be aware of your relapse triggers. Anything that prompts your mind to wander in an undesirable direction can summon the craving to return to your vice. Be conscious of anything that elicits a mental detour toward lustful thoughts or actions. Avoid the obvious movies and television shows which contain sexual content and nudity. Practice averting your eyes from explicit images to the point that it becomes a thoughtless reflex. Keep your Internet devices out of arms reach when you are not in dire need of them. The baseline themes of relapse triggers for pornography are more-or-less the same across the board, but everybody can have a unique trigger that differs from others. It is important to identify things that may trigger a relapse for you, specifically, and eliminate those things from your daily life.

Social media was a repository of relapse triggers for me, and I suspect because I often had my guard down when using such apps and sites as *Facebook*. I never knew what to expect or what would cross into my vision while I was scrolling—seemingly random images and posts, some of which would trigger an emotional response in me, lead my mind to wander, and result in an intense craving for a return to my vice. When I realized that social media was harming me more than it was providing any benefit to my life, I stopped using it for a long while.

Addicts often become professionals at hiding their problems, so give a trusted loved one unrestricted access to your devices and private bedroom to keep you accountable. My wife knows all of my passwords and can access my smartphone at any moment, uses my personal computer frequently, and my computer screen is usually within her view when I am using it, etc. If I were to suddenly deny her access to my phone or laptop or change my password without informing her, she would know that something was amiss, and I would be in big doo-doo.

Allow yourself some positive reinforcement while trying to quit! It helps to have and maintain a positive mindset when giving up a stubborn vice instead of a steady income of nothing but shame and disgust in oneself. Negative thoughts are not very motivating, nor are they productive in achieving an important goal, such as kicking a pornography habit!

One can make a sort of game out of quitting for some positive motivation. I know that the suggestion may seem odd or childish, but how has taking the issue seriously and with an intense, angry face gotten you? I suggest you keep track/score every time you say "no" to temptation—specifically one that pertains to your addiction or habit. Carry a small notepad or something equivalent to it that can serve the same purpose and, every time you push an inappropriate thought out of your mind, every time you avert your eyes from a potential trigger, or every time you refuse to visit a pornographic website, you mark a tally on the pad! Every time you say "no" to something, you get to watch the points add up! At the end of the week—or month, depending on which works best for you personally—add up the points and resolve to beat that goal during the next period! Even when you stumble, those times you said "no" for this period still count. Do not start over every time you make a mistake but keep counting the triumphs. You might be surprised how encouraging it can be to watch your victories vastly outnumber your defeats! And next time, you can aim to make those victories even more overwhelming!

Finally, and most importantly, when temptation strikes, and it will, stop and pray. Lean on God when the urge hits you to do something you should not do. Often, waiting 15 minutes before resolving to act on some impulse or urge makes all of the difference in the world! God tells us to seek Him out as our strong tower, so never hesitate to run to Him for shelter and deliverance from evil things.

Pornography, as with any addiction, is spiritual poison. Spiritual problems require spiritual solutions, and a spiritual poison requires a spiritual antidote. No matter what multi-step program or principles you may utilize to help free yourself from addiction, experts on the subject can agree that "in truth, [spirituality] is the meta-principle—the framework that holds the other principles together."[14] God is the core and source of all good, and His presence in your life empowers you to reclaim the good and reject the deplorable. You *will* need God by your side, so do not discount the stopping to speak with Him. When I was in the midst of struggle, trying to drop a terrible habit, I would often find myself talking to Him and reading 1 Corinthians 10:13 on repeat, being reminded that I will never be tempted beyond what I can handle and that God and the Holy Spirit is always empowering me to say "no" to evil things. Speaking to God before I did wrong always felt better than tearfully begging for His forgiveness after.

If you have struggled with pornography and masturbation in the past or present and feel discouraged because of what I am telling you, I have some wonderful news: if you stop doing it, you can and will heal. The damage can be corrected! If you quit the bad habit right now—today—in a year, your mind will mend, and your body will return to normal.

That being said, it would still be better never to have picked up the habit of addiction in the first place. If someone with a long-term cigarette smoking habit quits cold turkey, a year later, their body will heal, and their lungs will function normally and healthily again. At the same time, though, the former smoker will still carry scars. The alveoli (oxygen storing sacs in the respiratory system) in his lungs that died in the process of his smoking habit will not grow back; thus, his lungs, while

14   "Conclusion: Spirituality." *Six Essentials to Achieve Lasting Recovery*, by Sterling T. Shumway and Thomas G. Kimball, Hazelden, 2012, pp. 131–132.

healthy again, will not have the capacity they could have had if he had never picked up a cigarette.

God created miraculous bodies for us with the ability to heal in remarkable ways, but deep wounds, once inflicted, may still leave a scar behind. If you have deep self-inflicted wounds due to some addiction or habit, you *will* heal, and your body will recover, but it would still be better had the habit never taken root.

If you kick a porn habit and quit pleasing yourself cold turkey, your mind and body will function normally a year later. However, residual effects may arise, and you may occasionally struggle with your scars. The temptation to return to old habits may indeed occur. God will help you through it all, holding your hand every step of the way, to quit, to avoid relapsing, to heal, to stay on the right path once you gain your much-deserved freedom. All the same, you will find that it would have been best never to have gone down the wrong path to begin with.

I drive that last point home, not to discourage anybody, but to clarify the truth. There is always a repercussion for the mistakes that we make. God forgives and heals, but we must always be aware that the cost is there. It is never worth it.

The Gift of "No"

Many in the world today will try to convince you and all of us that we are no more than animals, that we essentially have no choice but to act on or live out our base impulses, that we *are* our desires. Of course, those people only attribute this logic to the realm of sex. By contrast, if you were to kill another human being, you would no longer be an animal or slave to your impulses; you would be held accountable for your actions. Only when it comes to sexual desires are we fed the nonsense that our desires are inescapable and must be acted upon. Many even espouse that the absence of moral responsibility and the abolition of rules surrounding sex is a form of freedom. I find the insinuation insulting and demeaning more than "liberating."

I am here to share the good news with you: you are *not* an animal! God created us specially—in His image. He set us apart from the other living creatures of the world by gifting us with "free choice." An essential part of free choice is that we have the capacity, ability, and freedom of being capable of saying one word: "no."

That's right, "no" is a gift. We have been given this wonderful gift, and God expects us to make good use of it, especially since a necessary feature of this gift is moral culpability. We are free to say "no," and we are held responsible for the result of that freely made decision. That means that we are not slaves to our every momentary desire, and we are under absolutely no obligation to live based on how we *feel*. We do have the free will to choose the path that our feelings pull us toward, but we can also use that will to choose another, better path.

The best definition that I have ever heard to describe maturity is the willingness to delay pleasure. In other words, mature, rational people know how to say "no" to doing things they should not do, no matter how much they may feel like doing it.

The culture that we live in in the 21st century tends to frown on the idea of maturity or at least that definition of it. Those who deny God would love nothing more than to do whatever they like, whatever feels good at the moment, and they would like for us all to follow suit, even as destructive as it may be to do so. You have the free choice to choose their way or the right way. Should you decide to do things contrary to the world's way, in favor of God's way, you will be doing right. If you choose God over the world, you may feel as though the world is against you, that you are going against the grain, that society will make an effort to make you feel out of place. Jesus said that you can tell if you are living God's way if you ask one simple question: "are you hated?" Other variations of that would be: "Does the world think you are crazy? Do people question you for your commitment to your lifestyle? Do you feel as though the culture is against you?"

Yes, the world may be against us sometimes. Society may be against us sometimes. Here is the thing, though: I don't bow to the people; I don't bow to society or the culture; I bow to God. That is how you know you're on the right track.

Who do you bow to? How will you respond when someone questions your faith or moral standard? What are you going to do when they try to pull you toward their practices and way of thinking? Are you going to stand tall or roll over and show your belly? Are you going to be courageous or cowardly? Are you going to stand with God and his standard—by Christian and biblical principles, or are you going to follow the world and jump into a pool of poop?

For Further Study:

Brody, Stuart, and Tillmann H.c. Krüger. "The Post-Orgasmic Prolactin Increase Following Intercourse Is Greater than Following

Masturbation and Suggests Greater Satiety." *Biological Psychology*, vol. 71, no. 3, 2006, pp. 312–315., doi:10.1016/j.biopsycho.2005.06.008.

Brody, Stuart. "Penile – Vaginal Intercourse Is Better: Evidence Trumps Ideology." *Sexual and   Relationship Therapy*, vol. 21, no. 4, 2006, pp. 393–403., doi:10.1080/14681990600891427.

Brody, Stuart. "The Relative Health Benefits of Different Sexual Activities." *The Journal of Sexual Medicine*, vol. 7, no. 4, 2010, pp. 1336–1361., doi:10.1111/j.1743-6109.2009.01677.x.

Eberstadt, Mary, and Mary Anne Layden. "The Social Costs of Pornography." *Analyse Economique*, 7 June 2013, analyseeconomique. wordpress.com/2013/06/07/the-social-costs-of-pornography/.

Meier, Sam, and Beth Meier. "Pornography's Effects on Marriage and Hope for Married Couples." *USCCB*, 2016, www.usccb.org/issues-and-action/human-life-and-dignity/pornography/pornographys-effects-on-marriage-and-hope-for-married-couples.

Romano-Torres, Mónica, et al. "Relationship between Sexual Satiety and Brain Androgen Receptors." *Neuroendocrinology*, vol. 85, no. 1, 2007, pp. 16–26., doi:10.1159/000099250

Chapter 15

Daring to Discuss Homosexuality

The topic of same-sex attraction and gay marriage is one of many subjects Christian are terrified of discussing with the general population. Even many pastors—dare I claim most of them—in western society today are petrified thought of tackling this subject amid a culture that is increasingly less moral on sexual issues, more desensitized to licentious behaviors, and ever more rabid when they hear a biblical view of same-sex relations. I understand that fear. Just a few years ago, in Canada, a pastor faced the prospect of criminal charges for simply stating that homosexual activity falls under sexual sin, and the angry mobs that can form when you do the same in the United States can be nerve-wracking.

In a society that demands tolerance for almost every immoral behavior, tolerance for voicing God's standard of living is going down every day. Christianity is under near-constant attack for daring to contradict the ways of the world. Christians are castigated for refusing to falter on moral standards that they did not set—for neglecting to change the Word of God, which is not theirs to change.

It is incredible how often I get called words like "bigot," or even the made-up words such as "homophobe," and get accused of hating gay people simply because I do not express approval for the behaviors they choose to engage in. It is as if people think there are only two options: approve of everything a person wants to do, or hate them? Nonsense.

I do not approve of the life choices made by any of the men whom I minister to in prison, but I still love them dearly enough to share the word with them, show God's grace to them, spend time with them, and desire the best for them. Of course, desiring the best for them means that I don't want them to continue the lifestyle that got them into trouble in the first place or that will cause them further harm. I feel much the same way when I speak out against sexual immorality, and homosexuality falls into that category.

None of this is to say that there have not been people in the religious community who have expressed malicious words and spiteful attitudes towards those who fall are *homosexual*. Many have been hurt by those proclaiming to be Christians, many who have been emotionally scarred by particular churches and their members. My heart breaks at the thought, and I will attempt to tackle that problem in this chapter, among others.

If you are reading this and you consider yourself gay or merely experiencing same-sex attraction, I want to offer you a vital message right off the bat: God loves you. I love you. I would not be writing this chapter in the first place if my heart did not go out to you. It is God's command for me and anybody else who claims to follow Christ to love you, and I am so very sorry if you have ever been hurt by people who have not lived up to that calling. You are a child of God, and He wants *all* of His children to come home to Him. Everything that a Christian does is supposed to be in the interest of bringing people closer to Him and not sending them running in the other direction. Sometimes we fail in that capacity. Unfortunately, we are still human beings with all of the flaws with such a condition. Please, do not think that it is God's wish for anybody to scold you or tear you down. Anybody who does that does not speak for Him. We are *all* sinners, and we are all in constant need of grace and forgiveness on some level. I pray that you can forgive anybody who has wronged you.

I fully intend to discuss this topic of homosexuality as kindly and lovingly as I can. I want to be kind in that I wish to be understood by anybody who considers same-sex attraction a struggle and considerate to any person who sincerely wishes to understand why God is adamantly against the gay lifestyle. I also intend to be loving, not only by making it clear that every child of God is loved and valued but by promising to be completely honest. I will not mince words, and I will not sugarcoat any piece of truth in this chapter, but rest assured that that is because I love you enough to tell you the whole truth. If I were to alter the truth to spare your feelings, as many people do to please the masses, you would have no reason to trust me or believe that I sincerely care for you. As Proverbs 27:6 says, "The wounds of a friend are trustworthy, but the kisses of an enemy are excessive."

Logs in the Eye

A friend of mine, some time ago, was having a conversation with me about his experiences volunteering with the church youth group. He brought up the subject of a young male teenager who had summoned the courage to confide in him that he was gay, or at least had only ever experienced same-sex attraction in the time since he had hit puberty. This brave young man was concerned about how his same-sex attraction would be accepted or perceived by members of the church's congregation, to which he was new.

My heart went out to the young man in my friend's story. I understood to a degree how hard it must have been to tell somebody about his dilemma. I could imagine that he was in the midst of a challenging and confusing situation—feeling predisposed to a particular form of sin that may not be widely accepted by the religious community of which he had only recently begun to consider himself a member. This young man was trying to pursue God but felt he had an additional handicap that most Christians do not share.

To clarify, I am not implying that this young man was broken or dysfunctional in *any* way. I merely empathized with him as somebody who has experienced my own unique struggles in my walk with God and sympathized with him for having to undergo a struggle that I have never specifically had to face. However, I have numerous loved ones who went through the same thing as him in their youth.

I asked my friend how he responded to this kid, who had so bravely confided in him one of the deepest struggles of his young life. My friend's response to my query made me uneasy: "I told him that the Bible refers to homosexuality as an abomination" was about it. My friend did not describe his process of engaging in a meaningful dialogue with the young man, tell me how he tried to relate to him, or even give any sign that he made an effort to help the teenage boy or show appreciation for the trust that had just been placed with him. This blanket reply to the young man's confession and confided confidence, while not necessarily incorrect, did not seem to be very helpful nor to be given with much love and compassion.

When confronted with homosexual feelings, coming out to somebody—anybody—represents a significant moment in a young person's life, not to mention a tremendous step of faith and courage. There is always that lingering fear that the recipient of the young person's confession will react with rejection or change their opinion of them to a large degree. If you are ever in the position of somebody making such a confession to you, consider the level of trust that is being placed in you, the significance that such a confession may have to the individual making it, and how hard it must have been for them to let those words escape their lips. It is seldom easy for a young man or woman to come out, especially for a young Christian whom such feelings would be considered taboo. Show appreciation to anybody who loves and trusts you enough to bring their inner conflict to light in your presence. Thank them for their honesty. Make sure it is clear to them that you still love them and that God always will, no matter what. This kind of validation will often put the confessor at ease and make them believe that they made a good choice in coming to you with their concerns. After that, take it a step at a time and walk with them through their struggle.

Back to the conversation with my friend about this young man who was confessing his thoughts and feelings of same-sex attraction, I pressed my friend for details in the hopes that he had at least ended his conversation with the kid by leaving him feeling loved or encouraged. Sadly, I was again disappointed. According to my friend, all he said to the boy was about how wrong homosexuality is and said nothing about simply having such feelings did not mean that he was any more broken or sinful than anybody else. In fact, by his admission, the kid had acted on none of his feelings.

I understand that my friend was unsure how to respond in that situation and that he was caught just slightly off-guard, as he had never been confided to in that way. However, that is no excuse when you consider the importance of shaping a young person's life and relationship with God. We all need to be witnesses and mouthpieces for Christ, which is especially important for somebody trusted with the church's youth. From what my friend was telling me, it seemed as though he was woefully unprepared for such an interaction. The fact that homosexual activity is wrong was the extent of his knowledge and understanding of the topic.

I said to my friend, "Let me ask you a question: do you feel the desire for sex, even though you are not married?" He looked at me with a slightly puzzled expression, as though he wasn't sure of the relevance of my query.

"Well, duh. You know I do!" he replied.

I followed up, "and do I castigate you for the desires of your body, even when you do not act on every last one of them?"

He let out a slight sigh as if he was starting to figure out where I was going with this line of questioning. "No, you do not," he answered.

"So, if this kid has certain attractions and desires that he ought not to act upon, even if they are different from yours, but he refuses to act on them, what has he done wrong?" I asked.

"Well, nothing... technically."

"No, not technically. He resists the temptation. You should have given him a gold medal! He should be lauded and celebrated for saying 'no' to the desires of his flesh, not being made to feel horrible for having them in the first place." Then, I pressed him a little bit further. "And what about that girl that you spent the night with last month? Should I be condemning you for that? And what if I were to take a gander at your Internet search history? So far, by all appearances, it seems like this kid has the most self-control between the two of you." I could see my friend starting to get visibly flustered and frustrated now, as though the implication that he was a hypocrite was not a fun thing to hear. Good.

I continued, "We don't get to pick and choose what is acceptable and what is not. You committed sexual sin. You do not get a free pass because those involved were female (opposite sex from you). That kid in the youth group confessed that he was struggling to resist the lure of sexual sin and was asking for guidance on how to live as a Christian with his desires in tow. I say, "'Good for him! I admire that.'"

My friend begrudgingly agreed with the things that I was saying to him. We continued to talk about it. We prayed about everything we had discussed, and, most importantly, we prayed for the young man in the youth group.

In all honesty, I do not have a perfect recall of this conversation. In recreating and paraphrasing it, I probably made myself sound a lot more articulate in the writing of this conversation than I sounded in real-time. Such is the way of the pen. I do not want you to get the wrong idea about my friend in this story. He is a work in progress, as are we all, but he has come a long way in his walk with God and his spiritual maturity since this conversation was had. He even holds me to account on occasion when I fall short or make a mistake, as any good brother ought to do. None of us are perfect, and we all need a course correction now and again.

We have stumbled upon why so many people in our western society get agitated with the Christian ethic. It is largely because so many of us are inconsistent. We are relaxed and too often permissive on issues of pornography and fornication but, if someone commits homosexual sin, we pull out the pitchforks and torches (or at the very least get very uncomfortable).

I am not surprised when people express that they think Christians act a bit crazy. We have grown so passive on fornication, sexual promiscuity, cohabitation, and other things along the sexually immoral lines. Yet, when we come across someone active in the homosexual lifestyle, "stop the presses! We have got to take a stand here!" Really? Now you want to stand for something, Christian people? Where was that enthusiasm with the *Christian* unmarried couple in the church who have been living together for two years and sleeping in the same bed? You haven't said a word to those people! Where were you then?

I honestly believe that one of the most significant reasons society is becoming more accepting of Islam while simultaneously becoming less tolerant of Christianity is that Muslims tend to be consistent on such social issues! You know where they stand on premarital sex and homosexuality because they tend to enforce both ethics to the same degree within their community. Most Muslims I meet would have no more tolerance for a fornicating straight couple than for a gay couple.

As Christians, everything we do is supposed to lead people *to* God, not away from Him. If a gay person becomes nervous when the individual he's conversing with refers to themselves as a Christian, we are doing something wrong on a wide scale. If anybody thinks that we hate them, we send them running as fast as they can *away* from God. That is exactly the opposite impact that we ought to be having.

My Christian brothers and sisters are called to share truth, but to do so with love. God *is* love. You cannot preach His word and spread His message with malice or contempt. It is just not possible. We are expected to hate sin, but we are never to hate the sinner.

I must confess that I did not always understand these things. As a young, stupid, immature kid, I sincerely thought that I was expected to hate gay people as I was the sins they were committing. That's hard to admit, but it is regrettably true. I am very thankful that that lack of understanding was short-lived.

My more mature perspective on homosexuality, in general, began to take form when I became a fan of a certain Christian comedian, Brad Stine, my all-time favorite comic. I find Brad the most shamefully underappreciated comedian in the 21st century. When I discovered Brad's comedy as a preteen by watching one of his DVDs, he said something during his act that drastically changed how my developing brain thought about the issue and became foundational to my philosophy moving forward. In response to the concern that gay marriage would be destructive to the sanctity of the institution, he responded: "You're right, [gay marriage] would be destructive to the sanctity of marriage, but let me tell you what's been the *most* destructive to the sanctity of marriage—who's done the most harm: heterosexuals who continue to get divorced at a 50% rate in this country; heterosexuals that continue to live with each other instead of having the guts to marry each other; heterosexuals who continue to have abortions because, 'a baby's not a miracle, it's a mistake'; heterosexuals that continue to believe that sex is just something you're supposed to enjoy because it's just for their narcissistic indulgence; heterosexuals that consider that it doesn't matter anymore to be committed no matter what happens, come hell or high water. In the '60s, we started the idea that marriage didn't matter and we're reaping what we sowed. So, the biggest problem is with the heterosexuals, and until we start getting our own home together, maybe we ought to start taking logs out of our eyes and taking care of our own house first."

Brad's statement, "taking logs out of our eyes," is, of course, a reference to Jesus' statement of not judging "lest ye be judged." It's a call for us not to reprimand others for their faults while we, at the same time, are committing analogous sins. Before telling our gay brothers and sisters what they are doing is wrong, perhaps we should look at how we live our own lives and be sure that we are not under the yoke of sexual immorality ourselves.

On the front of misbehaving Christians, tough love is real love. They generally know the standard that they are called to live by. If they refuse to try and live up to it, we are to call out the bad behavior. That is most definitely not restricted to homosexuals. Love does not simply mean, "accept me as I am." If you are acting horribly and destructively, and I just let you do what you wish in that case, then I do not love you enough!

There is a disconcerting growing normality in our western culture in which parents tend to believe that if you truly love your child, you will let them do what they want to do and be whoever they want to be, and act however they desire to act and that you shouldn't interfere but instead validate them and accept them how they are. This is why we are seeing parents today put their 6-year-old children through sex-change procedures and giving them hormone therapies and all of that other nonsense. Apparently, a 6-year-old knows what is best for themselves and should be making decisions that have permanent, irreversible consequences. Never mind that I have seen kids that age putting cat poop in their mouths. But, "if you don't validate that decision, you must not love that child enough, right?"

To any parent who believes such things, I have a challenge to present to you: the next time your small child wants to run out and play in the middle of a busy road with cars zooming by at over 50 miles-per-hour, validate their decision and let them do it. Prove that you "love them enough." If your teenager or preteen comes to you one day and exclaims, "I want to be a pimp," or, "I want to be a drug dealer," give them nothing but encouragement towards that life goal! Is that what a loving Father would do? I sincerely doubt it.

A loving father would want to keep their child from doing something that would harm or kill him or from doing something illegal or immoral. And God is the most loving of *any* father! He wants to protect us from making decisions and doing things that would bring us pain—things not in our best interest. He always has a good and loving reason for telling us, "no."

Born This Way?

We have all heard the famous line, "We have no choice but to be gay and live this lifestyle. 'We were born this way!' It's who we are!" That go-to line from the LGBT community is often followed by a similar propagandizing question, "if God is so against gay marriage, why did He make me gay?" I will be honest; I do not fully understand all of the factors that contribute to somebody experiencing same-sex attraction. I could run you through the entire list of supposed correlating factors (i.e., childhood sexual abuse, father absence, neglect, social isolation, etc.), but none would be likely to tell the whole story, and it would taste like a lie to claim that I have all of the answers to the question of how homosexual tendencies come to be. Nobody can give a definitive answer, though many claim to, and the claim that it is solely a genetic trait from birth does not seem to carry as much weight as it once did after decades of rigorous research being dedicated to the subject. It would also be foolish not to consider that there are social factors at work, given that the percentage of people who identify as gay, lesbian, or bisexual rises incrementally and generationally, depending on how socially acceptable or even celebrated LGBT identification is at the time amongst one's peers (Gallop, 2021). It is increasingly fashionable, for example, for a high school student to come out and identify as gay or bisexual nowadays. To identify as a member of the LGBT community in the 2020's often promises the attention that so many teenagers crave, and so it stands to reason that many will "come out" in some way just for the praises of their friends. Peer pressure can be an interesting component involved in skewing such data.

I cannot tell you, definitively and beyond a reasonable doubt, whether or not anyone can be *born gay*. What I can tell you is that I sincerely doubt that it matters.

Homosexual activity is not a sin of its own category. It grows from the same tree as any other sexually immoral act. The man who shares a bed with another man is no more or less guilty than a man who shares a bed with a woman he is not married to.

If a person comes out of the closet and confesses to me that he is gay, he has not committed some horrible act by his very essence. He has simply confessed that he has temptations, the same as me, albeit of a slightly different nature than those I struggle with.

We are *all* born into a sinful world, which is inseparable from being born with a sinful nature. Part of being human in a fallen world is that we are *all* predisposed to immoral behavior in some sense. Some feel an urge to steal more than others, some are compulsive liars, some are inclined toward addictive behavior and substance abuse, and most of us have a natural desire for sex that leads us to crave sexual sin. We all struggle with a desire to perform acts that we should not engage in—to do certain things that are outside of God's design and intention. None of us are free from the world of temptation. Even Jesus Christ, as a man, was tempted by the devil, though he never gave in to temptation. It does not matter if we were *born* with a predisposition towards a certain kind of sin or another, we are still accountable for our decisions, and we *freely* choose to make them.

I do not think that a married person alive has never committed adultery in their minds, who has never let their minds wander to places they should not. Unfortunately, the desire for the forbidden is a part of our fallen nature. Homosexual urges are no different. They are sexual urges that God commands His children not to pursue. Sexual acts have a place in only one context: inside of a marital commitment, between one man and one woman. Anything that falls outside of that guideline, including extramarital affairs, same-sex entanglements, pornography and masturbation, pedophilia, and bestiality, are all forbidden and not to be acted out. If it is not within marriage between a man and a woman, it is not of His intent and is, therefore, out of bounds. It is that simple.

God's Design and Why the Rules Exist

Secular culture claims that we must tolerate someone's immoral behavior if we truly love them because such behavior might make them happy. They say we should always want those we love to be happy under any circumstances. Of course, this argument only seems to extend as far as the world of sex. No rational human being thinks that it would be loving to tolerate or encourage a loved one's drug addiction because they know what detriment such behaviors could cause. There would, indeed, come an intervention at some point. As Frank Turek writes in his book, *Correct, Not Politically Correct*, "Love requires us to stand in opposition to behaviors that will likely hurt or kill our loved ones. In other words, it is unloving to enable or endorse destructive behavior."

Despite secular culture's attempts to convince us that sexual issues are beyond the reach of consequences, same-sex relations are not so different from any other "enabled" behavior. I would argue that I love my gay friends far more than secular society does because I do not want the detrimental consequences of the homosexual lifestyle to tear them down or destroy them. Any *happiness* they might experience from such behaviors would be short-lived compared to the fallout, and the result could be catastrophic.

God's design is intentional, and His rules for abiding by that design are never without reason. When we act out against His intent, the result is never beneficial. The facts and research support this fact.

Let us start with the mental and emotional cost of living a gay lifestyle. Various studies have concluded that those who identify as homosexuals are 150% more likely than heterosexuals to suffer from severe depression, anxiety, and substance abuse. Furthermore, the American Journal of Public Health reported that practicing homosexuals also statistically have a 200% higher rate of suicide when compared with straight people.

On the physical health side of the spectrum, homosexual practices are no more rewarding. For decades, it has been a prevailing and relatively consistent statistical trend that upwards of 78% of practicing homosexuals are affected by at least one sexually transmitted disease. While homosexuals only make up approximately 3% of the U.S. population, the USCDC found that the LGBT community still accounts for the vast majority of all syphilis cases, with 83% being attributed to gay or bisexual men, 60% of known gonorrhea diagnoses, and 75% of all occurrences of HIV. As recently as 2018, the CDC reported that gay and bisexual men made up 69% of all *new* HIV diagnoses. Beyond even that, in 2006, the CDC reported that over 82% of all AIDS diagnoses directly resulted from male-male sexual contact. Outside the scope of venereal diseases, men who engage in homosexual acts are also 17 times more likely to obtain anal or rectal cancer than are heterosexual men.

The physical cost of defying nature's design is nothing less than unsettling. The *Oxford Journal of Epidemiology* also reported that the average lifespan of a practicing homosexual man is no less than 20% (from 8-20 years) shorter than that of the average heterosexual man. Compare that to a lifelong cigarette smoker, whose life is shortened by a perceived average of 7 years. I guess the worst case would be a life-long smoking active homosexual. Given all of the physical and psychological health problems that result from homosexual activity, it can be estimated that only 1% of active gay men die of old age.

The authors of the study that concluded homosexual men's shorter lifespan, evidently, later wrote a letter to the editor voicing their displeasure with the fact that their research was being cited and used by "homophobic" Christians and groups as evidence for exactly what their research suggests—that living a sexually active homosexual lifestyle, by all available data, is not healthy by any means. Because they didn't want to let the evidence get in the way of their ideology, these researchers castigated anybody who followed the research to its logical conclusion and informed people about the implications. These scholarly individuals were angry that people like me were providing the public with their relevant research and daring to say, "yes, you are free to make your own decisions as to how you will live, but let them be informed decisions. Suppose you are going to choose to pursue a homosexual lifestyle. In that case, you are at least entitled to the knowledge that such a way of living is less healthy and potentially more dangerous than smoking a pack of cigarettes per day."

If you are a heavy drinker, doctors will tell you that you will damage your liver and shorten your life expectancy considerably, and thus recommend that you stop; if you smoke cigarettes, medical professionals will inform you that you are likely to develop lung cancer and again lower your life expectancy, and will recommend that you stop; if you are regularly engaged in homosexual sexual activity, however, no medical professional will say a word of warning, even though it presents more risk than either previous example, and in fact, would probably get into trouble if they did. It just seems rather incongruent—not to mention that it seems uncaring and unloving to withhold such vital information for the sake of political correctness.

The physical problems for women involved in homosexual activity are no more promising than that which men would risk. The Gay and Lesbian Medical Association reports that practicing lesbians suffer more breast and cervical cancers than any other subset of women worldwide. Beyond that, research has also shown evidence that gay women are also significantly more prone to bacterial vaginosis and hepatitis C.

Any man or woman who wishes to defy natural processes by pursuing pleasure through homosexual practices has the freedom to do so, though to their detriment. We all have the will and capacity to make bad decisions and do unhealthy things for ourselves. However, let us never convince ourselves that our choices are ever without consequences or fallout.

Indulgence indeed feeds and grows appetite. This truth is related to us in Romans 1:25-32: "They exchanged the truth of God for a lie and worshipped and served what has been created instead of the Creator, who is praised forever. Amen." "For this reason, God delivered them over to disgraceful passions. Their women exchanged natural sexual relations for unnatural ones. The men, in the same way, also left natural relations with women and were inflamed in their lust for one another. Men committed shameless acts with men and received in their own persons the appropriate penalty of their error."

"And because they did not think it worthwhile to acknowledge God, God delivered them over to a corrupt mind so that they would do what is not right. They are filled with unrighteousness, evil, greed, and wickedness. They are full of envy, murder, quarrels, deceit, and malice. They are gossips, slanderers, God-haters, arrogant, proud, boastful, inventors of evil, disobedient to parents, senseless, untrustworthy, unloving, and unmerciful. Although they know God's just sentence—that those who practice such things deserve to die—they not only do them, but even applaud others who practice them."

God will not force Himself or His way on us. that would defeat the purpose of the free will that He created us with. He loved us enough upon our creation that He essentially said, "I will give you so much free-dom that you may destroy yourself." We can choose Him, or we can choose our own way. If you truly wish to live by your own rules, God will grant you your wish and give you over to your desires, should you choose them over Him.

The earthly punishment for homosexual activity is much the same as it is for every other form of sin, sexual or otherwise: He gives us over to our desires, as well as the natural consequences of acting on them. When confronted with the truth and results of living their own way rather than His way, some people turn back to God and ask for forgive-ness, which He grants as He welcomes them back to Him with big hugs. When confronted with the same, other people blame God for allowing their sins to bite them. They harden their hearts like the Pharaoh in Ex-odus and dive deeper into their insanity. They continue to indulge their basest desires and only feed and grow their appetite for such things.

If indulgence does what I claim, logically, the result is what one might expect. The statistics support what I am telling you.

Men and women are designed to complement one another. There is something of a balance that occurs in a heterosexual relationship. Women temper the physical needs of men and pull emotional expres-sion from them. Men often sate the emotional needs of women—ide-ally without piling on any more baggage of their own. With this in mind, the logical and real conclusion of two members of the same sex engag-ing in a sexual-relational partnership is a lack of balance. Gay women tend to push each other to emotional extremes and cause psychologi-cal damage to one another, which no doubt contributes to the fact that they are as much as 167% more likely to divorce relative to straight couples, should they ever make a long-term commitment. In a similar yet more extreme manner, gay men cannot achieve the balance akin to a heterosexual union.

On the contrary, the mutual indulgence of their sex drive (absent the temperance of a female partner to provide emotional balance or to sexually satisfy in a way that a partner of the same sex physiologically cannot) results in their appetite being increased by exponential pro-portions! As a result, not only are gay men as much as 50% more likely to divorce than straight couples, but they are significantly less likely to commit in the first place. The Journal of Sex Research found that as far back as 1997, as many as 43% of active homosexual men have sever-al hundred sexual partners over their lifetime. Research suggests that almost 22% have as many as 500 sexual partners over a lifetime in the same journal.

When we chase cravings against our nature and well-being, no amount of indulgence ever seems to be enough. We can never be fulfilled by vice or a base lust, so we will always go out in search of more and more until it finally kills us, or we allow ourselves to be set free. We have the free choice to decide which comes first.

———————◆———————

Time to Digress: While the pleasant subject of sexually transmitted diseases is on our minds, I want to veer slightly off-topic for just a moment to make an important point. Everybody the topic relates to wants a cure for the STDs that they are contracting, though they seldom pay any mind to the behavior that got them in that position in the first place! Even the dumbest dog knows not to stick its nose where it hurts.

Whether members of the general population do or do not presently have a sexually transmitted disease, they *all* want a cure for the simple reason that their minds can be at ease while they are sleeping around with strangers and behaving horribly! Do not get me wrong, I don't want anybody to suffer from awful diseases, but it is not hard to figure out that if you do something wrong, immoral, or stupid, there will be negative consequences. Attempting to nullify the consequences with billions of dollars in research toward curing every STD known to man only gives people an excuse to continue the bad behavior and bolsters the moral rot in the culture in the same way that eliminating law enforcement and prisons would not solve the problem of criminal behavior.

Do you know what would be simpler, cheaper, and a whole lot more efficient than a vaccine, pills, countless condoms, and billions of dollars per year in medical research? Stopping with the behavior that gives you or other people sexually transmitted diseases! Yes, it is just that simple!

I can hear some people protesting, "Oh, but we cannot possibly expect people to be held accountable for their bad decisions! I mean, it's not as if everybody can control themselves, nor should they be expected to!"

To that, I say, "bologna on a rotten sandwich." Do you know what would happen if we stopped enabling people and started expecting them to behave properly and hold themselves accountable? Let them live with the consequences of their decisions? Those same people who "can't be expected to control themselves" might start considering their bad decisions' effects on themselves and others! Heck, we might get one step closer to cutting down on the narcissism of society because people would start thinking less about the urgency of their sexual desires and more about the people their impulses could impact if acted upon!

"Oh, but Zach, what you are saying is so radical!" Is that so? How is spending billions of dollars every year on contraceptives and stalemated "cure" research less radical and more rational than simply saying, "keep your pants on?"

I can think of two friends of mine from college, at the moment of writing this, who contracted "the clap." These young men happened to contract this STI by doing the same thing: a one-night hookup. All they both had to do to avoid a burning sensation when they pee was not to take a girl home whom they had just met and whom they would never speak to again! Do you think, after the diagnoses, that either one of them thought that the one-time momentary experience was worth the price? I think not. That thought would have been amplified if the STI in question was more serious and less treatable.

I lived in the same house as one of these men at the time of his infection. We shared a downstairs bathroom. When he went to the restroom to relieve himself, I could hear the screams! While I will admit that it was not nearly as amusing then as it might be now, I think the same thing now that I thought then: "you could have easily avoided that!"

If we could all practice self-control, if we could be the generation that collectively said, "keep your pants on," we would be the generation that ended the AIDS epidemic and wiped out sexually transmitted diseases! We do not need billions of dollars in cure research if we simply stick to the basics. A cure would be obsolete if we all chose the simpler and less expensive option.

Medical research is not a bad thing, and obviously, we should take care of the sick and the infirm. I do not mean my facetiousness to take away from that clear truth. All I mean to say is that some things are within our control and completely avoidable in most cases.

Love is Love?

There will be those who read the words of this chapter who call me all kinds of terrible names for telling the truth. There are those, even some who call themselves "Christians," who demand that Christians and the church compromise or change their moral standards to accommodate the secular world and the desires of the LGBT community members.

Such people will claim that we are "intolerant" to stand by our convictions, that we are "unloving" to say "no" to some behaviors that make someone feel good, that we cannot stand in the way of love because, as those who march in gay pride parades so elegantly put it, "love is love."

What meaning does that slogan truly have, anyhow? It says nothing profound or insightful. Do they think that they are citing a definition of the word *love* by simply repeating the word? If someone were to ask me, "what is a cat," how helpful or informative would I be to answer back, "a cat is a cat?"

Methinks that those screaming "love is love" do so because they do not have a firm grasp on what love is. Is it loving to let somebody you care about do something that you *know* will hurt them? Is it love to remain silent to spare somebody's feelings when you know that the information you have is vital? You may as well try to convince me that the true image of love is to come across a loved one trapped in a locked cage—one that is about to be dropped into the ocean—and hide the key to the cage behind your back because "they look so happy and peaceful in that cage."

Forgive me, but I do not see what is so loving about affirming my friend's homosexual lifestyle when I know that it is not good for his body or spirit for him to live that way. Furthermore, I do not understand how sexual acts that often cause pain, bleeding, and disease are considered acts of love in the first place. If your idea of making "love" involves hemorrhaging and painful, sometimes life-threatening infections, I feel inclined to recommend that you neglect to make that kind of love and reevaluate your definition of the term.

C.S. Lewis wrote: "It is for people whom we care nothing about that we demand happiness on *any* terms: with our friends, our lovers, our children, we are exacting and would rather see them suffer much than be happy in contemptible modes." The secular gay rights activist claims to love homosexuals because she wants them to do whatever they want; I would argue that I love them far more because I do not want to see them pay the price for doing whatever they want. I love them enough to say, "No, you should not live that way," because I do not want them to endure the pain that comes with it. The greatest gift that God gave us, I believe, is the ability to say "no," whether to ourselves or our loved ones.

Let me assure you that I have had many close friends who are gay or experienced same-sex attraction in my life, and I love them dearly. Some of those friends were not and are still not Christians; thus, I do not hold them to a Christian moral standard. They know what I believe about homosexuality and why I believe it, as I love them enough to be honest with them and do so in a kind-hearted way. I do not hold it against these people if they disagree with me or choose to live the homosexual lifestyle, as that is their choice to make as free-willed beings who do not have the Christian faith. I will continue to love them as best I can, be their friend, and pray for them. If my friends one day freely decide to come to Christ, I will be ecstatic!

But what of Christians who experience attraction to the same sex? What is their lot? It is, indeed, possible to be a Christian with homosexual feelings. I have several friends to whom this applies. Is there a way for them to live for God *and* have a loving marital relationship?

My heart will always go out to those who feel the conflict between God's morality and being exclusively attracted to the same sex, as there is simply no way to act upon those desires that is right before God. A sexually frustrated heterosexual individual can morally pursue their desires by getting married and being satisfied with their spouse, but alas, there is no way to make a homosexual union acceptable.

I have known friends to ask God to help them with this dilemma in a few ways. Somebody with same-sex attraction can change sexual orientation and develop an attraction to the opposite sex. I have seen it happen. However, such occurrences are not the norm. Not everybody who prays that their sexual attractions change or take steps to alter or customize their preferences will have such a thing happen to them.

The truth is that some people are called to a life of singlehood, though it may not always be the person's preferred solution. On occasion, I realize that singleness is treated within the church as a sort of affliction to be cured. However, it is entirely possible to live a very fulfilling life as a single person! Some might claim that, in some categories, the unmarried individual can be even more successful and fulfilled. The Apostle Paul (a single man himself) considered the single, unencumbered life a blessing, as one could freely serve God with no other obligation or distractions. He also advised that anybody who does not have a strong desire for sex remain single, as marriage is the only way to have sex morally, but it comes with its challenges and may not be worth the difficulty without the perks. Marriage is great, but it is not meant for everybody.

If you are a Christian with same-sex attraction, I encourage you to talk to God and ask Him what direction is best for you. If you desire to marry and have a sexual connection with somebody, you are welcome [if not encouraged] to pray for that opportunity. God may answer that prayer and grant a miracle. It has been done. Sometimes, though, our prayers are not answered in the way we would expect or prefer at the time. That does not mean that God is not listening. He may simply have something else in mind for you. There are many prayers that I have presented to God that were not answered as I had hoped, and looking back, I am so thankful for many of the prayers that He said "no" to. Those "noes" were some of God's greatest blessings upon me. Were God to grant my every wish like a Genie in a bottle, I would be an un-mitigated disaster today. There is always a very good reason for His answer, whether in the affirmative or the negative.

(For Christians wrestling with same-sex attraction, I often recommend two books by men with first-hand experience in this area: *Is God Anti-Gay?* by Sam Allberry, and *Single Gay Christian*, by Gregory Coles.)

It may not always be popular, but I will continue to say "no" whenever somebody asks me if homosexual acts are right or permissible, just as I would any other sin. I will continue to say "no" every time somebody tells me that the church or I ought to compromise our biblical values or *change* the moral standards handed down to us by our Creator.

The truth is that we believe in a moral standard that is far beyond ourselves and is a natural law that God determines and that is entirely outside of our control. We cannot change the moral or natural law to accommodate the world's desires any more than physicist Stephen Hawking could change the laws of physics to comply with his theories.

Once again, we do not bow before man, do not bow before society. We bow only before our Creator. We live in a world of His formation, which He stitched together His way. He knows the natural order of things far better than we could ever hope to. He intentionally put rules in place to assist us in navigating that natural order. He assists us in understanding how and why we are to live according to His design. Christians did not make the rules by which we abide, nor are they within our authority to change. You would not force a Muslim or an Orthodox Jew to ingest bacon, you would not force an Atheist to recite the Lord's

Prayer, and one ought not to attempt to force a Christian (or even still a Muslim or an Orthodox Jew) to celebrate or affirm same-sex marriage.

For Further Study:

Andersson, Gunnar, et al. "Divorce-Risk Patterns of Same-Sex Marriages in Norway and Sweden." *Institute for Marriage and Public Policy*, 2004. https://paa2004.princeton.edu/papers/40208

Center for Disease Control, *Cases of HIV Infection and AIDS in the United States and Dependent Areas, 2006 HIV/AIDS Surveilance Report*, Vol. 18, Apr. 2008. www.cdc.gov/hiv/pdf/library/reports/surveillance/cdc-hiv-surveillance-report-2006-vol-18.pdf.

Centers for Disease Control and Prevention, "HIV and Gay and Bisexual Men." *Centers for Disease Control and Prevention*, 16 Sept. 2020. www.cdc.gov/hiv/group/msm/index.html.

Dailey, Timothy J. "The Negative Health Effects of Homosexuality." *Free Republic*, Center for Marriage and Family Studies, 26 Dec. 2013, freerepublic.com/focus/news/3105393/posts.

Dunham, William. "Syphilis Rise in Gay, Bisexual Men Causes Worry." *Reuters*, Thomson Reuters, 4 May 2007, www.reuters.com/article/healthNews/idUSN0437305220070504?pageNumber=1.

Hogg, R., et al. "Modelling the Impact of HIV Disease on Mortality in Gay and Bisexual Men." *International Journal of Epidemiology*, vol. 26, no. 3, 1997, pp. 657–661., doi:10.1093/ije/26.3.657.

Hogg, Robert S, et al. "Gay Life Expectancy Revisited." *OUP Academic*, Oxford University Press, 1 Dec. 2001, ije.oxfordjournals.org/cgi/content/full/30/6/1499.

Hottes, Travis Salway, et al. "Lifetime Prevalence of Suicide Attempts Among Sexual Minority Adults by Study Sampling Strategies: A Systematic Review and Meta-Analysis." *American Journal of Public Health*, vol. 106, no. 5, 6 Apr. 2016, doi:10.2105/ajph.2016.303088.

Jones, Jeffrey M. "LGBT Identification Rises to 5.6% in Latest U.S. Estimate." *Gallup.com*, Gallup, 26 Feb. 2021, news.gallup.com/poll/329708/lgbt-identification-rises-latest-estimate.aspx.

King, Michael, et al. "Mental Disorder, Suicide, and Self Harm in Lesbian, Gay and Bisexual People." *Medscape*, BMC Psychiatry , 7 Nov. 2008, www.medscape.com/viewarticle/581741.

Poteat, Tonia. "Top 10 Things Lesbians Should Discuss with Their Healthcare Provider." *GLMA*, www.glma.org/index.cfm?fuseaction=Page.viewPage&pageID=691.

Rueda, E. "The Homosexual Network." Old Greenwich, Conn., The Devin Adair Company, 1982, p. 53

"STDs in Men Who Have Sex with Men - 2018 Sexually Transmitted Diseases Surveillance." *Centers for Disease Control and Prevention*, Centers for Disease Control and Prevention, 30 July 2019, www.cdc.gov/std/stats18/msm.htm.

"Sexually Transmitted Diseases Among Gay and Bisexual Men." *Centers for Disease Control and Prevention*, Centers for Disease Control and Prevention, 9 Mar. 2016, www.cdc.gov/msmhealth/STD.htm.

Van de Ven, Paul, et al. "A Comparative Demographic and Sexual Profile of Older Homosexually Active Men." *The Journal of Sex Research*, vol. 34, no. 4, 1997, pp. 349–360., doi:10.1080/00224499709551903.

Chapter 16

Virtue, Vice, and Everything Nice

In Milton's *Paradise Lost*, the epic poem about Lucifer's expulsion from heaven and the aftermath of which, Lucifer's arguably most famous line is when he exclaims, "Better to rule in Hell than to serve in Heaven!" When I read that line, I thought, *never before has more honest insight been stated into the sinful heart of man.*

Many (if not most) people have something that they might be willing to trade their joy for—that one thing in their life that they do not want to give up even if it keeps them separated from God, joy, and eternal life, and spouse and family.

For Lucifer, it was his pride and vanity, his insistence on seeing himself as greater and more beautiful than God, who created Him (of course, it is obvious that God did not create any being to be greater than himself). Lucifer was given the gift of an eternity in heaven but, rather than worship God in eternal paradise, he opted to rebel against God and be revered in the bowels of despair. His pride was more important to him than eternal joy, and God gave him what he wanted. Virtually everybody is faced with a decision like this at one point or another—to choose between God or that one thing that separates us from Him.

For many people, as with Lucifer, their separation comes from pride; for some, it comes from a bottle of alcohol; for others, it's an escape into the temporary high which comes from needles and pharmaceuticals; for some rich men, it might be money or earthly possessions that remove them from all things eternal (see Matthew 19:16-24). For all too many, true joy is stripped away by lustful pursuits, often in the form of sexual pleasure, easier to pursue and harder to let go of with easy access to pornography, which was the outward funnel of my joy for a long time. And, while I was choosing those pursuits and refusing to give up my hollow pleasures, I was keeping myself separated from my creator—building a hedge between Him and me.

God loves us enough to have granted us free choice. We can serve Him and have access to eternal joy, or we can choose the fleeting pleasures of a finite world and the self-serving desires that separate us from such rewards as joy. So, if we are deprived of joy and forever separated from God, we chose it. Whatever we choose, God shall honor that decision and reward us accordingly. God's way, or our way; Paradise, or Paradise Lost.

No one can serve two masters. Either you will hate the one and love the other, or you will be devoted to one and despise the other. You cannot serve both God and mammon" (Matthew 6:24). If a vice masters you, be it mammon (greed), drugs, alcohol, sex, pornography, or any other, then you are not free to pursue God, much less any other relationship. One master will not release you to serve another and will not allow you to serve another simultaneously.

The difference between the two primary forms of a master is clear. Your vice, whatever it may be, is cold and restraining. The positive feelings that it provides are hollow and meaningless, and they come with painful chains and shackles. The high fades, and you are left with nothing but an empty feeling and isolation until the next fix. It is a subtle, cunning, sneaky form of slavery but a highly effective one because it makes itself seem attractive and desirable. This self-induced vice gives us the illusion that it is a form of freedom.

Then, you have God, who loves you and wishes for you to love Him back but will love you regardless. And He is ready to embrace you any time. The feelings He provides are positive, free from hollowness, and filled with meaning. Love for God means that you can feel joy even in the hard times and for all of eternity after you've left the things of the world behind. There is no cheap high with God, just genuine love and an awareness of purpose.

Those are the two options before you, but you can't have them both. Many have tried, but it is simply impossible. One will always resolve to keep you separate from the other.

If your master is vice, pornography, for example, you are a slave in a cage for a truly heartless and abusive overlord. You can't pursue God or any other meaningful relationship if you can't get beyond the bars!

The good news is that Christ has smuggled the key to freedom into your cell. You can unlock the door and walk out at any time! If you accept the key and escape your jail cell with Him, the only catch is that you must leave the shackles behind.

In much the same way, if you wish to form a romantic relationship or even repair an existing one, you must first release yourself from the grips of your vice. As long as your heart belongs to the bottle, the needle, the unclean bed, or the computer screen, it cannot be freely given to a spouse.

By the same token, if your heart belongs to sex—if you form a physical connection with someone before a romantic or marital connection is established—then your heart does not extend to the individual you bond with. Sex is still your drug in that instance, and you are using your partner as a delivery system. Even if you become "official" with the partner in question, the fact remains, you are not giving them all of your heart. You can't because your heart is still beholden to your overlord. It sounds pessimistic, but a pessimist is what an optimist calls a realist. If a vice takes your heart, it doesn't make room for love.

In choosing our vice in preference to our eternal reward, we essentially become like Esau. He gave up his entire birthright—an immense fortune of money and property to be inherited from his father—in a trade to stave off his momentary hunger with a bowl of lentil soup. Esau chose to feed his appetite for a moment, but the cost far exceeded the reward so far as my mathematically challenged mind comprehends. We can choose our vice on earth over our freedom and the privilege of being in a relationship with God, but the value of the two options is far from comparable. After all, what is the value of a pack of cigarettes when placed on a scale alongside a beachfront mansion in paradise?

When faced with such a clear choice to be liberated from the trappings of sin or to remain trapped by our selfish infatuations, we all too often defer to clutching *the precious*. When we are asked, "Would you like an eternity of peace, love, and joy?" we respond with a rabid, "No!"

Stopping the behavior in question is the only solution. Our trappings must be severed, and our *precious* must be thrown into the depths of the fiery mountain. There is no shortcut or cheat code. If you have a sexual relationship with a person extramaritally, it is time to stop. If the other person involved doesn't want to stop, then it may be time to end the relationship altogether and do things *right* the next time.

Love or vice. The decision is yours to make. Just as God will honor your freely made decision, I am sure any wise human being whom you try to form a relationship with will as well. If you choose to love, you will be rewarded with joy and probably a spouse. If you choose vice, on the other hand, you will be rewarded with the lowest, sordid, hollow, and least gratifying pleasure, as well as a hollow relationship, should you attempt to form one.

It is Paradise or Paradise Lost. I pray you make a wise decision.

Chapter 17

The Religion of Sex

Emile Cammaerts wrote in *The Laughing Prophet*, "When people deny God, they don't believe in *nothing*, they believe in *anything*." God designed human beings for worship. We all crave meaning and under-standing and, when we deny God, we seek that meaning and under-standing elsewhere, whether we call it worship or not.

I have met an almost amusing (but mostly disconcerting) number of people who flatly deny the existence or legitimacy of God but, in the same breath, are willing to assign consciousness and intelligence to the Universe in a pseudo-spiritual way. For example: "the universe, in its ultimate wisdom, has a way of punishing people for doing bad things," or, "the universe seems to want me to be single for right now because all of my relationships are falling through."

By their own admission, an intelligent creator is *too much* for them to believe in or acknowledge, but empty, neutral, amoral space mak-ing conscious decisions about their personal life is perfectly plausible? That is known as the *pathetic fallacy*—assigning human characteristics or responses to an impersonal, inanimate force or object. The pathetic fallacy in this instance is just an empty attempt to sound spiritual or wise without having to submit to the authority of God.

Those who stick their noses up at Christians for believing in God because they, themselves, are "too smart" to believe in Him are all-too-often just replacing Him with proverbial idols such as Mother Nature, Horoscopes, mammon, or sex; all of which are rearing their ugly heads throughout western culture today.

Secular folk deny God and so tend to lack sufficient meaning in their lives, necessitating that they seek that meaning in anything else that they can find to fill that God-shaped hole in their hearts. Of course, the material and perishable things they attempt to find meaning in never sufficiently meet that need (at least not to the minimum necessary extent); thus, they always feel they need more of that thing. Suppose some individual seeks to satisfy their need for meaning with sex. In that case, as many often do, that person will continue to pursue that vice time after time, conquest after conquest, person after person, just trying to plug the hole in their heart. The ironic thing is that this only makes the hole larger, leading to feelings of depression and hopelessness. When we try to fill that void in our hearts with anything but God and His perfect purpose and meaning, we risk destroying ourselves.

The prioritization of physical pleasure above all else is nothing new or original to western culture or even to this century. We are merely repeating a trend of history—a trend with a far-extending tradition of brokenness: Sodom and Gomorrah, Ancient Greece, and Ancient Rome are all examples of societies consumed by the widespread pursuit of carnal desires, some to the point of destroying themselves. In some of those listed, sexual immorality was even seen as a form of worship to God or the gods. Today, however, sex has become its very own religion, and a man named Alfred Kinsey was its apocryphal messiah.

A False Religion's Founder

Alfred Kinsey is often referred to as the "Father of the Sexual Revolution." Quite the lofty title, I know. If there is any question that his admirers showed him a sort of religious deference, his biographer, James H. Jones, referred to him as "the high priest of sexual liberation."[15] Kinsey's first book, *Sexual Behavior in the Human Male* (to later be followed by its sequel, *Sexual Behavior in the Human Female*), published in 1948, was a bestselling culmination of research into—you guessed it—how men behave sexually. It wasn't quite as simple as an educational text, however. The book was primarily written to convince the culture that societal or personal restrictions on human sexual behavior were "unnatural" and thus immoral. It would be more accurate to label it as propaganda rather than education.

To get his questionable points across, Kinsey knowingly used skewed data and virtually fabricated statistics to claim that the majority of people were secretly engaging in crazy, unorthodox, and taboo sexual practices. I will avoid some of the more disturbing entries of his

---

15   Jones, James H. *Alfred C. Kinsey: a Life*. W.W. Norton, 2004.

book, for your sanity's sake, but a few examples of his false statistics are as follows:

- 50% of all married men commit adultery, often consistently or habitually
- 69% of white men have experience with prostitutes
- 10% of white men are exclusively homosexual for no less than three years of their life
- 95% of single women have had abortions

While each of these statistics, and more like them, have been widely refuted and discredited, largely because he gathered them by predominately conducting his "research" on sex offenders, they still went a long way with engaging the public's imagination and attitudes about sex. Lies and myths will often have such an effect when presented in advance to the truth.

Beyond Kinsey's disregard for truth, Kinsey dismissed all moral components accompanying sexual behavior. He preferred to keep his focus on the physical, material side of things, castigating the very idea of spiritual factors. You might say that he was a staunch materialist. Moral questions did not concern him. Kinsey spent a great deal of time and energy trying to convince everybody else to forsake moral questions as well and to think as he did. According to Kinsey, we should not hold ourselves to any standard different from animals, who never ask questions concerning right and wrong. Kinsey wrote: "Just as the birds do it, bees do it, so should we do it."

Kinsey abhorred what he referred to as "Victorian morality" surrounding sex—essentially the Judeo-Christian standards of decency, chastity, austerity, and virtue. The concept of purity, to him, would be inconceivable. Kinsey's goal in life was to disintegrate the moral fabric of the west, and he spent his professional career as an educator zeroed in on his primary target of sexual morality.

Alfred Kinsey's supposed Reproductive Anatomy and Physiology class was less focused on educating young minds on how the body physiologically works (as was the point of the course) and more focused on propagandizing to his students on what he perceived as the "evils" of chastity while walking them through, point by point, every stage of sexual intercourse in a combination of detachment and exaggerated detail.[16] In such classes, he claimed that rules surrounding marriage and sex were problematic and that "the danger to the family, then, lay not in sexual freedom but in sexual repression."[17]

Kinsey would even spend much of his time arguing against acknowledging differences between men and women, comparing reproductive organs of the two sexes in search of vague structural similarities to plant the seed in young minds that males and females were "essentially alike in their sexual anatomy."[18] consciously attempting to convince his students that distinctions between the two sexes are fictional and societally imposed and that homosexual sex made perfect sense with these bold claims in mind. I am sure that Kinsey would be proud of the transgender movement in 21st century America, which takes his propaganda just a step further.

To someone with Alfred Kinsey's worldview, morality has no place in the categories of sex and pleasure. By his estimation, "without society's demands of morality, choosing a partner would be like picking out clothes or dinner." Setting aside for a moment the fact that a "partner" is a human being, not some sirloin to be consumed and then forgotten about in the trashcan, Kinsey makes the mistake of assuming that morality is totally up to society—that there is no higher standard or authority than that which the masses, mobs, or state/government decide. Heaven forbid that the world's moral code is determined by mob rule!

The moral law goes far beyond society, and it is well outside of our control or influence. That is what Alfred Kinsey could not concede. He saw morality as a social construct—a dangerous proposition—and sought to mold it according to his own will. As we can see, his will was a cold, dark place.

According to Kinsey, an individual's personal history and sexual development should completely negate the need for moral constraints. The way he explains it, we cannot judge the actions of adulterers, fornicators, homosexuals, or pedophiles because we are not familiar with each individual's sexual background. In Kinsey's mind, no person is immoral for engaging in such acts; they have different "needs" because of their history with sex. This is circular reasoning, of course. The claim is

---

16   Ibid, p. 329.

17   Ibid. p. 328.

18   Ibid, p. 330.

that an act cannot be immoral because it was committed before, and thus that first act cannot be immoral either.

In other words, Kinsey writes in his book (and I am paraphrasing) that "there is no clear right or wrong. Sexual behavior naturally changes over time from one habit to another. It is not a moral issue, so we shouldn't judge people with different sexual appetites than us, no matter what that appetite is." Put simply: whatever feels good must *be* good.

The logical conclusion to Kinsey's argument is that rape, sexual assault, and child molestation should all be accepted because these people simply have different "needs" or definitions of what feels good. There's nothing immoral about any of these crimes if we stick to Kinsey's teachings. He exemplifies how little trouble he has in his conscience with such atrocities.

We already know that Kinsey did not like to link morals with sexual behavior. Still, the fact is that he also dismissed morality, ethics, and basic humanity altogether in favor of so-called "research." What do I mean? Alfred Kinsey devoted time and study to the sexual behavior of pedophiles (the results of which are recorded in his book). Not only did the man correspond with people who raped young children and babies, but he had his staff supply these rapists with stopwatches to be used during the horrific acts that they perpetrated and asked that they report on their sadistic experiences. In reporting on this "research" of Kinsey's, Sarah D. Goode rightly said, "there is a name for such behavior in civilized countries, but that name is not 'science.'"[19]

The man I am writing about did not belong in academia, and he most certainly did not warrant a position of influence. If anybody in the scientific community today had skewed research results as he had or, worse, engaged in his "research" practices, they would rightly be ostracized from the scientific community and hopefully presented with criminal charges!

A man who has such indifference—who sees nothing immoral about terrible acts being committed and, in fact, enables it to happen—has no concept of morality and cannot differentiate between right and wrong. As described even by his own admiring and lauding biographer, such a man has no guilt or shame—just cold detachment. That is the textbook definition of a psychopath.

---

19   Sarah D. Goode, Paedophiles in Society: Reflecting on Sexuality, Abuse, and Hope.

That was the initiator of the Sexual Revolution, the man whose doctrine many in our modern culture seem content to live by, and the founder of the modern Religion of Sex.

Discipleship of a Pornographer

Of course, the Religion of Sex did not stop with Kinsey. The false messiah needed a disciple to carry forth the doctrine. That disciple—the one who would take a primary role in spreading the teachings of a paganistic religious observance to pleasure—turned out to be none other than Hugh Hefner, the founder of *Playboy Magazine* and the father of the epidemical modern pornography industry.

According to the biographer, Stephen Watts, Hugh Hefner grew up in a strict Methodist home where silence appeared the prevailing family value. There was seldom any display of emotion or affection among the family and reportedly no passion to be sensed between his parents. The allegedly virtuous household was full of kindness but little else in meaningful human interaction. It might be easy to understand how a man who grew up in conditions such as this might later resent the idea of repression in any form, whether it be emotional or physical.

After getting married in 1949, Hefner gained a corrosive distrust of women and commitment in general after gaining knowledge of his [first] wife's one-time affair with another man. Over time, the resentment he carried for his wife would aid in his moral sensibilities being corroded away almost completely. This distrust and bitterness that he held onto with every cell of his heart was a toxic seed that could only grow a tree of deadly fruits. Like Saint Augustine said, "Resentment is like drinking poison and hoping the other person dies." Hugh most certainly guzzled down that poison, but it would toxify more than just him. Almost as if via osmosis, his poison would infect all of those he touched with his soon-to-be wide reach.

The dominoes soon fell. Hefner became angry with the very idea of sexual morality, viewing it as a hypocritical abomination against nature. His anger turned toward Christianity for forwarding the blight on society that was celibacy—for his perceived lack of freedom to pursue carnal desires. In Hefner's own words, "Man's moral life, as long as it does not harm others, is his own business, and should be left to his own discretion." Little did he understand that this statement is ultimately defeated by its own standard since immoral behavior is never perfectly unharmful to those around us, especially those of a sexual nature.

Just because he did not recognize the harm that he was inflicting on the women he used or the young men his influence would eventually reach does not mean that the harm was not there. I am again reminded of Walter Dean Burnham's quote: "A wise man does not tear down a fence until he knows why it was built." Hefner didn't know what was beyond the moral fence raised in his path, but he tore it down all the same.

At the age of 22, Hefner's convictions were furthered and cemented when he discovered a certain bestselling book published in 1948, *Sexual Behavior in the Human Male*, written by Alfred Kinsey.

Hefner was not shy about who his heroes were, "Kinsey had a tremendous impact on me. [His book] supplied the evidence that proved the things I had been feeling for so many years, which was that what we said about our sexuality was not what we did. That we were hypocrites, and out of that came a good deal of hurt."[20]

After reading Kinsey, Hefner came to such conclusions not out of intellectual honesty or the genuine seeking of truth, but because he had already been seeking justification for his denouncements of Judeo-Christian sexual morality and desire and permission to pursue all manner of sexual urges.

We often find the "truth" we want to find if we look hard enough. It is always easy for people to accept a lie that they hope or wish for. It didn't matter to Hefner that Kinsey's book was ultimately nonsense, widely discredited, and wholly immoral by any standard or measure in terms of the methods of research he conducted. Hefner wanted Kinsey to be right, wanted carnality to be virtuous (or, at the very least, morally neutral), and so he held on tight to that sophistic doctrine and spread the word of it far and wide!

Hefner's big accomplishment, *Playboy Magazine*, the foundation of today's porn epidemic, bears the mark of Kinsey's influence. *Sexual Behavior in the Human Male* was analogous to Hefner's religious text. The magazine he started was Hefner's unsettling version of ministry— all in the name of the Religion of Sex.

The magazine's first issue was released in 1953, containing provocative images of Marilyn Monroe, and sold 50,000 copies. By 1960, a million copies were flying off the racks every month. By 1970, that number had multiplied by seven. Today, millions of pornographic images and

---

20   Stephen Watts, *Mr. Playboy: Hugh Hefner and the American Dream.*

videos are consumed over the Internet every minute, poisoning the minds of our youth and giving them very wrong and unhealthy views of sex—something that God had intended to be a beautiful addition to His creation, not something to be cheapened or thought of as "dirty."

Sex is, unfortunately, the fastest-growing religion in the west, and people are sucking in its disturbing and perverse gospel with their eyes and letting it take a terrible toll on their minds and bodies.

For Hefner, satisfying the flesh was the only thing he pursued to grant meaning to his life—to fill his heart and satisfy his soul. Sadly, for him, lust is more parasitic than it is fulfilling, and his efforts could only make his heart brittle to the point of ashes and leave his soul malnourished to the point that, by the end, he was essentially a living husk. Anyone who seeks life-long purpose in the temporary things, the fleeting, the flesh, will find again and again that they only feel emptier still every time they indulge. My heart weighs heavy for anyone in such a position.

When Hugh Hefner died on September 27, 2017, secular culture and media mourned loudly for the loss of their great disciple—praising him as "a great man who contributed so much to the world and had such a profound impact." I was there, and I remember these tributes vividly. This icon of theirs is the same man who:

- Would take advantage of a pretty, young, impressionable girl for self-gratification and bragged about having slept with over 1000 women throughout his life—all of whom were all little more than tools of pleasure for him, names to add to the list he could boast about later.
- Profited from taking naked pictures of some poor father's naïve teenage daughter and showing them off to the whole world.
- Made his fortune by painting women as mere objects to be used for quick gratification and then discarded at the literal turn of a page.
- Founded an industry that destroys lives and crushes souls.
- Blurred the lines between what is moral and decent and what is evil.

The same people who claimed that Hefner was a great man were also the ones complaining loudly to the entire culture about how awful men are, how they are all sex-crazed pigs, how they see women as objects. Do you sense a trend? Do people ignore the fact that Hefner and the industry he built had a great deal to do with the fall of men into this ditch, or are they just completely oblivious? Hugh Hefner was the reigning champion of all things that the man-critics complain about, personally and professionally. Many feminists, who ostensibly live for the empowerment of women, praised the man for making them feel powerful and beautiful, when, in actuality, what he did was rob women of dignity and respect, not to mention hiding the beauty of their hearts and minds by getting men to focus more on their bodies.

The Religion of Sex (R.O.S.) proves itself time and time again to be without sense, consistency, or logic. Emotion and desire reign supreme in this doctrine! To heck with rational thought! We are, after all, talking about a religious practice that mocks God yet bows down to the misuse of something that He invented. God designed sex with a purpose and gave us instructions on how best to be used and enjoyed. The R.O.S. steps on His intention, deciding that they don't want to live by His rules, even though those who live by them tend to have better, more fulfilling lives and love-filled hearts. Fences are put up for a reason.

When you try to fill your heart with fleeting pleasures and carnal pursuits, it will never be enough, and you will end up far emptier by the end than you did when you began that pursuit. When you fall into a pit such as that of sexual sin, the last thing that you want to try is digging that hole deeper. If you want freedom, you have to get out of the pit, and for that, you must look up.

Never Enough

The Sexual Revolution, which officially took place in the 1960s, wasn't enough for the sex worshippers, so they had to keep going, keep fighting for more, they had the "right" to sleep around without the "oppressive" institution of marriage getting in the way, normalizing promiscuity and destabilizing the American family. Now they needed to redefine marriage and gain the right to same-sex marriage. Does anybody else see the tragic irony in that? They fought to make marriage obsolete, only to make it the central pillar of the homosexual agenda.

Same-sex marriage became nationally legalized in the United States in 2015. The followers of the R.O.S. *needed* churches and pastors to affirm this Biblically immoral behavior by declaring that homosexuality is not a sin. Of course, pastors and other Christians did not set the moral standard. Thus, it is not within our power to alter. If Christians invented their own moral code, I suspect that the strictures on sexual behavior and other stuff humans like doing would not be nearly as strict. In fact, I guarantee that the moral standard to which we are held would not be even remotely close to what it is in the Bible were we to develop the rules for ourselves. Without God's guidance, we would destroy ourselves.

When same-sex marriage was nationally legalized, I was in college, and my friends and college peers thought I was crazy when I explained that it would not stop there because issues of sex always escalate: the porn addict gradually begins to crave more taboo offensive material. Everyone who has had a pornography habit that has lasted for over a year has had at least one moment when they said quietly to themselves, "I never thought that I would look at something that depraved and like it." The sexually indecent always begins to need more perverse practices and sex acts, etc. He is overstimulated and eventually becomes bored with acts that range from normal to detestable and seeks a new thrill to keep things interesting. Overindulgence in pleasure never fails to *reduce* the occurrence of pleasure and satisfaction in the long run. There is never any satisfaction when it comes to sexual immorality, only an increased and more depraved appetite, and so I was sure that things would continue to escalate. My theory was that pedophilia was next in line.

It turns out that I was not as crazy as my peers believed. Shortly after that, proponents for the legalization of pedophilia began to gain confidence and express their beliefs on very public platforms, attempting to convince people that child sexuality ought to be normalized and that "love" has no age. While I find it hard to imagine this movement gaining any meaningful momentum, as even the most fringe people I know find it abhorrent, the R.O.S. crowd has been moving their agenda along in very rapid, aggressive, ferocious, borderline rabid velocity over the last decade.

Even after the attacks against the Biblical morals of the church, the R.O.S. sought to go beyond same-sex marriage by attempting to render gender obsolete altogether. They did this by teaching children in schools that gender is a social construct, that biology is a myth, and that a 5-year-old boy should choose to transform into a girl and vice versa surgically. This topic requires a whole stand-alone book to describe and refute. However, anybody with a healthy brain and the ability to think critically can see how dangerous this specific ideology is.

Beyond all of this, the followers of the Religion of Sex feel the need to make sure that nobody contradicts the nonsense they are preaching (or, more accurately, spewing). They tear down all of these moral fences but give no thought as to what awaits on the other side, why those barriers exist in the first place—no critical thought toward the consequences that will inevitably come.

R.O.S. observers seek purpose in their life, but they have denied God and thus have difficulty finding it. They cannot, by nature, believe in nothing, so they must open themselves to believing in *anything*.

Every time the sex-worshipping subculture gains ground, they get more and more greedy, wanting to claim more land and crush more opposition—not dissimilar to how a glutton's appetite grows the more he indulges and stretches his stomach. They claim that it is all in the name of "tolerance," which is the central premise of the R.O.S. doctrine. By their estimation, one can only truly love somebody if he tolerates their every behavior, belief, and decision. Of course, no rational human would call it love to tolerate a loved one's behavior of shooting heroin daily and living in drug addiction.

The followers of R.O.S. claim that everyone should "tolerate" the beliefs and behaviors of those who believe or live differently than they do. Then, those same followers turn around seconds later and criticize Christians for believing differently than they do! I suppose tolerance only works in one direction. Apparently, Christianity is intolerant because it doesn't conform to the ways of a worldview that demands tolerance, and tolerance can only work if you do not tolerate those who don't believe in the same "tolerant" worldview as you do! Whoa, my head hurts from how self-defeating that whole philosophy is!

(Feel free to read that last paragraph again, as I said "tolerance" a lot.)

One cannot demand that people be tolerant of their lifestyle and belief system while insisting that my contrary beliefs are wrong and must be changed. It is logically inconsistent to believe that you can take a side on an issue without opposing the other side of the argument. If you stand for one thing, you stand against another. I stand for sexual purity and thus against promiscuity. Others stand for promiscuity and "liberation" and thus against purity. To sum it all up, it is impossible to live by the modern code of tolerance without being intolerant to some degree.

No matter how far the sex-worshiper goes, it is never enough for those who engage in it, and it will never be enough to satisfy. The purpose that followers of the R.O.S. have chosen to pursue, the gods they have chosen to revere and serve, the rituals they have chosen to partake in will never bring satisfaction. I, as a follower of God alone, only

Page 171

wish to share God's love with people, which will allow them the chance to experience true purpose, meaning, and satisfaction. And I love them enough to tell them that God's standard is the best way to live by—that living the way they are is not good for them—even if they may hate me for it.

Unlike sex, God is worthy of my worship. Woe to him who bows down before the created things in place of He who created them.

For Further Study

Kinsey, Alfred Charles, et al. *Sexual Behavior in the Human Male.* W.B. Saunders Company, 1948.

Marcuse, Herbert. *Repressive Tolerance,* Boston: Beacon Press, 1969, pp. 95–137.

Watts, Steven. *Mr Playboy: Hugh Hefner and the American Dream.* Wiley, 2009.

Chapter 18

You Will Find the Kind of Spouse You Seek

When we are applying for a job, most of us plan for the interview process accordingly. If you are pursuing a high-paying dream job and making your way to the job interview at a fancy law firm or another black-tie workplace, would I be wrong in assuming that you would dress appropriately? If you are pursuing a job in which the general attire is a pressed suit, you will wear a nice suit to the job interview. If you want a job in a small retail establishment, you would dress respectably for the job interview! Khakis and a button-up shirt would be the minimum requirement. If you dress inappropriately for an interview, your chances of getting the job are next to zero percent.

Your appearance, how you carry yourself, and dress make a difference. It does matter. Body language makes up approximately 83% of communication, so yes, how you present yourself is of consequence. If you slouch, you appear weak and timid, but standing up straight, chest out, and keeping hands out of pockets sends the very opposite message. If you walk into an interview with a straight back and make eye contact when you speak, that makes more of an impression than anything you verbally say during the interview. Body language is the most crucial face-to-face communication in any professional, social, or casual setting.

As you may have guessed, part of your body language is the clothes you wear. Your attire always has the benefit (or hindrance) of projecting an image—a message about your personage. Your clothing at an interview can say a whole lot about how serious you are about a job prospect. Whether professionally or socially, how you dress can say a great deal about your personality and lifestyle. People can paint you as a serious or fun person, rich or poor, neat or sloppy, proper or lewd, etc. What message is your attire sending about you?

I enjoy funny T-shirts—clothing bearing a humorous message that can draw people's laughter. However, I noticed something about people who wear funny shirts. Generally speaking, when a guy wears a funny shirt, the shirt has more personality than he does. The joke on the shirt is the extent of his sense of humor and his social skills, though that is not true in every instance. For my part, I choose not to wear funny T-shirts very often anymore because I want my fun side to manifest and be exhibited in my personality, rather than be limited to my attire. I do not want anybody to glance at my shirt and think I need to wear it to compensate for some lack of charisma. I think similarly about women who dress in very revealing clothes. It often seems as though they are trying hard to gloss over their personality or lack thereof by hyper-sexualizing themselves. Is it any wonder that the only men who seem to take an interest in women of such habits are wooden and sleazy?

One way or another, a person's character is expressed through how we dress and present ourselves. Why not express your character in the best possible terms? If you would dress properly for the job you want, would it not make sense to treat the dating world as a job interview and dress for the kind of man you want?

I can hear the sound of some women's eyes rolling right now. You are all bracing yourself for what is coming. "Oh great, another Christian boy is going to try to tell me to dress subtly and conservatively!" Yes, yes, he is. However, let me first disclaim that I am not a fan of legalism in the slightest sense, and I do not claim that you or anyone else is a good or bad Christian based solely on how you are dressed. Should you choose to wear revealing clothes, I will not condemn you, and I can assure you that God does not love or value you any less if you happen to rock a halter top or show off your midsection.

I will tell you that you are doing yourself no favors by advertising yourself in such an unfavorable light or fashion—by dressing provocatively. God's concern in this category is for *your* wellbeing—the condition of your heart, keeping the eyes of men with bad intentions off of your body, and keeping virtuous men with good intentions checking out your big heart.

I love Muhammad Ali's advice to his daughter in this area. I wish I had been the one to put it in these terms: "Hana, everything that God made valuable in the world is covered and hard to get to. Where do you find diamonds? Deep down in the ground, covered and protected. Where do you find pearls? Deep down at the bottom of the ocean, covered up and protected in a beautiful shell. Where do you find gold? Way down in the mine, covered over with layers and layers of rock. You've got to work hard to get to them."[21]

A woman is more valuable than any diamond or pearl, and she should value herself as such. She should be hard to get to. A man should have to work and labor to reach her heart and pay the highest price that he can to have her. If a man wants something worth unfathomably more than any quantity of gold, he must be willing to value her as such and commit the rest of his life to her as payment. If he is unwilling to pay what God has charged for her, he ought not to have her. Ladies, if you do not make a man work and labor to see you and have you, you do not value yourself the way your God does. Your value is beyond counting and demands just compensation. You were not meant to give yourself away for free. "Your body is sacred. You're far more precious than diamonds and pearls, and you should be covered too."[22]

Here is the problem—one of many—with attracting a partner by using your body: your body *is* going to change. You *will* get older, put on weight, get gray and wrinkly, and the body you used to attract that man with will no longer exist.

To use your body to attract a man is to reel him in with the temporary. That will ultimately make the relationship temporary. While a nice seasoning, physical attraction cannot make up the whole meal. It does *not* fill a person up or satisfy. It does not make for a sturdy long-term relationship. A meal needs substance and nutrition more than just seasoning, or one is likely to starve. Hotness, money, and sex all have an expiration date! They will not sustain either partner forever. It will end badly, with broken hearts.

In a single statement, if you attract a man with your body, you will likewise repel him with your body. Proverbs 14:1 says, "A wise woman builds her house, while a foolish woman tears hers down by her own efforts."

I am sure you are familiar with the old classic children's tale, *The Three Little Pigs*. All three little pigs built themselves an individual house: one built his house out of straw, the second out of sticks, and

---

21   Muhammad Ali, *More Than A Hero: Muhammad Ali's Life Lessons Through His Daughter's Eyes*

22   Ibid.

the third built his with brick and stone. Only one of those three houses was still standing after the Big Bad Wolf huffed and puffed and blew the house down. The brick house was built from the sturdiest foundation. As a result, that house withstood even the harshest wind. The first little pig did build a house, but he did not do so with a strong foundation or sturdy material. His house could not remain standing when the wolf blew on it, but the little pig tore his own house down long before that—in its poor construction. His own effort ultimately destroyed his house.

When a woman attracts a man by dressing provocatively with her body, she is building a house of straw, and even that is only if the house manages to be completed (if the man she attracts chooses to remain for more than one night). That woman did not lay down a strong foundation of character, virtue, and love that a stone base consists of but instead went with the straw walls of lust and sexual sin. The Big Bad Wolf called Time brings with it many winds; age, sickness, pregnancy, etc. Any one of them can blow a straw house to nothingness. Of course, most of the men whom a woman snags by utilizing "straw tactics" will not even stick around long enough to make a commitment and build a shaky house.

If you are using straw tactics—attracting men by dressing like an exotic dancer and seducing them with your flesh—do not complain that the men you end up with are pigs, so to speak. If you attract men that way, you shout that you are weak of character. As a result, the men you attract will be very feeble as well. You tore down your house before it was built. If you want better men, practice better behaviors.

You might say, "Well, men should treat me like a princess, with dignity and respect, no matter how I am dressed or how I act!" Of course, they *should*. Bad men *should* do a lot of things. Bad men *should* avoid lying, cheating, and stealing. They *should* live life pure and virtuous. They *should* treat you with respect and love. But the fact is they will not. That is not what bad men do, and bad men are exactly whom straw tactic behaviors will attract. You can fully expect bad men not to behave badly, but it will not change the state of reality. Bad men, sadly, will not magically behave like good ones because you wish them to.

Good men will treat you with love and respect no matter what, but good men are not the ones you will lure to your side with tight-fitting clothes, exposed flesh, and a seductive attitude. If a man is wise, he will not date a woman who carries herself as such. Do not complain about the character of men if your character shows to be in shambles.

And, do not tell me that if you attract a bad man, you can be the one to change him! Bad men do not become good men for bad girls! In my experience, "bad girls" are just weak-willed women who put on a show because they're lonely and want to give the "bad boys" what they want. These are the women whom bad men think they can use. A man will not change his immoral ways for a weak-willed woman who gives him anything his flesh desires and attracts his attention by showing off her body or presenting the allure of commitment-free sex. If a man is only interested in you if you wear pants that accent your butt and a shirt that leaves little to the imagination, stay away from that sad, sorry, pathetic excuse of a "man!" Run!

I can assure you that dressing subtly works in your best interest. The first thing that caught my attention when I laid eyes upon my beautiful wife for the first time from across a crowded dance floor was how self-respecting she seemed—how conservatively she was dressed compared to the other girls in the establishment with their half-shirts and their short pants that extended a length of about 3-inches from the waistband. Not to mention she sat out every song played accompanied by people on the dancefloor grinding on one another (seriously, how is that considered dancing? I felt the overwhelming urge to contact law enforcement and report mass sexual assault).

My wife's character was reflected in her appearance and how she presented herself to those around her. That's how I knew I had to meet this woman. She attracted me, not with her body, but with her persona. When I spoke to her, I wasn't staring at her surface features. I was digging for the diamonds hidden in her heart. This woman knew how to build a sturdy house. She was building out of brick.

A Bad Boy is a Bad Man

In the children's animated Disney film, *Wreck-It Ralph* (a solid scholarly choice for a life lesson, I know), there is a scene in which all of the villains from all of the video games gather in a circle as a sort of support group in which they collectively cope with their lot in life as scripted antagonists. Ralph, the main character, no longer wants to play the bad guy and confesses as much to the group in this scene. To comfort him, one of the other villains in the circle says to him in a thick Russian accent, "Just because you are a *bad guy* does not mean you are a bad *guy*."

While that statement is nice for a kid's film and might be true in Ralph's case, since he's just a nice guy who was cast for a role as the antagonist of a video game (in effect, around-the-clock actor), it is not all too applicable in real life. Unfortunately, that seemingly innocent line represents how many real-life women view the very real-life men they choose to date.

In our modern-day culture, most people tend to watch many movies and television, and a minority even read a lot of romance novels. In so many of these fictional works, there is always a male character with rough edges whom the women always seem to fall for. This character is often portrayed as a tough guy, a womanizer who sleeps with many women, a cold yet confident man who acts like a jerk towards people, and perhaps somebody who drinks too much. But the women in these stories, and the women watching or reading them, always seem to fall in love with this man because, "deep down, beneath his rough exterior, this man has a heart of gold!"

No, he does not.

Outside of the fictional world, out here where reality reigns supreme, the men who do immoral things and have immoral habits are not going to be the heroes of your story. They are simply immoral men who do bad things. That is the kind of man who tends to make a real woman's life hell on earth. Bad boys are exactly that: bad.

A bad guy who puts on the heart-of-gold act is a wolf in sheep's clothing! Jesus says in Matthew 7 that you can recognize a wolf in sheep's clothing by the "fruits that they bear." Good fruit does not come from a rotten tree, and bad fruit does not come from a good tree! In other words, if a man regularly does bad and immoral things (fruit), then you can be assured he is not an overall good man (tree). No one wants to gorge themselves on the apples from a rotten and moldy orchard.

If you want a good man, ladies, then avoid men who have tendencies to do the following things:

- Lie
- Cheat
- Steal
- Go out and get drunk
- Try to get you drunk
- Do drugs or own a bong
- Talk down to you

- Skip out on his responsibilities and obligations
- Curse at you or call you profane names
- Treat you like his servant or doormat
- Look at porn or ask *you* to look at porn
- Masturbate
- Put his hands on your breasts or private parts
- Try to get his hands in your pants or under your shirt
- Pressure you into sex
- Try for alternative forms of sex as a loophole (i.e., oral or anal)
- Sends pictures of his private body parts
- Ask you for inappropriate pictures
- Pursue you or other women who are known to have a boy-friend
- Date multiple women at the same time
- Pursue any woman wearing an engagement or wedding ring
- Ask you to live with him outside of marriage
- Hit or threaten you
- Excuse immoral behavior by saying something to the effect of, "I just can't help it," or, "I just have to be myself."
- Is a slave to his urges and desires, sexual or otherwise

If it looks like a snake, moves like a snake, sounds like a snake, and acts like a snake, you are about to get bitten!

A good man does good things and develops good habits. A bad man does bad things and develops bad habits. It is not that hard to figure out. Jesus died on the cross to free us from the bondage of sin, not to give us an excuse to sin as much as we please. It is very simple. Have as much love and respect for yourself as your creator does. He wants what is best for you, and a serpent is not it.

I know that there are those among you who are thinking, *we are not supposed to judge people, but that is what you are telling me to do!* If that is you, I will ask you to engage your critical thinking capabilities. But, before I do, I have some news to break to you: Jesus simply did not command us not to judge. The words "do not judge" are certainly in the Bible and in that word order—again in Matthew 7—but that is not the whole of the message. One cannot simply pick those three words out among the rest; take those three words alone out of context and just cast aside the whole rest of the passage.

In Matthew 7:1-5, Jesus says to us, "Do not judge, lest you too be judged. For in the same way that you judge others, you too will be judged, and with the measure you use, it will be measured against you. Why do you look at the speck of dust in your brother's eye and pay no attention to the plank in your own eye? How can you say to your brother, 'Let me take the speck of dust out of your eye,' when all the while there is an entire plank in your own eye? You hypocrite, first take the plank out of your own eye, and then you will see clearly to remove the speck from your brother's eye."

So, now that we have read the whole passage, we can see that the often-misquoted message is not simply, "do not judge," but rather, "do not judge *hypocritically*." Jesus did not say to remove the plank from our own eye and then leave your brother alone to drown in his sin. He said that we should not look at and acknowledge his sin without recognizing and answering to our own.

In other words, don't tell your friend to stop drinking beer while you are holding a bottle of whiskey. Do not judge a girl for being sexually promiscuous while having a different sexual partner every month. We cannot live in a functional society without making moral judgments! You do so every time you are lied to, when someone cheats in a board game, when an individual drives recklessly on the road with no concern for the safety of anybody else, and when one commits a horrific crime. We are commanded to use wisdom and make moral judgments for good reason! However, we are not to exempt ourselves from the moral standards that we hold others to. That is Jesus' command to us.

Time to Digress: In truth, how I have thus far explained the "do not judge, lest you be judged," is only half of the truth behind what we can conclude that Jesus was saying. Yes, Jesus is telling us in Matthew 7 that we ought not to judge hypocritically, but there is still another meaning. Beyond hypocrisy alone, we are warned against judging people unjustly or unfairly, such as in the case of those individuals who are just now being exposed to the ways of Christ, people who are new to the church, and those who have yet to undergo sanctification. If we cannot expect a non-believer to live as though he believes in God, would it be any fairer to admonish somebody for falling short of Christian standards of behavior when said individual has yet to learn what those standards are or how to apply them to everyday behavior? You cannot expect an infant to stand and run on its first day, should you not expect a newly born-again individual to be the picture of Christian virtue immediately after accepting Christ—or worse yet, expect that every guest at your church (who may not yet be a believer) conform immediately to the church doctrine.

Hypothetically, if I invite a young woman to church who has had an unpleasant upbringing, a questionable past, or a disreputable career (an exotic dancer, for example), one can probably assume church would be a new experience for her. She does not know the etiquette, probably doesn't have many Sunday best clothes in her closet, and might have a slight habit of saying words that Christians are not supposed to say. Such a woman might be nervous about attending church for the first time, and the last thing she needs is the added pressure of judgmental attitudes and glances being directed her way. She is a guest in God's house and should be treated with dignity. We are not to scare away those seeking God by showing them grief about such menial things as their attire and making them feel too ashamed or alienated to return. Let such a person come to God as she is, and let Him do the rest when she is ready.

If we were commanded not to judge at all, in any capacity, then we would have to ignore a lot of scripture from the Bible. Not the least of which is when Jesus tells us to beware of wolves in sheep's clothing. If we cannot judge people in any way, then how are we to separate the sheep from the wolves? We could not.

With all of that being said, I am advising you to judge people based on their actions, as it is a telling reflection of the condition of their hearts. You have to make certain moral judgments about a person before you consider dating them, much less marry them. To make a judgment is to tell the good from the bad. You would be foolish not to.

If you are hiking and come to a rope bridge that extends across a long and deep canyon, but you notice the bridge is made from frayed rope and rotted wooden planks, you reasonably judge that you cannot trust that particular bridge to get you across the canyon safely. If you trust the bad bridge, it is likely to break and send you falling to your death. Instead, you would be wise to find a good and sturdy bridge to get you across.

In the same way, you should be wise enough to judge whether a man is good or bad. If the man were a bridge, would he support your weight or cause you to fall? If you meet a man who drinks excessively, acts like a jerk, and pressures you into sex, it is better to avoid him and keep looking. You cannot trust an immoral man to be any better for you than the analogical bridge that will drop you.

If you meet a good Christian man but discover he occasionally views pornography, back away! That is not what a good man does, much less a Christian man! Trust me on this one.

I know what it is to fall into the bad man category. I was that nice young man who occasionally guzzled alcohol and secretly viewed pornography in college. No woman who dated me was better off for it with such poison coursing through my character. Neither of those habits, which many of my peers would have considered harmless, are anything you want to have involved in your relationships in any situation.

A good man does good things, and a bad man does bad things. No man is perfect, obviously, but there is a stark difference between a man who makes the occasional misstep and the one who succumbs to immoral habits. To my male readers, if you are involved in any of the habits brought up in this chapter, I would advise you to stop it. I mean it when I say that women should not date—much less marry—a man who engages in such things. No one expects you to be without flaws, perfect and blemish-free in every way, but you had best hold yourself to a high standard. Jesus certainly does, as will any good woman of strong will. And you want a good woman.

Seek, and You Shall Find a Bad Girl

A wife of noble character, who can find? She is worth far more than rubies. (Proverbs 31:10)

When I wrote about seeking out a good man, it was inevitable that I would also have to pick on the women. I already know that many of my acquaintances will resent the material I include in this section. Still, this entire book is filled with material that many will object to. The truth is often offensive; that's how you know that you're at odds with it. Let me assure everyone that my intention is never to offend people maliciously, but the offense is unavoidable to those who speak the truth. So, let the blight of my likeability begin!

Men cannot be excused from making poor choices in women any more than women can for making poor choices in men. We are no less fallible. And, while we may be motivated differently in our bad decisions than women are, we no less fall prey to the "follow your heart" delusion. Of course, as I have said, following our hearts is exactly when we tend to initiate the worst of our life decisions.

A good woman can indeed be hard to find in our fallen world. I know this well. I desperately searched while living on a college campus to find a woman of good character. Of course, where you look does matter. As the old real estate cliché goes, "Location, location, location." And a fraternity house party was a poor location for my search.

As men, we are motivated not just by our hearts but by our eyes and the desires that our testosterone gives rise to. This can tend to make us stupid if we allow it to, as I did when I thought I could find a good, marriageable woman at a frat party. We men are visually stimulated and, as the wise Ben Kenobi put it, "your eyes can deceive you, don't trust them." This is not to say that we should look for a woman blindly—quite the contrary—but where our eyes go and what they focus on can make a significant difference. Suppose a man chooses to meet women at a party flooded with loud music, alcohol, and morally questionable people. In that case, his eyes are likely to fixate on the wrong things. If he chooses his location more wisely, such as a church function or a morally neutral public gathering, his eyes are at less risk of being pulled to the wrong things.

A man's eyes alone cannot see into a woman's heart. If your physical sight is all that guides you, then good luck seeing beyond a pretty face and a shapely body. It sounds corny, but if the outward appearance is all you see, then you are blind.

A man is called to use wisdom when making any decision, and seeking a marriageable woman is indeed an important one. We don't just want an attractive woman; we want a beautiful woman from the inside out, whose character outshines her appearance. A good woman with whom we can get along and share life. But what does a good woman look like?

Many men fall into the same trap as the women I was addressing in the previous chapter: seeing a pretty face who behaves badly but imagining that she has a heart of diamonds buried beneath the coal on the surface.

At the risk of sounding somewhat redundant, a good woman of noble character does not generally:

- Lie
- Cheat
- Steal
- Dress provocatively
- Drink heavily
- Do drugs or own a bong
- Look at porn or claim it's alright if men do

- Sleep around
- Try to get men into bed outside of marriage
- Engage in alternative forms of sex, seeking a moral loophole (i.e. oral or anal)
- Move-in with a boyfriend
- Let men touch or grope her breast or buttocks
- Send you naked or suggestive pictures
- Seek to attract men primarily by using her body parts
- Use sex as a means of finding love
- Tolerate men who curse at her or call her profane names
- Hit or verbally abuse you
- Date men who are married
- Pursue any man with a wedding ring
- Try to come between a man and his girlfriend
- Try to get you drunk
- Pressure you into immoral behavior
- Flake on you (let your yes mean yes, and your no mean no)
- Need a man like you to *save* her from her own life choices
- Date men who habitually do the things on the last section's list.

As with a good man, a good woman does good things and develops good habits. An immoral woman with immoral intentions does the things on the list above. By no means can you expect to find a woman who has never made a mistake in her life. On the other hand, whether or not someone is actively engaged in immoral things is a sure way to see what is in their heart. You will not find a heart of gold in a woman who tries to sweet talk you into sexual immorality.

The Bible tells us in Proverbs 31:30, "Charm is deceptive, beauty is fleeting, but a woman who fears the Lord is to be praised." Don't let a woman's pretty face and smooth words distract you from what might be a heart of coal. A good, moral, God-fearing woman will not lead you down an immoral and destructive path. A woman who encourages good habits is the kind of gold that you are digging for.

Bad Company

If you want a good visual of what bad company keeps looks like, look no further than Jezebel, the most wicked woman in the Bible. Jezebel, who was said to be beyond physically beautiful, became the wife of King Ahab of Israel to cement good relations with the foreign nation of Sidon, of which Ethbaal, Jezebel's father, was the ruler. Jezebel was not the wisest choice of wife for the Israelite King, who was expected to serve God.

Jezebel proceeded, over the years, to impose her will upon the people of Israel and, as a prerequisite, over her husband, the king. She convinced her husband, through many methods, to promote the worship of her pagan gods, specifically Baal. Whenever Ahab tried to disagree with her or, more accurately, disobey her, he was thoroughly emasculated. Jezebel had a habit of doing this to men. If she did not kill them, as she often did, she would strip them of masculinity—often to the point of cutting off their manhood and making them into eunuchs. The prophets of God whom Jezebel did not manage to have killed eventually fled to escape her, including Elijah.

A brief summary such as mine hardly does justice to the evils of Jezebel, so I do encourage you to read about her in I and II Kings. The short of it is Ahab led his kingdom to ruin and horror at the behest and under the influence of a woman with a pretty face but whose heart was as far from virtuous as one can get. She was evil and was not content unless her man joined her in it. She was not above appealing to his pride or questioning his manhood to do so, though I suspect seduction played a large role in her influence over him as well. Jezebel knew that Ahab would be forced to choose between serving his wife and serving God, being her ways were contrary to God's. So she used every ounce of influence she could impose upon him to turn his eyes away from God.

Keeping bad company always has the potential to be destructive. No matter our intentions for being around immoral people (such as hoping to be a positive influence on them, etc.), good intentions always have the potential to backfire when acted upon by strong negative influences. Few things make a man fall faster than a pretty woman, and few things make a woman fall faster than a charming man.

Years ago, when I was working at a bar as a bouncer, I was all-too-often exposed to worldly influences: alcoholic beverages, smoking, objectionable music, dirty dancing, attractive girls, you name it. This was not the environment in which to meet virtuous people and, in fact, I never expected to. One woman who frequented this bar, we shall call her Lana, was near tireless in her pursuit of me. I say this not to boast or to paint myself as some ladies' man, but to present a picture of what some women (or men. I am just speaking from my point of view for this story. Interpret based on your case) can be like and to put you on your guard.

Maybe it was because I was yet uncorrupted, or perhaps she genuinely found me attractive and appealing, but, for whatever reason, this Lana found me appealing. She flashed me a mischievous smile every time she was in the bar while I was working, touched my arm while she talked to me, and was not at all subtle about her desire to "go home" with me. One night, in a group conversation with my coworkers and some patrons, she overheard that I was a virgin. Her response to this revelation? "Well, we need to fix that!" as if it was something that made me broken. She gazed at me long and hard while saying those words, shooting a coy smile and staring me down with knowing eyes. Of course, the fact that I was still a virgin *on purpose* was of no consequence to her.

After that night, she was at the bar more often, trying to get and keep my attention, trying to make me fall for her, or simply attempting to make me fall. You see, some people, man or woman, don't want your heart—it's not a prize to them. Some people just want to see if they can *corrupt* your heart. It's like a game to some of them. Some women and men simply do not want love and commitment. Some just want to see you fall to their level—to see you surrender your moral standards, cross that line that you cannot uncross, and watch you crash and burn. I will not lie to you about this; Lana was physically attractive and alluring. On more than one occasion, I came far too close to falling for her charms.

At one point, I tried to convince myself that maybe I could pursue something meaningful with this girl if my intentions had a positive influence on her—to win her heart to Christ and change her life. I quickly realized that that was a bad idea, born of a mind influenced by emotion and desire. My honest motive was not to win this girl to the Lord, no matter what I told myself. I just wanted an excuse to be around the pretty girl who was interested in me (albeit that her interest was not actually in *me*, so much as what she could do with me). And, even if I had intended to "date her towards Christ," it would not have ended the way I planned. I was burning with desire already, and she would have gladly broken me down, and I was fooling myself if I thought otherwise.

I Corinthians tells us very plainly, "Do not be deceived: bad company corrupts good morals." Lana was bad company, for sure. Had I allowed myself to date her or even spend time alone with her, I have doubts my morals would have gone uncorrupted. Had I let my guard down, she would have breached my defenses without a second thought. She knew my stance on premarital sex (and I am not the one who set that stance); she didn't care. Or, if she did, it made her want to be the one to break me.

II Corinthians 6:14 says, "Do not be yoked together with unbelievers. For what do righteousness and wickedness have in common? Or what fellowship can light have with darkness?" Beware, you cannot expect the non-Christian girl to respect your Christian values, and you particularly cannot rely on them to respect your boundaries when it comes to sex. But beware even more of the one who *claims* to be a believer in God but does not live like one. At least non-Christian girls are generally honest and consistent with what they believe or do not. You can trust them *not* to hold themselves to a Biblical standard.

On the other hand, a person who claims the title of "Christian" but lives as though they have never heard of Jesus or the Bible is far more deceitful. They will openly call themselves followers of Christ, flaunt their Bible verse tattoos, maybe even go to church. Then, you may find that they habitually attend crazy parties and get drunk, treat sex about as sacredly as would a hippie at Woodstock, and try to convince you to join in on the *good times*. "Don't be such a prude; live a little; the world isn't the same as it once was; stop living by outdated rules; God's not going to condemn you for having a little fun." And, I must say this in response to these things I commonly hear: the world is just as sinful as it always was, and God's rules and standards do not expire when the culture says so.

I have heard it all before from those who claim to be believers. So did Paul. He wrote in Romans 1:32 (NLT), "They know God's justice requires that those who do these [immoral] things deserve to die, yet they do them anyway. Worse yet, they encourage others to do them, too." People seldom sin out of total ignorance of God's rules. They know God's standards in their hearts; they know when they do wrong. That wrong is only amplified tenfold when such people praise and encourage the sin of other people, probably because having somebody join them in their wrongdoing makes them feel better about the things they do—the things they know they should not be doing. It might be a little easier, at that moment, to give in and compromise your values and do what the crowd wants you to do, but it is also a whole lot harder to live with.

Watch your step around those who claim to know Christ but act as if they've never heard His name. I honestly wish that such individuals would stop telling people that they are Christians! I know that suggestion sounds harsh and uncaring to some of you. But, when we know God, when we accept His grace and forgiveness, we are called to live by His standards to the best of our ability. There is little point in claiming to know Him if we continue to act as though we have never made His acquaintance. Those who act out their "Christianity" that way are not only slapping our Father in the face, but they make all other Christians look like hypocrites who are full of rubbish, and, most importantly, they make it look as though having Christ in your heart makes no difference and God is irrelevant. That is a vile message for an outspoken Christ-follower to convey to the world!

We are called to make disciples and win people to the Lord so that they can share in His gift of eternal life in paradise. How does implying to people that the Lord has no impact in your life advance that purpose? How does that lead to a growth in the future population of heaven? If you are one of those professing Christians who live like a pagan, I implore you to stop and think about how you are living and representing God. I beg you to either live according to God's word the best that you can or stop calling yourself a Christian.

Yes, both believers and non-believers can negatively influence you to be corrupt. The responsibility rests on you to determine how you will be influenced. This means you must use wisdom in determining who you choose to spend your time with and what kind of woman (or man) you pursue. A virtuous woman will build you up, be constructive in your life, and walk with you down a good path. The other kind of woman, the kind who lets the spirit of Jezebel whisper in her ear and lend her instruction, will corrupt your heart and destroy you.

If a woman such as Lana or Jezebel cannot manage to corrupt you, she will try to make you feel emasculated—convince you that you are not a "real man" because you stand firm in your convictions and possess self-control. That is what Jezebel does. Moral people have no place in her world and must be destroyed. If you don't worship the idolatrous gods of sex and evil, you must be torn down, dehumanized, and destroyed. Just ask Lana, who, upon my resisting her attempts to get me to sleep with her, said something to the effect of, "Let me know when you are finally ready to be a man."

Let me be clear: a "real man" sticks to his guns and stands by his moral convictions when things get hard. The real men are the ones who are willing to lay their lives down in the name of what is right and good, something which is never easy. If somebody questions your manhood (or even your womanhood) based on your unwillingness to compromise your commitment to God's standards, you are in good company. Turn and walk in the direction that leads you the furthest away from that someone. That individual wants to tear you down, decimate who you are and who God intends you to be. Stand tall as you refuse to cower or bow before Jezebel and her disciples.

Do not hate those who treat you in such a way, however. As Jesus said when He was dying for their sins and yours on the cross, "they know not what they do." I doubt that many of them even understand their own motivations at times. Even if you have to draw a hard line, you can be kind and loving toward people who criticize or belittle you and be stern in your resistance to their attempts to break you. You are commanded to love them. You cannot and will not win people to Christ through hate and spiteful words. If they treat you with malice and contempt, it does no one any favors for you to return fire. Anger will get you nowhere with such people. Make your moral standards known, live them out, share them with whoever will listen (without being boastful), let God work in your life, and all the while be loving and kind to those who think you are crazy. And some will. It's up to them to decide if they will allow themselves to see that God's way is superior to their own.

If, by some chance, you find yourself faced with a similar situation which I faced with Lana—somebody trying to pull you away from your moral convictions, and you being even slightly tempted to oblige—I would advise you to love them by giving them a wide berth. I know the suggestion may seem odd how you can love somebody by staying away, but nothing is loving about risking a fall into temptation with such a person. It would be counterproductive to show them that God is not the determining factor in your life, providing them with a reason to believe that their way of living is better than His. You will be enabling them to pull further from God, themselves, as you succumb to their influence.

Do not leave those most in need of God's love out in the cold, as it is not the healthy who need a physician, but the sick. On the other hand, keep good company, and do not think it wise to risk compromising yourself for somebody you know who has the potential to influence you negatively and pressure you into things that you should not do.

For Further Study

Ali, Hana. *More than a Hero: Muhammad Ali's Life Lessons Presented through His Daughter's Eyes*. Coronet, 2001.

Chapter 19

Guilt and Shame Are Not Inherently Bad

As I have pointed out before, premarital sex and pornography have become so normalized in western culture that they are practically viewed as traditions. Sadly, this is not restricted to secular circles. Even Christians are far too often living lives of casual sexual immorality, often without giving any second thought to the lifestyle. It's as if everyone thinks that a girl sleeping with her boyfriend, a young man sleeping with anyone he meets, or a teenager spending hours per day viewing pornographic material is no big deal because "that's just how everyone lives nowadays."

Church leaders have often caved to the societal pressure and compromised on this front, resigning themselves to act as though sexual immorality is just a lost cause—a battle that can't be won. They have forgotten the limitless God they serve. Some have gone so far as to claim that we can't expect people, especially teenagers, to control themselves when it comes to sexual desires, so we may as well encourage them to practice safe sex and use condoms instead! They act like *self-control* was merely added to the Fruits of the Spirit list by accident or some excusable mistake! Or as though sex is the only category for which self-control does not apply! Apparently, unbeknownst to me, lust just cannot be contained. God is up in heaven throwing His hands up, exclaiming, "Well, I obviously can't count sexual sin against you or allow it to have any negative consequences because I designed you to be incapable of resisting lustful appetites, thus ensuring that you would always fail to remain sexually pure! That's why no one in the history of time and humanity has ever pulled such a thing off!"

Does that sound silly? Because it ought to.

So, what? Should sexual sinners get a free pass? Should we just let it go because we mistakenly view sex as a *need*? I, for one, love you all enough to give you more credit than to presume that you can't control yourselves and to hold you to a higher standard than that which the average degenerate might measure up to. As does your Creator—significantly more so, in fact.

1 Corinthians 10:13 says, "No temptation has overtaken you except such as is common to man; but God is faithful, who will not allow you to be tempted beyond what you are able, but with temptation will also make the way of escape, that you may be able to bear it." You are not trapped! God will never let you be ensnared by an allurement you cannot cope with or let you suffer a situation you cannot possibly manage. You are always stronger than some people will give you credit for, especially with Him at your side.

In earnest, we cannot begin to view certain sins as a *necessity* unless we wish to throw ourselves down a steep slope that will inevitably lead to a hard crash. Or do we honestly believe that giving ourselves a free pass in the pursuit of one category of sin will not result in us branching out and compromising other moral values? If you let a tumor grow in one organ unchecked, cancer will eventually spread to other areas of the body! And the cancer of sin can spread from the sexual organs to the heart and brain in no time at all.

A lack of accountability is a dangerous domino effect. Suppose we decide that it is permissible to make concessions for one moral blunder or another. In that case, we will eventually convince ourselves that adding one more to the list of exceptions is no big deal. Then we add yet another to the list, and the file keeps growing longer and larger, and, before you know it, it's so comprehensive that you need tabs to navigate it.

So, why is it that Christian leaders and many in the congregations have become so lax in the department of sexual morals and seldom even address the subject? I am inclined to believe that much of the reasoning has to do with the fear of making people feel guilty or ashamed.

Oh, we wouldn't want to make anybody feel bad about doing bad things; what a horrible prospect! Funny, we used to call that conviction, which was the first step on the road to repentance and forgiveness of sin. To fix a problem, one must first recognize that one exists in the first place. To be forgiven, one must acknowledge that they have sinned and need forgiveness. For someone to accept Christ and be absolved of their transgressions, they usually need to feel conviction first.

In a modern culture that reveres the great and powerful "feelings" and "self-esteem," society tends to shun anything that doesn't make us feel good. We can't encourage competition in little league sports because we don't want children to feel like they've lost and failed at something, so we have to have participation trophies to avoid the risk that kids might dare think that there may be a need for them to get better at something and develop a skill! On the same token, we do not want anyone to feel bad about doing something morally wrong or self-destructive. We do not want them to feel like they have to change something about themselves (such as behavior) to become better than they are! Thus, we cannot allow anybody to feel guilt or shame.

I will bang on this gong as loudly as I possibly can: Guilt is not a bad thing! Shame is not evil! These things are how you become aware that you have done something you should not have done! Guilt is the result of a moral conscience. A conscience is a handy tool given to us by God to make us aware of the notions of right and wrong and keep ourselves accountable when we do something sinful that He would not approve of. By crucial design, we have this ability—this great power!

If you do something bad, you ought to feel bad. I never thought that such a basic suggestion would make me sound like a legalistic radical to some people. If you lie, you ought to feel guilty about it. If you commit a murder, you had best feel ashamed, and the jury would be in the right to find you *guilty*! This is what is often referred to as a *consequence*. An individual who never feels remorse for wrongdoings and sees no reason to adjust their behavior accordingly is the very definition of a *psychopath*—something that I am sure you do not want to be. If you experience guilt when you screw up, rejoice! That is solid evidence that you do not belong in an insane asylum.

When we make a mistake, we should, indeed, regret that mistake. Then, we free ourselves up to ask forgiveness for it and, finally, resolve not to repeat that mistake. We must understand right and wrong and learn from our missteps if nothing else. That is a crucial part of the human experience, and guilt and remorse are crucial parts of the process.

Once we have felt the consequences of our sin, we may ask the Lord to forgive us for what we have done, as well as anyone else whom our sin may have affected. That is when we can be set free from our shame.

The potential problem with shame only occurs when we do not feel free of it after we have reconciled and atoned. When God forgives us—and He always does—we are set free. We *should* be, and we should feel as though we have been. When we confess our sins, God doesn't hold them against us. He does not hold them over our heads as leverage or continue to torture us with reminders of our past mistakes. God grants us grace and, in His eyes, our sins are forgotten.

If you confess your sins to God and ask to be forgiven but still feel the weight of that mistake on your shoulders, that is not from God. That's from the other side—the one who wants you to remain in a state of hopelessness and loves for you to remind yourself of any and every reason why you may not deserve freedom, grace, and love.

Here's the truth about that hopeless feeling: none of us *deserve* grace. That's what makes it so amazing! We are broken and sinful beings, yet God offers His love and clemency to us freely! He knows our fallen nature. He knows our hearts. He knows our faults, yet He freely chooses to love us more than we can comprehend! This is why Jesus dying on the cross as payment for our sin is such an incredible act of love and sacrifice! Because we deserve to pay the price for our crimes, but He said, "Don't worry kids. I'm coming down there," and He took up the cross that we deserved to carry. Our Lord, who was clean of sin and any reason to feel shame, suffered in the worst ways and paid the cost of our transgressions for us. Oh, what an amazing Father we have! And He did not endure all of that for us just so that we would feel trapped in our shame for mistakes that He has already wiped clean from our record.

There have been times when I have made very big mistakes—the kind that I would be convinced I could never forgive myself for—that I asked God for forgiveness, and He gave it to me. And yet, I somehow refused to accept His forgiveness of these particular mistakes. I did not accept a pardon from Him, nor did I dare to grant it to myself. And so, the shame followed me around like a raincloud over my head, keeping me in a near-constant state of doom and gloom.

That is not God's wish for any of us.

I asked God to forgive me for the same mistake again, and again, and yet again. But His forgiveness is not what I was lacking. God forgave me the first time I asked. He had long forgotten my mistake. The problem was that I had neglected to forgive *myself*. I was in an emotional prison of my own making. I had not given myself permission to be human, which implies making human errors. I had failed to allow myself the same grace that God shows to us all. He had freed me. That means that I had only to let the past stay where it was. I needed to thank God for His love and understanding and tell myself that I am forgiven by Him and me. I no longer allow myself to be tortured by any particular error that I have made, even if I still have the knowledge that it happened.

Shame allowed me to understand that I did not want to repeat my mistake. It only became a problem when I refused to let it go. There is no wisdom in claiming that we should refuse to feel shame or allow others to do so. Grace is not a get out of jail free card that excuses us to do whatever wrong things we like. That is the problem with a society that stresses a perverse and misconstrued version of "tolerance," in which everything goes (with the apparent exception of Biblical values). If tolerance is our priority, then consistency would logically conclude that the only behavior that is off-limits is remorse. Apparently, that is supposed to result in some form of utopia. Oh, yes, a world populated entirely by psychopaths who know nothing of shame! Sounds like a paradise.

Can we set a slightly higher standard for our culture, please?

We need incentives against immoral behavior. Shame is an essential part of that incentive. If you do something immoral, do not rebuke the guilt that rises in you, and don't shrug it off or run from it. Let it perform its proper function, deal with the consequences, repent, resolve not to make the same mistake again and, finally, forgive yourself.

Chapter 20

The Lost Art of Resisting Temptation

A common challenge believers hear from non-believers and skeptics goes something like this: "If your God exists and He is so good and loving and all-powerful, then why does He allow evil to exist, and bad things to happen to good, innocent people?" It is a valid and understandable question and one that I will attempt to answer to the best of my limited ability, as simply and concisely as I can.

When God created the world, He made it a paradise, absent evil and death. Then, He created humanity, upon whom He bestowed His likeness. For a man to be truly made in His image, however, man had to be given a powerful mind, capable of all kinds of thought. And so, God lovingly gave His creation the gift of free will—the ability to think for ourselves and make our own decisions free and independent of direct influence. However, one thing was still missing.

How just would God be if He had granted us free will but denied us the opportunity to exercise that free will? What good is a gift that one cannot use? Would it be love if He gave us the ability to freely choose Him and His ways without allowing us an alternative? Would that truly be freedom? If I were a skeptic, I might argue that free choice with no choices is simply the indoctrination of a "free" mind.

So, God presented the first two people with a choice besides Himself. They could choose God and His ways and live in eternal paradise, or they could choose to go down their own path, turning their back on God and following temptation—allowing sin to enter and dominate their lives.

In the beginning, God loved us enough to grant us free choice, along with different choices to choose from. He knew all too well that the choice to bring evil and sin into the world wasn't good for us, but free will would ultimately be useless without that alternative to Him and His path.

Out Father loves us so much that He said, "I am going to create you in my likeness, and thus I will give you so much freedom that you might destroy yourselves. Sadly, we do tend to be rather self-destructive with that freedom. That is the choice He gave us.

Love is something that, by nature, we must *choose* to do. We are granted the freedom to love God and follow His perfect ways, or we can choose to waste that love on earthly or carnal desires. By its very nature, love is a choice, and God chose to gift that choice to us out of His affection for us. He knew we would often choose to pursue temptation over Him, as He allowed us that freedom. On the other hand, we are free to resist temptation and temporary delights to *send our love freely to God instead*! When we do such a thing freely, it means more to Him! After all, which would your earthly parents prefer: that you do something for them because they told you to, or that you do something for them because you love them, and you want to show it?

Forcing us to love Him by denying temptation would hardly be just or loving. He had to give us the ability to be tempted along with something to be tempted towards. Sometimes, it doesn't feel all that loving because resisting the temptation to do something wrong but desirable can be very difficult—sometimes bordering on excruciating. Resisting temptation is a challenge and a skill that must be learned and honed.

Picture an overbearing mother who shelters her child from the rest of the world. She forces this child as a teenager to go to church and get involved. The child has no choice in what he does with his time as far as church and social exercise is concerned. Perhaps this mother takes it a step further and castigates her child every time he questions his faith and asks important questions, thus stifling his critical and free-thinking. So, he can never challenge the thoughts and ideas she imposes upon him and is not prepared to defend his own thoughts and beliefs, because he barely knows how to think for himself. Now his faith and moral spine are fragile.

Taking it yet another step further, say this hypothetical mother seldom allows this now teenage child to go out with friends or visit their homes because they could *potentially* be a negative influence or say something that the mother doesn't want her child's delicate ears to hear. This is not to say that a parent should never have a say in who her child hangs around, but there comes a point when such restrictions only smother and suffocate. No perfect friends exist, but early friend-ships are indeed important—as is exposure to a diversity of thought.

This same hypothetical teen is disallowed from dating even as he approaches 18-years-old because the parent is far too worried that he might be *exposed* to sexual temptation. No Internet access is allowed, television, media, nothing that could expose the child to a negative in-fluence or an idea foreign to the parents' philosophy. All divergence must be cut off before it makes contact with the child.

While I do not wish to question whether or not this hypotheti-cal parent loves her child, the question must be asked: Is that what true parental love is supposed to look like? The examples that I gave do seem rather aggressive and overbearing. I am sure that someone would claim she loves her child too much, but I would argue that her love toward that child is defective, not excessive. I would have hated to grow up that way, and I can only imagine how such an overbearing stagnation would have negatively affected me.

Furthermore, that kind of mother's love certainly does not meld with God's template of what love looks like—at least not as He exempli-fied it. And, since God *is* love, I would assume that He knows something about the topic. God loved us enough to grant us free choice *as well as* the chance to choose. Beyond that, he allows us to be tempted, so we may be given a chance to either choose our love for sin or learn how to say "no" to it and choose to love and follow Him. And part of that free-dom to choose the second option is that we must be allowed to *learn* to do so. One must *learn* to say no to temptation.

It is hard to learn to resist temptation if you are never exposed to it. If you never see a stunning person of the opposite sex, or if you are never allowed the opportunity to experience lust, then you will never learn how to reject it. Thus will have a hard time refusing sexual temp-tation when inevitably presented with an enticing situation.

One should never play with fire, of course. I am not encouraging anyone to put themselves in situations to be tempted intentionally! But you should still know that the fire exists. A kid who knows nothing of fire and has never seen the flames will not know how to give it a wide berth or put it out. A child needs to be aware of the existence of fire, the potential dangers or benefits it may pose, and how to extinguish it if need be. Sin is part of life, and temptation will eventually find us. We must be aware of how to approach that fire. We need to exercise our free will if it is ever to be strong enough to help us win.

Since I am so fond of analogies, let us say that we are a soldier, our will is our sword, and exposure to temptation is the whetstone used to sharpen it and keep it battle-ready. Normally, God might be the sword or the stone in an analogy such as this, but that doesn't quite fit our purposes here, so let us say that God is the blacksmith who crafted our sword (will) and gifted it to us.

To effectively fight our enemy, the edges of our sword will need to be sharp. Just as you sharpen a sword by gently pressing it against the grindstone, your will is sharpened when it is *gently* exposed to temptation. However, improper or excessive use of the sharpening tool can damage the blade or grind its edges away, much like how diving head-long into bad situations and flooding our senses with enticing images can erode our will. Overuse the whetstone, and the sword will be damaged, possibly a liability in battle as it may break, but neglect the maintenance of the blade, and the sword will be blunt and useless.

Our will and sword are wonderful gifts, but they are also a great responsibility. We must keep our free will maintained and sharp and ensure that we do not misuse it. As with any weapon, free will can be used for good or evil. Ours is to make the best choices about using that weapon, but we must be allowed to make them.

My mother is the opposite of the aggressively overprotective mother mentioned before. She loves her children more than life itself and wants the best for them, but she knows she cannot dictate how they think or every action they take, especially when they are out of her house. Even if she could, she undoubtedly understands that it would be less than loving for her to rob her children of their freedom. She raised her kids the best she could, taught us moral values in the hope we would choose to live by them, but she knew that ultimately the way we live when we are not under her roof would be entirely a matter of choice on our part. So, while I was living with her as a teenager, she allowed me the freedom to make choices. Of course, if I did something wrong, there were consequences, and she utilized discipline—though I was pretty well-behaved by my teen years after the discipline she incorporated in my younger years. My mother always provided me with moral guidance, and then she would let me go out with friends and pray that I lived by what she had taught me.

My little brother is still a teenager living at home with my mother at the time of this writing. Just recently, she permitted him to go to a bonfire with his friends on private land, and, to his credit, he was honest enough to admit to her that he had reason to believe people would be drinking alcohol there. My mother is a wise woman, and she recognized that each of her children is different in personality and would have to adjust her parenting methods accordingly. However, her central premises and themes would not falter. We all had the same foundation; each underwent a slightly different approach. My mother knew that if she flat-out told my brother he could not attend the bonfire and kept him cooped up in the house all night, it would make him more rebellious. So, she permitted him to go with his friends to the bonfire!

I did not agree with this parenting decision when I heard about it, probably because my mother telling me not to do something would have worked like a charm on me because I tended to like rules and structure. I was not as rebellious. However, I was not my brother's parent, so the decision was not mine to make. My mother permitted my brother to go out with his friends to this event but, before he went, she gently talked his ear off about reasons she didn't think he should drink, what kinds of things to be wary of in that environment, how he ought to be careful, and laid on thick that she didn't know what she would do or how she could cope if anything bad were to happen to him. That last dose of motherly love had the deepest impact.

My little brother still went out to the bonfire that night but, before he left, he told my mother at least 1000 times he loved her and was almost hesitant to leave the house at all. But she let him loose to exercise his free will. Not only did the kid not drink and drive, but he did not drink at all. In fact, he took it upon himself to make sure that anyone who did drink made it home safely to their own mothers. That was *his* choice at work.

My mother gave my little brother the freedom to choose between right and wrong, and, ultimately, he chose right. One could argue that it would have been better for him to have chosen not to go to the bonfire at all, but then who knows what might have happened? Would someone at the event have chosen to drive their car under the influence of alcohol if he were not there to ensure they did not? Would all of those kids have made it home safely without him loving them enough to take care of them? We cannot know, but whatever you might think, I am proud of my brother's choices under the circumstances. He could just as easily have gone the other way with his decisions, but that's freedom for you.

I am not yet a father, so feel free to take my thoughts here with a grain of salt, but I know enough from learning from those wiser than myself that the goal as a parent is not to raise great children but to raise good children who eventually become great adults (loosely paraphrased quote, Dave Ramsey, *Legacy Journey*). A picture-perfect kid can grow up to become a disastrous adult, especially if the first time he tastes freedom and experiences any level of personal responsibility is in adulthood—when he is no longer under the watch or influence of parents. Young people need room to grow, a certain level of responsibility, and the freedom to fail at something. If one is a good—perhaps slightly lucky—parent, the biggest moral blunders that their child ever makes will be the ones they make while living under the parents' roof.

Even God, the perfect Father, does not have perfect children on this earth, with the marked exception of Jesus Christ, of course. We are all His children and will make poor decisions, and our Father knows it. He gives us the guidance we need and sets the values and rules to live by, but, ultimately, the decision of whether or not to follow them is ours. He would hardly be a just God if He gave us free choice, but no choices to make. For His children to possibly make good decisions, they must be presented with an alternative, and they are not always going to make the right call. God knows this as a father—as The Father—and it's the best any parent can hope for without controlling their kids' actions via remote control.

Young Christians are leaving the church in hordes, often the instant they leave home and taste pure freedom. They were sheltered beneath their parents' wings in the home—drifting behind the momentum of their parents' faith and values. As soon as they go off to college or transition into living on their own, they no longer catch the overflow from their mother or father's intellectual cup, and they no longer know what to think or believe because their parents are no longer making their decisions for them.

If that kid enters a college classroom, that impressionable young mind will fall under the new wing of secular professors who will be the ones telling the kid how to think or what to believe, and the new things he is taught will not always be good. His mind becomes unfermented clay, ready to be shaped by anyone willing to mold it, and that kid is going to accept whatever he is told to because that's all that he was brought up to do! Without freedom of choice under some manner of parental tyranny, he did not learn to think for himself or form critically thought-out conclusions.

Again, I am not yet a parent. I can only tell you these things based on what I have seen with my own eyes while living on a college campus and witnessing this phenomenon first-hand. A person, young or old, needs moral and intellectual guidance and room to grow and form their own conclusions. We all need to be allowed to make our own decisions. It is in our nature to do so—it's how our Creator designed us.

In order for any person to learn to make good choices and avoid or deny temptations, they need to be aware of the alternatives; because the alternatives will present themselves at one point or another. A person will not always make the best moral decisions, but we need to be trusted to do so at some level, or else no "decision" is made. Our Father and our parents on this earth can only do their best to implement the right values and allow us to put them into practice, and sometimes we will fail. But, if we don't get any practice before we are tempted in the most intense ways, our chances of success are not all that high.

You would not expect a high school basketball player to be a superstar athlete if he never practiced the craft or had never been exposed to physical basketball. You cannot expect an adult who has never been exposed to any manner of temptation or practiced resisting any particular lure to be a moral saint when things get tough.

Take, for example, a man who has never said "no" to a pretty face. Every time this man has been presented with a chance to be sexually involved with a woman, he says yes. Given any opportunity to sin, fornicate, this man does not attempt to resist. Say this man finally decides he likes a girl enough to marry her. Shortly after that, this now married man is tempted with the chance to have an affair—it's new, it's exciting, and it only feels natural to pursue this chance. There is very little stopping the man from saying "yes" and cheating on his wife with the new woman who has presented herself. Why? Because saying "yes" to temptation is all he ever practiced at. He never learned to say "no" to the things that tempted him.

We often become very good at what skills we practice and naturally stagnate where we do not train. If one does not practice resisting temptation, or worse, practices at indulging carnal passions, one remains very unskilled at the opposing skill. We need to practice saying "no" while the cost of failure is not so high.

Once again, I am not suggesting anyone go out in search of strong lures that may cause them to fall or allow themselves to be put in avoidable compromising situations. One of the most effective ways to fight temptation is never knowingly putting yourself in a compromising position. However, you still have to leave your house at some point and live your life, and tempting situations will find you; thus, no one should be oblivious to the factors and hardships of a fallen world full of sin. When confronted with temptation and challenges, we should bear in mind what our Father would think we should do and remember the doses of Fatherly love He gives us every day and the reasons He has for wanting us to do right.

Chapter 21

Legendary Willpower

I tend to read just about everything I can get my hands on. Admittedly, I was not always so eager to read and grow in knowledge, but I developed an appreciation as well as a passion for reading and expanding my mind over the past five years or so. More recently, I resolved to read and bring myself up to snuff on the classic works of literature, such as Dostoyevsky's *Crime and Punishment* and Milton's *Paradise Lost,* which I referred to in an earlier chapter, though I must confess that poetry is not the easiest genre for me to read or understand.

One of the classics that I recently brought myself to read—at least for the first time since I was in school and the first time I cared about reading it—was *The Odyssey*. It is a fantastic story—well worthy of its position among the other classics of literature. Widely believed to have been composed by Homer almost 3,000 years ago and told verbally for centuries before being recorded on paper, the fact that it has survived this long is a testament to the story itself. However, it may not have near the significance of the Bible. This epic piece of Greek mythology contains drama, warriors, powerful beings, phantoms, cyclops, and sirens. The sirens are a particularly interesting aspect to me.

Odysseus was a famously wise and cunning man. During the Trojan War, a story told in the Odyssey's prequel, *The Iliad*, he had the idea to build the famous Trojan Horse; a trick used to infiltrate the heavily fortified city of Troy and victoriously end the war that is believed to have endured for a full decade.

After winning the Trojan War, Odysseus sets sail with his crew toward his home in Ithaca. Homer's Odyssey tells the many episodes of this decade-long trek.

During this expedition, Odysseus and his crew pass by the island of the sirens, creatures of the sea who resemble beautiful women and who are known to lure men to their deaths with their seductive singing voices.

Knowing what was to come, Odysseus ordered his crew to fill their ears with wax so that the sirens' song could not allure them. As for himself, Odysseus ordered his men to tie him to the mast of the ship and leave his ears open and clear so that, though he could still hear the deadly melody sung by the sirens, he could not be lured to his death by them. He wanted the knowledge that came with hearing the song that had led to the demise of every man before him to hear it, but he was not willing to bet his life on the strength of his willpower. Odysseus was brave and strong of will, but he was not stupid by any means. He knew there was no wisdom in relying on his strong but mortal willpower alone. So, he put a system in place to prevent it from being his only line of defense.

Willpower, by itself, is weak. I do not care who you are, your self-control has its limits, and those limits are not as hard to meet as you might think. The same is true for all human beings, from the best of us right down to the very worst. That being the case, if you put yourself in positions that require you to resist temptation, most especially sexual temptation, the sirens will win at one point or another.

We will eventually slip up and burn the house down when we play with fire. I have known my fair share of Christian folks practicing abstinence and wanting to stay sexually pure until they're married, as they should. I have also seen far too many of those young Christians vastly overestimate their willpower (or even that of their partner). A young man puts himself in a compromising situation with a cute girl, kissing behind the closed and locked door of a bedroom, which turns into making out, but all the while, he's thinking, "it's alright, I'll know when to stop." And then he hears the sirens' song, the harmonic allure of temptation, and now he is relying entirely on his own resolve to keep from walking off the edge of the ship to his demise. The call is strong, and it only takes a moment's breach of his willpower, a single moment of weakness, for him to tumble over the edge. And once he is in the sea, there's no going back.

I don't want to hear from you or anyone, "I have practically super-human self-control! I can handle it!" That is a lie! You do, indeed, have self-control that you ought to exercise, but it is a lie to say that you do not need to be smart or utilize wisdom because your will can handle any allure. Don't think for one second that you are the Chosen One!

The Bible says in 1 Corinthians 10:12, "Take heed when you think you stand, lest you fall." In other words, it's when you think to yourself, *I'd never do that*, that you are at the highest risk of doing *that*. You get to thinking that you can enjoy yourself without going too far because of your "strong will," and so you stop thinking critically, stop being careful. You allow yourself to be alone with someone of the opposite sex for a while, start making physical contact, things start to get passionate, you get to thinking that you will hit the brakes before things end up going too far, but the line marked "too far" gets gradually farther away as you go. Then you end up doing something that you cannot take back, all because you thought you would withstand the call of the sirens.

When you most confidently think you stand tall, that's when you fall.

Spending extended time in private (behind closed doors) with someone of the opposite sex you are not married to is about as safe for your sexual virtue and health as playing catch with a stick of dynamite is for your face. You may as well be standing on the plank of a ship, on one foot, one foot hanging over the edge, ears wide open as you sail toward the island of singing devourers.

You need to, as Odysseus, tie yourself to the mast. What do I mean? I mean, take preventive actions to avoid falling into traps of temptation. Sooner or later, temptation will come, the sirens will start to sing, but you need not rely on willpower alone to avoid falling overboard and being dragged to the depths.

Do not put yourself in potentially compromising situations, even if it seems relatively harmless at the time. If you are in high school and a girl asks you to come over to her house while her parents are not home, do not put yourself in that obviously precarious situation! Just say, "no," and that's the end of it. "No" is your best friend. If you get invited over while her parents *are* home, you don't go up to her room and close the door! Keep doors open at all times! Doors and barriers are not best buddies with your sexual virtue! They are more partnered up with their pal, promiscuity.

If you are a woman in college, you do not go up to a guy's dorm room for "privacy." Good things do not happen when college kids hang out in dorms. I have been to college, I have lived in a dorm building, the walls are thin, I have heard things that one cannot unhear. Don't do it!

To the adults, do not end a date by inviting someone into your home for a drink or accept the same invitation. Don't snuggle up on the couch for a little one-on-one late movie night. Have fun if you want to do it in a group setting, with other people around to keep you accountable! But that can be far too intimate a setting for a couple of unmarried people alone.

Are you sensing a theme here? The truth stays the same no matter your age or alleged maturity level: you avoid potentially compromising situations by avoiding intimate privacy. If it is just you and someone of the opposite sex, in a private place, in close quarters, getting personal, the sirens are singing at the top of their lungs! Be together in public or a group, by all means. Go on group dates, watch movies with friends, be one-on-one in a relatively public setting with other people around who can see you. But there is no need for an unmarried pair to be alone behind a closed door.

If you struggle with temptations linked to pornography, it is just as important to put systems in place. When I was struggling to quit this unfortunate habit, I would turn off my smartphone and other Internet-capable devices and keep them far away from me when I went to bed at night. This way, I was not easily tempted to get on the Internet if I ended up lying awake at night, and I avoided triggers. I even deleted and avoided all social media for a good long while, as previously mentioned in the section of this book on pornography regarding relapse triggers.

Finally, as the classic saying goes: "nothing good ever happens after 2:00 a.m." You may have heard that statement before, and it rings true. The later it is, the more tired you are, the less energy you have. If your energy is low, so are your inhibitions! If you have had a long day, are sleep-deprived, or are just plain tired, it is not the time to be socializing with the opposite sex. The more tired you are, the more your capacity for good decision-making is compromised. It is a similar effect to being intoxicated. Heaven forbid if you are tired after having been drinking alcohol! If it is late, the odds are that your resilience to pressure and temptation is essentially diminished. Just call it a night and go to bed.

Overall, putting systems in place to avoid certain temptations or bad situations takes a little bit of common sense and critical thinking: what might you be tempted by? What kinds of things will test the limits of your self-control? Are those situations or triggers at all avoidable?

What can I do to avoid them? Make a plan, execute, stick to the system. The sirens will not reach you if you tie yourself to a mast.

Chapter 22

Best Interests

When it comes to dating, it seems obvious that you want to have the best standards possible when choosing a potential life partner—at least, I hope it is obvious to you. You want to find somebody with character who has high standards for how they should be treated and how they should treat others. There is nothing more attractive to a mature person than an individual who puts the needs of others before their personal desires.

It's always good to find someone who does not enter a relationship for purely selfish reasons, though admittedly, most romantic relationships are entered with one self-serving reason or another in mind. Everyone has something self-serving that they want out of a relationship; otherwise, they probably wouldn't bother getting involved in one. Relationships would seem too much of a hassle if there were no perks. But if a woman enters a relationship solely because she wants attention and physical affection, giving little thought to how she can serve her partner and do what is best for him, it may be time for a man to run. A romantic relationship is beautiful and has many personal benefits, but it does not work selfishly. Marriage, while fantastic, is an act of sacrifice: of giving yourself over completely to another person, ignoring selfish desires, forsaking all others, and committing your life to serve and love somebody. Love is sacrifice. It leaves no room for conceit. And this leads me to my topic: love means doing what is best, not *just* for you, but for your significant other as well.

I worded that last statement with intent because I want to clarify that while you should think of others before yourself, *your* best interests still count. That is still half of the message.

Sometimes, when it comes to premarital relationships, you must consider what is in your interest, your partner's, or the both of you. What the heck am I talking about? I am referring to the potential situations in which it may be necessary to pull the ripcord on a relationship, jump ship, or dive out of the car (and let me be clear that I am speaking solely in terms of premarital relationships in this case. I am in no way advocating divorce here).

Not all relationships are healthy. Sometimes the people involved are incompatible (i.e., have religious or moral differences), sometimes one or both people involved in the relationship are in an emotionally unhealthy state, sometimes the timing of the relationship is bad, sometimes one person is narcissistic, and sucking the life from their partner. There are various reasons romantic entanglements are not always good news. Thus, a relationship may need to end before somebody decides to make it permanent via marriage.

In a relationship, you have to think about what is best for you or, just as important, what is best for the other person. Ask yourself: "Am I really what is best for her/him?" "Is this someone whom it is wise for me to be with?" "If dating is the easiest stage of our relationship, will I be content with this person for the rest of my life?"

Before I met my wife, I dated other girls. But, none of them lasted longer than five weeks. And no, that is not because I was shallow or kept deciding that I just wanted a new girl. It was because, by using common sense and critical thinking, I generally knew early whether or not this was a person I could marry one day. That is, after all, the end goal of dating. If you are dating for fun, let me suggest that that is neither beneficial nor healthy for either person involved. People are not here for your time-killing enjoyment purposes: not their hearts or bodies. Dating can and ought to be fun, sure, but the fun is not why it exists.

The thought process of asking, "Is this someone I could marry" is not one to be practiced through emotions alone. Had I relied on how I *felt* when making these important decisions, the decisions would have been made poorly. I know that I would have stayed with some women for far too long and gone down paths I should never have gone down. Most people use the "follow your heart" strategy when making big life choices such as who to marry, though the term "strategy" is being generous. As I have implied before, that goes a long way in explaining why many people in our modern western culture are emotionally unhealthy.

Answering the question "should I be with or stay with this person?" should be made rationally and logically. At best, emotions are a secondary factor and do not take priority when considering important, life-altering decisions. Determinations such as those concerning who you spend the rest of your life with (or even the next year of dating with) demand a sober and steady mind if one has any hope of achieving the best possible outcome.

As I stated before, my dating relationships never lasted longer than five weeks. That is generally how long it took me to conclude whether or not I had the realistic potential of marrying the girl, though it sometimes did not take even that long. Many possible factors can play a role in such decisions, but here are a few examples for reference as to why a relationship might justifiably end:

- This person I am dating does not make God a priority in her life. She is not a believer or claims to be one, but her actions and habits beg to differ.
- This person keeps trying to pressure me into premarital sex. I am only human. If I stay with this person, my willpower *will* fail, and I will do something I regret later.
- This person is not emotionally or mentally ready to be dating *anybody* right now. She goes into a panic whenever we are not together and refuses to be happy unless she's in a relationship. A codependent person is never genuinely happy or satisfied and will likely make me miserable in the long term.
- I like her, but I am not the best thing for her. She might be better suited to a man with different personality traits than mine. I need to set my desires aside and do what is best for her, even if it hurts one or both of us.
- She is gorgeous, but she is very self-involved, and her outlook on life is askew or shallow. A materialistic woman might not make a good spouse.
- This person has no intention of ever having children and starting a family, but I want to have kids.

Nobody is perfect, so don't think I am suggesting you seek the perfect person. But, if the other person does not show any qualities that would be present in a good, life-long spouse, their values are broken or absent, they are habitually selfish, show a propensity for unsavory behavior, do not respect you enough to wait until marriage before having sex and try to pressure you into it, move on quickly. Look inwardly as well. Are you putting your needs first all the time? Do you stand by firm moral principles? Are you influencing them or pressuring them toward immoral behavior? Are you what is best for the person you are with right now? The sword has two edges, so be sure that they are both sharp before you consider plunging them into the marital scabbard.

Dating relationships are easier than marriage—there is no question about that. When you are dating, that is as light, simple, and carefree as your relationship is ever going to be. That is why I find it inconceivable that some boyfriend/girlfriend couples bother to seek out relationship counseling and couples therapy when their relationship is not going well! Dating is going to be the easiest time in your relationship. If a couple is having problems that demand the aid of a third-party professional, that is an undeniable sign that the relationship needs to end ASAP! When you hit the kind of turbulence in the fun stage of a relationship that necessitates the help of a therapist, that plane is destined to crash! It will not get better from that point, and permanence will most definitely not improve the situation! Find a parachute and jump out while you still can!

History and Baggage

Everybody has a history—events from their past that they can look back on in either a positive or negative light. We all have past deeds we are proud of and past sins we are less than proud of. This poses whether or not you are familiar with your partner's past and *comfortable* with it. The same goes the other direction as well, of course. It matters how much or how little one's partner cares about one's past deeds and misdeeds. If one person in the relationship was sexually active with several people before coming to Christ and entering their current relationship, for example, in that case, that is something the other member of the couple must reflect on and decide if he is comfortable with. Sexual history impacts current and future relationships, so one must be aware of and comfortable with such things if considering marrying an individual with an indiscreet past. Some are all right with taking on such a challenge, which is perfectly alright! I prefer that they understand there will be difficulty associated with this factor.

If one party has a past drug abuse or addiction, his partner should know that and be aware of who she is getting involved with and what factors are at play. A history of addiction is vital information for somebody who is romantically involved with the individual in question, as it has the potential to impact their future seriously, so it is fair she is made aware of this so she can decide if she is comfortable with it to commit her life to a man. That assumes the addiction is in the past, and the person is in recovery. If the individual is still using drugs, that is an immediate disqualification for dating, much less marriage! Say goodbye!

If one is not completely comfortable with the history of the person they are involved with, it is not only permissible for them to acknowledge it, but it is responsible! It almost doesn't matter what the aspect of their history is, specifically. Barring anything too shallow, if it makes one uncomfortable, it matters. If your boyfriend likes *Star Trek*, that may be an insurmountable hurdle that you cannot overcome, and you would be perfectly justified to move on and find a man who prefers *Star Wars*! If your girlfriend is not okay with the fact that you used to watch *Friends* on repeat or spend entire evenings playing *Gears of War*, that may or may not be a deal-breaker for you. I'm honestly surprised that might wife still agreed to marry me after discovering my fondness for playing a particular board game, *RISK*, and just how involved I could be in a game with my brothers. Some way, somehow, she decided that she could live with that.

Everybody has baggage. It is entirely up to your discretion whether or not you are alright with what the other person is carrying because that baggage does not get left at baggage claim in the airport. It will follow you home. Your partner will be carrying their baggage for years to come, and part of marriage involves you helping them carry it. That is important to point out, so I will repeat it: whatever baggage one of you carried into a marriage, you will both end up carrying it! It is not shallow or closed-minded to confess to being uncomfortable with an element of your romantic partner's life. It is your responsibility to determine whether you are comfortable enough with this person, as they are, to spend the remainder of your life with them. If the answer is no or you are struggling to rationalize a way to make it a yes, then it may be time to terminate the relationship and move on for both your sakes *before* you commit to a marriage. It is a simple matter of using your best judgment.

It Runs in the Family

Speaking of baggage, it is important to discuss the main source of baggage in the known universe: the family. Contrary to popular opinion, her family does not simply evaporate when a boy marries a girl. They are going to be around for a very long time. In essence, when you marry one person, you marry their family too, and they are now *your* family. They are going nowhere, so you had best be comfortable with the family of the individual you choose to spend your life with, and they had best be alright with yours.

Do you have a crazy family? When you bring a boyfriend or girlfriend home to meet the parents, does he or she hear Mad World playing in their head? Do you have to warn people about your uncle well in advance before they encounter him? Are there certain family members that you avoid bringing up in casual conversation? Do you expect the police to show up at any family function? If the answer to any of these questions is "yes," then welcome to the very large club!

Everybody has at least one oddball in the family, but some families are just downright scary! My wife and I both married into varying levels of insanity, but we knew that going in, and neither of us ever complains about the other's bloodline. I love my in-laws, to be sure, but some men might not have been completely comfortable with the whole extended family picture, and that's alright; I was comfortable with it, and so I gladly agreed to marry into this family.

If you marry the individual, you marry the family. They are not going anywhere, so you had best be content to be a part of the unit. These are the people you will spend holidays with and the people your children will be held by. If you have reservations about the family of the individual you are considering for marriage, I suggest you think long and hard about whether or not you can stand a lifetime of relating to these people. If you conclude you cannot stand these people or do not fancy the notion of sharing a room with them for hours (going on days) at a time; then it is time to move on and find somebody whose family is more to your liking. I know it sounds harsh to break up a relationship with a girl and break her heart because her family is from the land of Insania and probably lives on Meth-Head Blvd. None of us can control where we come from or who we are related to, but if you marry into a family that you abhor, you and the person you marry are *both* going to pay the price for it in misery.

If you are comfortable marrying into a crazy family, do so by all means! It certainly makes life interesting. However, do not be deluded into believing that the family does not matter. I do not know what factors might be stumbling blocks to you, specifically—what signals might give you pause and necessitate a reevaluation of the situation. But if there are any factors that you have reservations about when it comes to a family you might marry into, and decide that said factor makes you uncomfortable, break off the relationship for your sake and the other person's. Find someone with a family you like and let someone who is okay with the rough areas be the one to share this life with the crazy people!

If you are the one with the crazy family, then the same rules apply: if the person you are considering for marriage hates your family, then that person must go! Unless you plan on never associating with your family again—which I seldom endorse, much less find practical outside of extreme circumstances—then whoever you marry is going to be a part of *your* family. Once the vows are said, it's her family too, so she had best be willing to associate and get along with them. If that seems unlikely, then it is time to move on and find somebody who can appreciate your animated gene pool.

Do Not Waste Your Precious Time or Theirs

I do not think it takes very long to gauge whether a romantic relationship has potential or not—assuming that one does things right and does not physically join with a person and remains capable of thinking rationally. Before meeting the woman who is now my wife, my dating relationships never lasted longer than five weeks, and there is a reason for that. It is not that I kept track of the days on a calendar and decided, "this day, exactly five weeks from the day we started dating, is when we either break up or get married." No, I knew why I was dating (for the purpose of getting married), and five weeks is generally the longest it would take me to conclude that I was not going to marry the girl I was currently seeing. If I was not going to marry her, then I would not continue dating her. It was as simple as that.

I did my best to think rationally about a relationship early on because I did not want to waste my time or anyone else's if the relationship would not end in marriage. Time is a valuable commodity that cannot be replenished, so it stands to reason that we do not whittle it away frivolously. Premarital romantic relationships are an investment of our time, and sometimes that investment needs to be cashed out before our losses are too great. I certainly did not want to wait until one or both of us was so heavily invested in the relationship that to break up would be utterly devastating. Thinking about romance rationally might not seem too sexy or romantic, but sparing yourself and others from avoidable heartaches and emotional scars seems worth the effort.

I did not always do things right as a single man, mind you. I do not need to remind anybody that no person is perfect. I made mistakes and sometimes broke hearts. It's not a good feeling, nor is it a noble pursuit, but sometimes it is a necessary struggle. If a man is in love with a woman, or vice versa, but the relationship is toxic, unhealthy, or simply lacking a clear destination, it is better that one person should have their heart broken than for both people to exist in a destructive or empty relationship.

You Do Not Still Have Your Pride, Nor Do You Want It

Just as I have broken off relationships with good intentions, some women either rejected me completely or broken things off with me for what they perceived to be good intentions. In their eyes, we had no future together for one reason or another. Maybe they did not find themselves very attracted to me, as does happen to someone as inhumanly and magnetically attractive as myself (disclaimer: the last statement is a joke), or maybe they had some reason more profound than that. There is no way to know for sure, and it hardly matters in any case.

Some people do not take rejection well. Some let it do more than temporarily depress them but utterly ruin them. On the other hand, some people use rejection as a reason to say, "well, if they cannot see how high quality I am, then perhaps they do not deserve me! I can do better than someone like that!" I am betting that a fair number of people reading this have said something to that effect at one time or another. And, while I do not deny you have quality, one should be careful not to fall off of the ledge you're on when you let that state of mind run rampant: the metaphorical ledge being *pride*, and the fall is fairly self-explanatory.

Pride—which can be described as an overinflated, deep-seated satisfaction with oneself and found to be synonymic with conceit, vanity, and arrogance—is commonly known as the sin that leads us to destruction quickest. It was the first sin of humanity, after all. Adam and Eve did not think it was *fair* that God limited them as humans and wanted to be more like Him. So they ate the fruit that the serpent—later identified as Satan—offered, thinking they deserved more than the deal they had been blessed with. By its very nature, pride separates us from God and all that is good, including anyone else who may love us. Pride *separates,* and thus nothing can be gained from indulging it.

It is better to be humble and recognize we are not the whole package; we have faults, that maybe it was not the other person's blindness to our wonderful traits that made them less inclined to date us, but their subtle awareness of our flaws. Maybe pride was among the things they saw. The first step to fixing any problem is realizing that there is one, so let's acknowledge the serpent in the room.

Forget what the marching masses of the Gay Pride Month Parades are shouting in the streets; pride is not a virtue. It is the sin that led to the downfall of mankind at the beginning of time and, before even that, the sin which got Lucifer ejected from heaven. Lucifer was a beautiful and talented angel once upon a time, and he believed himself to be the "whole package." This thinking led him to start believing that he, the creation, was even greater than God, the Creator. He, in his pride, wanted to exalt himself to God's level and perhaps beyond. We all know that Lucifer's pride did not pay off, and now his level is in a fiery pit beneath our boots.

Pride was the motivation behind the Tower of Babel as well—mankind's attempt at building a tower that would stretch to the heavens and bring them to God's level, which seems a common theme where pride rears its head. God put a stop to that, of course. The insistence of "gay pride," it would appear, is our modern Babel. Our people want to exalt themselves to God's level by trying to to dictate the moral and physical laws of nature. That is an impossible task, to be sure, and as long as our pride leads us to attempt to play God, we will never truly know Him.

Furthermore, as long as we are attempting to use pride as a tool to find love, we will never truly know love either. Again, pride cannot help us to find *anything* good. It has only the power to separate.

Sin and virtue, not surprisingly, are opposite. As such, pride and humility are opposites. It's all well and good to care about oneself, but it is a very different story when one starts endowing themselves with laurels.

Proverbs 11:2 (NIV) tells us, "When pride comes, then comes disgrace, but with humility comes wisdom." When you take pride in yourself, you blind yourself to your faults and raise yourself above others in your mind (often looking like an idiot while doing so). Not only is this an impeccably unattractive trait to have, but it perpetuates the lie that Satan has been feeding us since he appeared before Adam and Eve in the Garden of Eden. Pride has *always* been the quickest path to destruction and not often the most subtle. So, not only will pride destroy a person, but they'll have an audience while they do it! It was the thread that Satan pulled on to drag mankind down into the dumps with him, just as it was the source of his evil that got him cast from paradise in the first place.

To display oneself with pride is to portray the worst traits about oneself to the public eye. It makes a person look foolish and unattractive to an astronomical degree. How do I know? From first-hand personal experience, how else? It used to be that, as a single man, any time a girl rejected me, my strategy was to stroke my ego to infuse myself with confidence. My self-applied balm took the form of statements like: "Oh, she doesn't know what she is missing by not having me around," or, "she just proved that she's not worth my time or attention because it makes no sense for her to reject me." Did you find those statements at least a little bit repulsive? Hopefully, you did. That is a sign that you understand the toxicity of the condition I was afflicted with. Ironically, I did not realize that this made me less attractive inside and out and gave girls even more valid reasons to reject me. Confidence is attractive, but pride is not its synonym. I would argue that the two are very much opposite of one another. Pride, at its root, is grown from the soils of insecurity.

Shamefully, those statements and others like them are exactly the kinds of things that I said and thought to myself in the face of rejection—even sometimes beforehand to give myself the boost of false courage to approach a beautiful girl. Little did I understand that my sad exercises just perpetuated the very traits that got me rejected. My pride made me ugly as much as miserable, and it was noticeable.

It's not until you view yourself through a humbler lens that you afford the wisdom to see your imperfections. There is yet more irony to be found in the fact that when I finally began to let go of my pride and blind self-image, I ended up a far more confident person as a result. A certain level of humility made me more attractive to the people around me and, as a result, made me more confident than my moronic pride ever did. Of course, I had to check myself so that my newfound confidence would not boomerang back into prideful thoughts, but it was easier when my geyser of confidence did not rise from a spring of conceded boorishness.

I like to say that the smartest people in the world think that they are idiots, and the dumbest people in the world think they're geniuses. Socrates is known for saying, "All I know is that I know nothing," and no one calls Socrates a dufus.

The wise call themselves foolish, and the foolish call themselves wise. A generous man has never given enough charity by his own estimation, but a greedy one has given enough for a lifetime. I can go on for a while with examples of how pride distorts reality.

You will never meet a good man worth admiration who makes pride a personal virtue. There are no wise prideful men. A wise person doesn't boast about how wise he is. And you will never see a truly humble person make a fool of himself. It's hard to make humility look unattractive. You might think that someone who lacks confidence is an example of unattractive humility, but you would be wrong. Humility does not contradict confidence. Lack of confidence is not the result of excessive humility but a defect. In its truest sense, Humility radiates and demands confidence, making a humble person all the more attractive. If a woman brags about how attractive she is, that is pretty unattractive. But the girl next to her, showing love not to herself but the people around her and making them feel special, without a word about herself, that girl is a priceless gem.

Chapter 23

Unhealthy Relationships

Some time ago, while I was hard at work in the workshop at my place of employment, I happened to spot a phenomenon that I normally would have overlooked and dismissed as mundane, but I felt compelled to pay close attention to some reason

There was a spider web in the corner of my workstation. The creepy crawlers loved our shop building. It was like their own 24-hour nightclub. A small yellow jacket had flown into my work area as well. He buzzed around my head, and I did that little dance that so many of us do when being faced with a flying stinger, trying to avoid it while at the same time trying not to freak out. After the yellow jacket was satisfied with how much he had made me look like a freakshow to my coworkers, the winged yellow demon flew off and put some distance between him and me, heading straight toward the corner where the eight-legged fiend lay in wait to trap its prey.

The yellow jacket floated around the spider's corner for a moment until finally getting snagged on the web. The jacket was ensnared in the trap of doom. At that, the spider leaped into action. He glided down the web to where the yellow jacket was struggling to break free and went to work, attempting to wrap the little winged creature in an imprisoning cocoon of webbing to be eaten.

The yellow jacket wriggled and fought against foe and web, evidently not ready to die by a stranger's fangs. Miraculously, and to the good fortune of the jacket but the immense disappointment of the spider, he managed to break free of the spider's web, now able to fly away to freedom.

Unfortunately, the yellow jacket did not seize this opportunity to fly away to liberation. He kept close to the same corner, hovering near the web from which he had only just escaped, testing fate. It had been free to leave, to fly far away from its adversary and torment, but it just would not leave the short radius of the spider's web. The yellow jacket finally got caught in the spider's web for the second time, and there would be no escaping it then. It went right back into that hazardous, unhealthy situation but could not fly away a second time.

I realize that that story seems mundane. After all, it is only a bug being caught in a spider web, which happens every day. However, the minor details that I observed in this particular instance fascinated me. Like that yellow jacket, many human beings get trapped in bad situations, often in the form of abusive people and unhealthy human relationships. The extent of the unhealthiness of a particular situation can vary, but it is always best to avoid such hazards and people. Sadly, once a treacherous individual lures us in, it can feel like we are caught in their web. Sometimes it seems hopeless to resist the snare, so we put up little fight, and other times it seems that escape is within sight, but it is not quite reachable. It is always possible to break free of such people and hazards (if not always easy). Still, once one does manage to break free, we must get far outside of the spider's radius, hovering far outside of the danger zone, and not allow ourselves to be reeled back into madness. If you go back to an unhealthy situation or relationship that you were blessed and brave enough to escape, the end is not likely to be pleasant. Sometimes it can be fatal.

I have a list of friends and loved ones who have been hurt by toxic—sometimes very abusive—relationships. Often, there is no difference between the two. Some walked away with severe mental and emotional scars; some walked away with physical scars; a couple did not walk away at all. One such girl, a friend from high school, had her life cut short because of one such relationship. I take the subject of abuse very seriously, and I wince at the idea of anybody being caught in an abusive situation, mistaking the vindictiveness for some form of love.

Love does not harm. There is absolutely nothing loving about cuts and bruises. Nothing is loving about malicious words and actions that leave no physical evidence but can run just as deep, if not deeper.

If someone you care about or "love" hurts you, get away from them and stay away. Do not be afraid to tell somebody (a parent, a trusted teacher or mentor, a school counselor, any pastor you may know, or even one you've never met before) that they have hurt you, especially if you still have lingering fears. If the person who hurts you is a parent or someone of authority, talk to the authorities or law enforcement, I implore you. Tell *somebody*. Do not let something like this eat away at you or chip away at who you are.

God loves you; He wants what is good for you; He has surrounded you with people who are willing to love and care for you whether you are aware of it or not. Talk to God, and talk to somebody else about your situation. One way or another, you will see what *real* love looks like.

Believe me; I know that this chapter might be heavy and potentially hard for some to read. It is not one that I particularly wanted to write. However, I have witnessed far too much abuse and experienced it, if only a relatively minor case, in my two decades and some change on this earth to neglect this vital topic. It would not be loving for me to pretend that this stuff does not occur. I want everyone to be prepared to handle such things, be willing to walk away from hazardous situations and relationships and have the courage to recognize that you are loved by your all-knowing Savior and Maker and have far too much value to be willing to endure such treatment. What I write here is not particularly substantive, nor is it a substitute for getting counseling by any stretch of the imagination, but perhaps it is at least consequential.

Your God knew you and loved you before He even formed you in the womb (Jeremiah 1:5), you are fearfully and wonderfully made (Psalm 139:14), and He has great plans for you, plans greater than you could know (Jeremiah 29:11-13). You are intended to be loved, adored, and treated as something precious. I want to be very clear that God's desire for you is not that you are subjected to ill-treatment. You are His child, and like any Father, He wants to see his child handled with care.

I know, all too well, that it can be difficult to reach out to people for help and guidance when you are in a bad place, particularly if trapped with a bad person. Feeling stuck in place with somebody who does not wish you well is suffocating. To feel trapped by somebody who seems to actively wish you harm is terrifying. I do not wish it upon anybody to feel unloved or unsafe in their own home, as I used to.

I cannot presume to speak too much on behalf of my siblings, but we all carry our psychological scars from a past spent with our father. My sister developed ulcers from the stress he caused her and had to be hospitalized; I suffered almost daily panic attacks for what felt like ages and was in a deep, mind-fogged depression for years. I will spare you from having to read about the worst of the details for now, as I will spare myself from having to write about them.

What I can tell you is that I withdrew from the world, genuinely convinced that my mere existence vexed everyone in my life. I remained largely isolated because I did not wish to trouble my friends and loved ones by presuming to obligate them to help me through my petty problems. I hid from everyone who cared about me because I sincerely believed that nobody could bother to love me beyond a surface-level expression. I even doubted for a very long time that my Heavenly Father could be bothered with the likes of me.

My only flesh-and-blood example of a father was cold and distant in the best of times, seeming to show me affection on a conditional basis. My understanding of fatherhood—at least subconsciously—was that I had to earn love and affection. I worked hard in sports to earn my earthly father's attention but, as far as I could tell, I had done nothing nearly worthy enough to warrant the positive attention of a Father in heaven.

Of course, I only thought that way because my perception of fatherhood was confused and distorted. I had imprinted on my dad as a father figure, and thus I had pasted his image onto the very concept of paternal love itself. However, the standard of love comes from our Father in heaven, and it is a far stronger love than we can even imagine, much less feel capable of expressing ourselves. The defective sub-standard version of love that I experienced under my dad is a pathetic attempt at imitating the real thing. My dad's love was damaging and tainted with pain, but my Father's love is life-giving and limitless—not to mention unconditional. If only I had understood that sooner.

While I do not dismiss the impact of what they went through, what my siblings and I endured at our father's mercy is nothing compared to what our mother suffered. The image of "love," if you can call it that, which my father portrayed toward my mom, was something out of a Steven King novel. I either seemed to be oblivious to most of what went on behind closed doors, or my adolescent mind had instinctively blocked it out or suppressed the comprehension of matters. Although, I suspect that I caught on that something was going on because I was acutely aware that the environment in our home would darken whenever my father returned home from his long trips, and I began to prefer when he was out of town.

My dear mother was psychologically tortured for years. Her emotional state began to manifest in her appearance as her face went gaunt, and her hair started to thin and fall out from the anxiety. I once watched from the back seat of a moving vehicle while my father was driving as my mother opened the passenger-side door, leaped out of the moving car, and started running. That is how afraid she had become of the man I called "dad."

My mother is a very, very strong woman—the toughest person I know, beyond any doubt. At the time that this was all going on, though, she did not know what to do—who to talk to and how to be free of her situation, along with her children. There were more factors than just her safety that she was considering, and she didn't feel she could even talk to anyone or do anything without serious fallout.

My dad seemed like the ideal husband to the outside world, the church congregation, and even my mother's parents. He was well-respected and well-liked in the public eye, and he always seemed pleasant to his peers. The spider (my father) had her wrapped tightly in his web. He had tortured her mind and was sucking the life out of her, which became apparent by her stress-induced physical appearance. He never beat her or any of his children, did nothing that would leave clear physical evidence of torment, but not all (or even the worst) abuse is physical.

We were living in a silent, secret, psychological hell. Here's the thing, though: we were only in it as long as we allowed ourselves to be—as long as we kept quiet about it. I only wish it hadn't taken so long to open up about it.

I can assure you that my father, like any abuser, definitely did not want anybody to know what he was doing and how he was treating those he was supposed to love. If everyone found out, he would have been dealt with, and the hell would have ended abruptly. If the entire church knew, if both sides of the family knew, if family friends knew, if his dark deeds had been brought into the light, the coward would have crumbled.

Eventually, my mother talked to someone and got help, got a good distance away from my father, and even rediscovered God, whom she had admitted to spending years resenting. She found hope and new life in Him. I took a little bit longer to find peace with Him, not because I was hurt more (I wasn't), but because I was stubborn and less receptive to Him. But I eventually laid out all of my pain, hurt, and guilt before God and asked for His help and healing. Eventually, I began to ask for the strength to forgive those who had wronged my loved ones and me.

We lived in a bad situation, but the way out was always there. He was always there. We relied on our waning strength to get us through and endure for a long time, but it was not enough. We were lost. We did not know what to do, where to go, or who to seek help. We were trusting in ourselves too much and trusting in God too little.

"Trust in the Lord with all your heart and lean not on your own understanding. In all your ways acknowledge Him, and He will make your path straight" (Proverbs 3:5-6). Once we brought our fear, frustration, anxiety, and hopelessness before Him, it did not seem so hopeless. I do not want to sound overly simplistic or give the impression that my mother, siblings, and I had all of our problems evaporated. The hardships and pain did not cease to exist when we walked away, to be sure. We had to put distance between ourselves and our abuser, and sometimes he tried to reel us back into his web. I confess that I was once the yellow jacket who hovered around the danger zone too close to the web, and eventually, he trapped me again, as well as my little brother, who sadly never had the chance to escape the web, to begin with.

When I was leaving the university, my car had just croaked, and I had no money to my name, so my father put me in a room in his rental house. Without a job or transportation to drive, I had to rely on help, and he knew it. It was common for him to offer help—particularly money—as a hook to get his children caught and at his mercy. Abusers often like to incorporate financial pressure to make their victims feel trapped with them, and any tool they could use to exert control over one of us would utilize. My brother and I lived in his house for months, which was unpleasant. My brother ended up needing to go into rehab and, while I will spare the details, it did not take me long after that to suffer a complete mental breakdown. In pseudo-desperation, I skipped town and moved to the first place in which I could find a job which, fortunately enough for me, was near the good side of my family.

It is bad enough to be caught in an abusive situation, to begin with, but when you do manage to escape, make it a complete break and getaway. Do not hover about the web waiting to get caught again. I urge anyone beneath the heel of abuse in any form, please, place your trust in God and seek help and counseling.

I do not hate my father. I hope that God works in his heart and that a miracle takes place, but that does not mean I have to be around him and his abusive behavior waiting for such an event to occur. I have not seen or spoken to my dad in years, and he has yet to meet my wife. That is not because I hate him (again, I cannot emphasize enough that

I do not hate my father), but because he has not changed and perhaps needs a form of motivation to do so—some manner of deterrence from his present state and habits. Bad behavior must be confronted, and walking away is a rather effective form of indirect confrontation that keeps me and my loved ones out of harm's way. I will never return to abuse, whether mental, emotional or otherwise. Once the bee escapes the web, he would do well not to stick around and get caught again.

You should *never* stay in an abusive or toxic situation. Get help, get free, and do not return to the spider's hunting grounds.

If my father tried to prove that his heart had been transformed, I would *reluctantly* give him that chance to prove himself, being ever-so-wary and prepared to walk away should his claims prove less than true. I would grant him that opportunity because he is my father, like it or not. He also no longer has any sway over me or any hooks with which to draw me in, be it financial or otherwise, and I can walk away at any moment if his claims prove to be false.

On the other hand, I would *never* recommend extending the same courtesy to a former abusive romantic partner! No commandment says, "honor thy ex-boyfriend who beat or harassed you." You owe that individual absolutely nothing of yourself. Once you walk away from a hazard like that, stay away and cut all ties—all potential lines of communication with him (or her, as the case may be). It is not your job to "save" him from himself or help him be a better person! An abuser will *not* accept such help from someone they abuse, no matter how hard that person tries! Leave the saving and the heart transformations to Jesus. Pray for that person, if you will, but stay far away and never go back.

You never want to go back to your abuser, but that does not mean that you cannot or should not be open to forgiveness. As long as you hold on to resentment for what was done to you, that person who did it will always have power over you. You essentially become their slave when you enable them to determine the terms of how you move forward with your life, how you feel, and what you think, even if it is all negative toward them—especially so. Until you can pray for those who hurt you, freedom will feel out of reach.

I know that it is hard to forgive when you have been wronged in such a profound manner. Sadly, virtuous things, which we are all called to do and the most worth doing, are seldom easy. Doing such challenging but worthwhile things is what sets us apart as true followers of Christ. So, while you should still maintain an indefinite distance and lack of contact between yourself and the abuser of your past, it is equally important for your heart and spiritual well-being to eventually be willing to pray for those who have wronged you and find it within yourself to forgive them in your heart.

If you need a little bit of additional motivation to leave a bad relationship than you already have, consider this: the abuse does not hurt you alone, but also those around you and those who love you. Please, do not take that as an excuse to distance yourself from loved ones and friends, as that is the worst thing you could do! I am, after all, imploring you to seek their help in getting out of bad situations if you are in one.

I am saying that those who know you and love you will be hurt by knowing that you are being hurt. In the case of physically abusive partners, things can escalate beyond that, and people can be physically affected if a bad partnership is not broken off completely. Nobody wants to see you hurt, but the one in the bad relationship must be the one to make the break.

I used to be a bouncer in a bar during my time in college. During my employment at this establishment, I met a very pleasant and charming young woman—we'll call her Grace— who had recently moved to town with her boyfriend. As I have stated, there are many reasons why such cohabitation is a very bad idea, but add this story to the list.

Grace eventually started working as a bartender in the same bar. She became a joy to have as a coworker. I began noticing, though, night after night, that this boyfriend of hers was *always* in the bar while she was working. Not only that, but he was always lurking in some corner off by himself with a drink, just eyeballing her. With the way he stared and never broke focus on her, it was a wonder the intensity of his gaze didn't set her on fire. This often went on for the full extent of Grace's shift. Outside of the initial creepiness of this inherently obvious behavior, it signaled he might have been a little overbearing and possessive.

One night, this boyfriend came into the bar again while Grace was working, and it was clear that he had already been drinking and quite intoxicated. Naturally, my job as a bouncer demanded that I disallow him from entering the building under those circumstances, and I tried to bar him from entry and even offered to get him a ride home. The man immediately was aggravated and aggressive, which is never a good omen and was even more cause to ensure that he did not stay on the premises. Just as I was about to eject him from the bar forcibly, however, my boss (who had a close friendship with this headcase) approached the scene and told me to let him in, assuring me that she would keep him on a tight leash. That claim of hers would later prove to be nonsense, but I begrudgingly conceded to my employer's demands. So, this guy departed from my side to go and sit at the bar where he could once again "keep an eye" on Grace while she worked.

Later in the evening, Grace had just served a male customer, and her boyfriend immediately called her over to his corner. I witnessed from my podium at the other end of the crowded bar as he proceeded to grab her by the back of the neck and yank her ear to his mouth so that he could sternly speak into it. It was as unfriendly and aggressive as a gesture could be.

Now, not much will provoke me into a rage, as I am a pretty calm individual with a long fuse and a soft temperament by nature, easily averse to most confrontation. Be that as it may, a man touching a woman in such a malicious and unkind way is one of the few and quickest triggers that will put a fire in my eyes and make me fume with rage. I mean, the moment I saw what this man was doing, in my mind, I was already smashing him into a paste.

I approached the couple just as the boyfriend released Grace's neck and tossed her violently aside. She stormed out the front door of the bar, attempting quite unsuccessfully to hide the fact that she was crying. I opted to go outside and check on her rather than physically assaulting her boyfriend. As I exited the building, I found Grace slumped over on the curb of the parking lot, sobbing.

As I attempted to help and offer comfort, Grace confided in me that she had just moved over six hours away from her hometown and family to come here with her boyfriend and, while he scared her sometimes, staying with him seemed better than being alone. That's how abusers often work: they isolate you from any support structure that you might have, family or friends, until you are utterly dependent on the abuser alone for human interaction and some manner of "stability." This makes it hard for you to leave, and they know it.

Grace defended him by claiming that "he's only really bad when he's been drinking." Even if I believed that for a second (which I did not), the fact is that he knew how he was when he drank, and yet he still did it. He drank alcohol quite frequently. He was not going to give up this destructive behavior, even if he was physically hurting this woman whom he claimed to "love."

That is *not* love. Not even close. Love is patient and kind, and, by its very nature, it does not harm! Suppose a partner of yours is ever engaged in destructive behavior such as alcoholism or drug abuse, especially to a dangerous extent. In that case, they do so knowing the harm that it can cause. That person loves their drug of choice more than they do their "loved ones." Stay away from that person.

In Grace's case, her boyfriend was providing her with all the evidence that she needed to be assured that he was willing to choose the bottle of whiskey over her safety and well-being. She yet remained undeterred from her opinion that he loved her "deep down." She honestly believed that the right woman could transform a devil and that she could be his angel—never mind the detriment that her crazy over-romanticized opinion might have on her safety.

This was a terrible situation. I took Grace back into the bar through the back door and let her stay in the safety of the backroom while I firmly tossed her human scum of a boyfriend out of the front door and told him not to return, else I would have him arrested without a second thought. My boss was noticeably upset with me for treating her little buddy so harshly, but I did not care. He had to leave.

Unfortunately, after closing time, with just me, Grace, and three other bar employees there, the jerk returned, and my genius of a boss unlocked the door for him. She even took it further and told Grace to "work it out" with him.

Can I offer a little piece of advice from somebody with a brain? Never try to "work it out" with somebody who hurts you! Cut ties and run! Grace should have cut and run from the start. My lunatic boss should never have suggested she attempt to have a rational discussion with her drunken abuser—much less that she should try to mend the relationship with him.

Between the time of this abusive madman showing back up at the bar and the police showing up at my request, this guy had punched a hole into the bathroom door, screamed and cursed at everybody in the building, physically assaulted someone, and pulled out a knife. This was far from a good night to be a bouncer and certainly not worth the meager salary I was being paid.

Miraculously, nobody was seriously injured. The police eventually showed up and put the crazed man in handcuffs but then allowed him to go free because both my boss and even Grace testified that he had done nothing wrong. Yes, if one allows abuse to go on for long enough, it has enough psychological effect that one can do something that senseless in defense of their attacker.

I told my boss, without hesitation, that I was finished working for her. I made it clear that I refused to work for someone who holds the safety of her employees, of Grace, of myself, and in fact of anyone in such low regard as to enable that scumbag to walk away freely, and who would consciously enable the clear abuse of a young woman to continue. I never stepped foot back into that bar.

Last I heard, Grace was still with that ghoul, though that was years ago. Despite my best efforts, there was no way I could help her if she was unwilling to help herself. No amount of rational convincing would force her hand. She had an opening for escape but chose to return the power to her tormenter. As heartbreaking as it was, all I could do was pray for her. My love and prayers go out to anybody in the midst of such horrific circumstances.

Those circumstances can be changed, but nobody can change them for you if you do not allow them. Abuse and harmful relationships are terrible things. They hurt not just the abused but those around them and all those who love them.

If you are ever in an unhealthy or abusive situation, I once again implore you to tell somebody and get help. Spread the message covertly, but far and wide if you have to! When others know what is happening, that abuser's perceived power is stripped from him. If you fear your safety, you can talk to law enforcement and get a restraining order. In extreme circumstances, protective custody can also be an option. Failing that, it helps to have friends or family to stay with. If you are isolated enough by your abuser that that does not seem like an option, you can ask for help and guidance from members of a local church, should you be willing to confide in them. I know that most people in my church would have protective arms around you before you had the chance to ask.

Nobody should suffer in such a way as Grace or my mother. Nobody has to. Even if you are unaware of it, some love you and want what is best for you. There is He who loves you and wants what is best for you. If you allow people to love you and help you, they will. If you bring your struggles before God, He will be there right beside you. Nobody is greater than Him. No abuser is a match for Him. And He can heal all wounds and quell all evils. "The name of the Lord is a strong tower; the righteous run to it and are safe" (Proverbs 18:10). If you are ever in a bad situation, He has a place for you in His tower. Run to Him and find relief. He will post guards around that tower in the form of friends, loved ones, law enforcement, clergy, and anyone else who you allow to love and care for you. Trust in Him, trust in *real* love.

"Love is patient, love is kind. It does not envy, it does not boast, it is not proud. It does not dishonor others, it is not self-seeking, it is not easily angered, it keeps no record of wrongs. Love does not delight in evil but rejoices in the truth. It always protects, always trusts, always hopes, always perseveres" (1 Corinthians 13:4-7).

Never settle for anything less. You are *always* loved by Him who created you and wants what is good for you.

My love goes out to you as well. That is why I have written this for you. I may not know you personally, but you are in my heart. These pages were written for you. God bless you.

Chapter 24

The Model Prisoner

We have discussed the plight of spiders in the relational world who trap people in their webs and do them harm. In addition, we have driven home the need for anyone trapped in the web of abuse or mistreatment to talk to someone, talk to God, and make their escape. I suppose the question now becomes, "How do we avoid getting close to the 'spiders' in the first place? How do we preemptively sidestep the need to get help and talk to somebody?"

When considering forming a relationship of any kind, one must always have standards in mind! Know what qualities are important in a partner and what traits are unacceptable for a prospective spouse. Know your deal-breakers before you attempt to date anybody and stick to them regardless of the circumstances. No girl gets lax treatment and escapes the purge of standards because she is extra pretty. If you set the standard that you will not date someone who uses swear words out of habit, then walk away when the girl drops an F-bomb; if you resolve not to date anybody who drinks alcohol, smokes, or utilizes any other substance, walk away when you see that pack of Marlboros in her hand.

I cannot decide for you what your standards should be for whom you will date and potentially marry, but I hope you use this book's advice, and more importantly, the Bible, as guidelines for your list of criteria. I would also recommend you set a goal and write down your guiding principles. It never hurts to have a hard copy of your standards readily available for reference, as well as to keep you accountable for sticking to your guidelines.

If you recoiled at the suggestion that you should write something down, I understand. However, suppose you do not have a hard copy detailing the traits you are looking for in a romantic partner, visual evidence of the standards you intend to hold firm to, your standards *will* be malleable and subject to change on a whim—when your emotions take over. You become discouraged and desperate or blinded by how "cute" someone is. I know what is liable to happen because I have done this, and I am not the only person who has bent his own rules and compromised his standards to avoid being alone. There is no winning in that scenario. The last thing you want is for emotion-driven moments to lead you to compromise on your principles and make avoidable mistakes.

So, write down what you are looking for in a partner and what traits you should turn away from. Make a list of good qualities for someone you date to have and bad qualities that you do not want them to have, and refer to that list often when deciding whether a particular individual is a wise option for you. Think of it as a contract you make with yourself. If you meet a girl that you think you might like, but her character conflicts with an essential item on your list of standards, then do not breach your contract by pursuing her. It is that simple.

The standards you set for the kind of person you will date do not have to be complicated. Determine your value system, make a list of those values, and look for somebody who shares your values. I, for example, wanted to find a girl who believed in the biblical principle of abstaining from sex until marriage, and straying from that standard seldom led to good things. If you set the principle, you must stick to it. You do not want your standards to be set unreasonably or impossibly high, such as seeking a man who has never told a lie or a woman who has never made a bad judgment call. Please do not think I am advising you to be stingy or prudish in your decisions, but it is essential to find somebody who shares your value system. I would argue that setting standards too low would result in a far worse situation.

You want to do the best you can when making decisions about forming relationships. This means having good standards in place for those you consider, and it especially means that you have no business starting a relationship with someone you think you can "fix" or "change." That approach to dating and relationships is not healthy for *anybody* involved, and only stupid people date that way. You are not stupid, so do not do it! If the individual in question is, for example, a heavy drinker, a recreational drug user, a drug dealer, a convict, or a womanizer, no touchy! Leave those people alone if you know what is good for you!

You cannot fix who that person is. If they wanted to be fixed or changed, they would do it themselves! Only a weak-willed person can be convinced that a person engaged in bad behavior would be willing to change their bad behavior *just for you*! A strong-willed person has high standards for who they date from the outset and subsequently sticks to those standards. Therefore, it follows that those who date with the hopes of "changing" the person they date are weak-willed and therefore malleable. Bad men love weak-willed women because they are easy to reel in with the over-romanticized idealism that says, "he can change," and once reeled in, she is often easily manipulated. A malleable woman can be heavily influenced by an individual who has bad intentions and thus can be hurt by the one they wanted to "change" or "fix" in the first place.

I do not care how many fictional romantic movies say otherwise. Unrepentant and immoral men are not changed or *saved* by nice girls with good intentions. And men, that works in the opposite direction too! I do not care how nice or cute they might seem. Remember, again, Jesus saves, and the Holy Spirit changes hearts. You are neither one of them. You do not.

I believe in grace and in second chances at doing life right. The Lord redeems, and people are indeed born again. However, until such a time when that happens, the person's past and present matter, as it reflects the condition of their heart. You cannot and should not bet the rest of your life on someone who walks in the park with their demons.

The Model Prisoner Phenomenon

I have spent a lot of time around inmates in the prison system. No, I was never a convict and have never worn an orange jumpsuit. I do prison ministry, and I have given many sermons to these men and have had engaging, often emotional, conversations with many who have had questionable pasts. Many of these men knew nothing of Christ before going to prison, and it is a privilege to talk to them about Him. Jesus said that it is not the healthy who need a physician, but the sick. There is no better place to find those who need God's medicine than in prison, and many of the inmates I speak to are convinced that, had they been exposed to Christ and scripture in school, they wouldn't need it in prison because they might not be in there.

Being involved in this ministry has, unquestionably, been one of the most fulfilling experiences of my life. I can tell you, firsthand, that God moves in many of these convicts' hearts clearly and drastically—making them unrecognizable from the men who entered the prison in handcuffs. It's often easy for these men to accept the prospect of hope in Christ when their situations seem hopeless. God loves his children, and He wants them *all* to come home to Him, so He sends men like those in my ministry to show His love to those who may have never felt it but need it. Thankfully, many of the inmates I meet are ready and willing to open their hearts to God and experience true joy despite their circumstances. These men often leave prison truly changed.

One man involved in my ministry, a man we'll refer to as Adam, was once a convicted criminal himself. This guy was tough, hardened, and angry in his day. Hearing him talk about his past life tends to make people sweat out of fear of who he once was, though that fear is dulled by the foreknowledge of seeing a glowing example of a man of God he has become.

When I first saw Adam give his testimony, I was truly stunned. For a moment, it almost seemed like he was reliving his past life, and I felt a quiver run up my back. This man told the story of how he accepted Jesus Christ into his heart while behind bars, through the influence and genuine love of a fellow inmate whom Adam had, just moments before, actually beaten to the edge of death just for speaking the name of Jesus. Adam, this hulking and imposing figure of a man, broke down into tears in front of 50 hardened criminals as he told them that he accepted Christ over the broken and bloodied face of the man who refused to stop telling him that Jesus loved him. That is a harrowing yet incredible story.

Today, Adam is a far cry from that man with violent hate in his heart. He has truly been born again, and it is made clear through his actions, behavior, patience, the way he honors and loves the people around him, the way he honors and loves his wife, and how he passionately pursues God and proclaims His love to anybody who will listen.

Adam is not the first violent criminal to be changed inside and out through the love of Christ, and he is far from the only one. Sadly, men like him are not the norm—more like exceptions to the general rule.

The more common pattern for men exiting the prison system is considerably less inspiring than stories like Adam's. They often come out worse off spiritually than when they went in. That is a logical conclusion that we can expect when these individuals spend all their time surrounded by bad people who have done heinous things. The group-think in these close proximities can be strong. Making matters worse, individuals in such an environment often feel that the best way to survive in the system is to submit to some level of conformity—to act like the criminals they are surrounded by. This is a big reason I find prison ministry so vitally important; making these guys feel loved and hopeful has a profound countereffect.

That being said, one relatively consistent pattern of behavior seems to hold true for a high percentage of inmates and ex-cons: they get proficient at hiding their dark side when they are being watched. This skill can be obtained and practiced whether the one watching them is a security camera, prison warden, fellow citizen, or an attractive and well-meaning member of the opposite sex.

When a convict is inside—as a prisoner—he is under near-constant surveillance. Someone is always watching and waiting for them to misbehave. Inmates know that acting out will result in punishment and possibly an extended prison sentence depending on the offense, so they often put on the "model prisoner" show. They keep their head down and avoid acting out. They act like the ideal inmate, worthy of receiving a trophy engraved with the message "most reformed" or "best-behaved inmate." It is how a prisoner acts when they are *not* being watched that is the concern. Sooner or later, the individual is released from prison and back into society, and we see if they can keep up the act. Often, the act does not stick, and they end up being arrested again.

Now certainly not everybody who has ever been to prison and behaved well is putting on a show, and I do not mean to beat up on ex-cons. This is not the "do not date men who have made mistakes" chapter. As I have said, I have a lot of love for people inside, and I try to show them grace whenever possible. I know a fair number of men who have been to prison for offenses ranging from minor to serious, who were born again and are wonderful people today. I am merely using the illustration of convicts to make a finer point. As I call it, the model prisoner phenomenon does not apply solely to convicts. That is precisely the direction in which this is going.

Men and women put on the model prisoner act every day to get what they want. A player and womanizer makes himself out to be a well-meaning guy to an unsuspecting girl, only to show his true colors when he gets what he wants out of her and breaks her heart. Abusers put on the model prisoner act by seeming like the ideal boyfriend or husband while the world is watching, only to drop the act and reveal the monster inside when behind closed doors.

These are extreme examples, I grant you, but I hope the point is clear. The façade that an individual puts up is generally not the whole picture. We are all guilty of this to some degree, I'm sure, but the depths to which a façade goes can vary drastically between characters, and it's that depth that matters. If somebody tries to act a little bit like you and your friends in a misguided attempt to be liked, that's one thing. When a person wears an entirely false persona and tries to get you to fall in love with them under false pretenses, that is another thing entirely. While there is no fool-proof method to see into the depths of everyone's heart, how might we look out for those putting on the "model prisoner" act?

The thing about acting is it is relatively easy to fake an expression or an *action*, but it is significantly more difficult to fake or hide a genuine *reaction*. Acting is easy for those who have a talent for it, but our reactions to emotional stimuli or even physical pain tend to be a bit more authentic. Just look at a blooper reel of any television sitcom such as *Friends*. Observe as these professional actors break character and start laughing when something unexpected happens on set.

When I was doing the dating around thing, trying to talk to girls, get their phone numbers, and take them on dates, I would often attempt to fake (or act out) large chunks of my personality. I am not proud of it by any means, but it's what I did. Most of the time, though, I do not think I was even aware of what I was doing. From a source of insecurity and nervousness, I would impersonate somebody I would have liked to be more like—an actor who played confident characters or such—and try to simulate some personality trait I thought a girl might find attractive but that I didn't embody at my core.

If I tried to act more confident than I was when talking to a beautiful woman, deep down, I thought, *what would Tony Stark say*? It was not hard for that girl to peel back my phony mask. All she had to do was test me a little bit. If she teased me or made fun of me in any way, I looked flushed and embarrassed; if she neglected to laugh at something I said, my face betrayed the fact that I felt expectant, timid, or defeated. I would *react* to certain things in a way that made me appear different than how I had been *acting*, and the girl could often see through me almost immediately. My *reaction* was the only yellow flag she needed to tell her I was not sincere or candid with her and that something was off about the person I was portraying myself as.

That, in effect, is what *you* want to do when chatting somebody up—watch for and be aware of those reactions and signs that tell you, "This person is not being genuine with me. They are hiding something."

A person can act all they want, but it is challenging to act while reacting. How a man or woman responds to inconveniences or minor annoyances is a far more telling indication of what's in their heart than the way they act around you in general or when they know that they are being observed.

Look beyond how a person of interest acts and pay closer attention to how they react to certain things, be they big or small:

- Do they get defensive when you ask them personal questions?
- Do they become rigid when someone inquires about their Internet search history (I fully endorse mentioning it on the third date)?
- Does their body temperature change when you ask about text messages from/to other members of the opposite sex?
- When someone bumps into them on the street by accident, is their response, "I'm sorry, please excuse me," or is it closer to, "watch where you're going, moron?"
- When a minor inconvenience occurs, do they take a deep breath? Or do they instead start spewing curse words?
- Do you feel safe and secure in their presence? Or do you sometimes feel uneasy, scared, or demoralized?
- Do they respect your boundaries? Or do they occasionally try to push them? (i.e., do they respect your wishes to remain abstinent, or do they look for excuses to enter a bedroom with you or try to touch you inappropriately?)
- If someone were to get confrontational with them, would they attempt to resolve the situation peacefully? Or would they be quick, if not eager, to physical aggression?
- Do they exhibit jealousy to the point of blind, borderline violent rage?
- Do they try to get along with your friends and family? Or do they make attempts (whether subtle or obvious) to isolate you from them?
- Are they slow to anger like a pot of water gradually approaching a boil? Or is it more like flipping a light switch?

The model prisoner act is exactly that—an act. Acts fade. How a person *reacts* is a more reliable indication of who you will end up with if you date or marry the person. If you want to be careful and intentional about who you spend your time with, then it is important you pay attention to more than their voluntary words and actions, and do not dismiss their less voluntary responses because they are absolutely relevant. Character is truly shown with what we do when we think no one is watching.

Chapter 25

Why Wait?

We are generally patient when waiting on marriage for a generation of people who want everything now! I am being facetious, of course. It has nothing to do with patience, though fear might play a key role in one's willingness to wait indefinitely for this key step of maturity and responsibility.

For many young people, getting married and having a family has become something of an afterthought—a consolation prize they begrudgingly accept when they have done everything else in life and want to try something new. Some men tire of being single, wasting time, living promiscuously. Hence, they figure they will finally get hitched while still having some attractive years remaining and can still get a girl's attention.

Some women want to get their career out of the way first and reach the top of the ladder before they dare consider the daunting prospect of sharing their life and success with another person. Heaven forbid they should later brave the unfathomable sacrifice of time and energy to spend loving a child or two.

In our culture, both men and women sometimes seem to be convinced that the goal of life is to be completely self-interested. That is, more or less, the way we have been trained in this most recent generation. Most of us have grown up hearing those messages repeated in our ears: "Don't even think about getting married until you are 'old enough' (whatever that means) and as mature as possible; wait until you have enough money (can I get a number?); wait until you have finished your education (I still haven't finished mine, nor do I intend ever to stop learning); wait until you have been dating the person long enough to know absolutely everything about them, perhaps 8-17 years (that one is my favorite to make fun of); in essence, wait until everything else in your life is *perfect* so that you can endure the absolute horrors of marriage! You wouldn't want to be added to the 50% divorce rate, so you should do the same things that everybody who gets divorced does!"

Am I the only one commenting on how insane people sound who say this kind of stuff? Sometimes it feels like it. It's no wonder that many folks my age (mid-20s) are afraid to get married and are content to wait until approximately 40 years of age. For crying out loud, that may very well be half of your life that you'd have spent waiting! Or were you under the impression that you were going to live forever? I am so sorry; I did not mean to fracture the illusion.

As far as I can tell, people are hysterical about the very idea of marriage because they have been conditioned to fear the mythical 50% divorce rate, which gives them a misguided sense that marriage is doomed to fail. Yes, I did indeed say *mythical*. It is not real! Half of all people who get married *do not* get divorced! Psychology Today and many other scholarly sources openly confess as much! When you look at first-time married couples, their success rate is a far more staggering 75-80% average! When we look at repeat offenders—those who get divorced and re-marry—we see the divorce rates climb. Funny enough, second and third marriages have a statistical 75%-80% failure rate, parallel to the first-marriage *success* rate. Those who get remarried often tend not to change old habits that led to their marriages ending; they just changed spouses and hoped that would fix things.

So, the small population of serial divorcees who cannot stay married for more than five minutes makes the marriage failure rates look scary. Those are often the same people who enter a marriage virtually *expecting* it to end in divorce. The real divorce rate for first marriages rests somewhere closer to the 25% range. That is still not fabulous, but it is very different from a full half. Those who do not make it an option have far less to worry about. In my house, the D-word is forbidden. We are not allowed to say it any more than we are allowed to do it.

I am here to tell you that the society-wide fear of marriage is not only unfounded but counter to our best interests as individuals and as a society. We cannot continue normalizing the trend of waiting until we are in or around our middle age to get married! How long do you think you are going to live? Furthermore, for the women involved in this craziness, how long do you think that your body will allow you to wait before having children?

On average, by the age of 29, most women reflect having a ball-park of 12% of their eggs remaining. This means that 88% of their capacity to conceive a child has passed them by, and their body has a harder time getting pregnant. Women only have a finite quantity of eggs in their body and, once they run out, that's all folks.

It is a fact that women are at their peak physical health and capability while in their early twenties. With that being the case, young women have an easier time conceiving children, childbearing, physically recovering after giving birth, and correctly nursing an infant. Women over thirty years of age, by contrast, not only have a harder time conceiving children, but pregnancy for them is also associated with "increased risk for miscarriage, stillbirth, diabetes, hypertension, placenta previa, placental abruption, cesarian birth, and pregnancy-related mortality."[23] That is if they can conceive at all because, with age, comes the degradation of a woman's eggs, which also, in turn, can result in a list of birth defects for the child. Difficulty with conception and pregnancy can also be amplified if the aspiring mother has been on birth control medication for an extended time.

Today, women are postponing having a family for a later date to do what? Have a little extra money beforehand? Then, these women finally get married in their mid-30's and start trying to have kids, but may discover how hard it is to get pregnant at that age. Many such women begin spending a fortune on fertility treatments and surrogacy—tens of thousands of dollars, minimum—and there goes that extra money they had been saving. That is to say nothing of the fact that many women who wait until their 30's to try for children realize that this is also the time that their careers are starting to grow legs, so they may end up wishing that their children were older than infants and didn't need constant attention. Quite the list of ironies, no?

Having so many people wait until later in life to get married and neglect having children does have consequences that outweigh any perceived benefit. More children are born outside of wedlock and into broken homes than ever because people do not marry, but they still want sex. More couples in my generation live together in sin than marry one another, resulting in more broken homes, more broken hearts,

23   Alden, Kathryn R., *Maternal Child Nursing Care*, 2018, pp 94-95.

and less societal stability. Since the 1970s, shortly after the rise of the Sexual Revolution, the United States' birth rate has generally been below birth-level rates. The millennial generation is not the first American generation that will not have a birth rate equal to or greater than before. Still, we are certainly seeing record lows in these recent years—in other words, our population is dwindling because people do not have families. Again, the kids born without two loving parents are in the picture.

I have said it before, and I will not stop saying it: marriage is the single most vital stabilizing agent that society and culture have. Take it away, and history suggests nations crumble. In the interest of keeping our culture breathing and making it healthy again, I want to dispel some primary reasons people tend to postpone marriage and children.

Addressing Maturity

I catch a lot of flak from naysayers when I praise and support young marriage, and of course, that does not stop me from doing so. I am quite convinced that people should get married young and build their lives with their spouse as a unit if they have that chance, instead of attempting to build a solitary life and bring an outsider into it later. The latter situation seems to be a recipe for avoidable tensions and pain.

On the flip side of this issue, I also firmly believe that it is best for young people not to get involved or invested in romantic relationships until a year before they are old enough to marry legally. The longer two people date, the harder it is for them to keep their hands off of one another—particularly in the case of hormonal preteens and teenagers. I simply cannot find the wisdom in allowing 13, 14, and 15-year-old kids to develop passionate feelings toward one another, only to tell them that there is nothing they can do about those feelings until they get married. Not to mention many of the same parents who let their kids date at an early age do not want their kids to get married even when they are old enough for the same reasons that I am presently writing to debunk! It is ridiculous to put young people through that! Under such conditions, is it any wonder Christian teenagers tend to fail at sexual purity? Give me a break.

It is a simple rule that I believe in and stand by: if you cannot legally marry the person you are dating in approximately a year from the time you start going out, you should not be dating. If you are old enough to marry but do not intend to do so as soon as reasonably possible (such as within a year after your first anniversary), then why are you dating the person?

So, yes, I believe and support marriage as young as 18 years of age and fresh out of high school. Call me radical, but it was not until recent decades that such a concept became an abnormal consideration. It was only after, for example, casual sex became a societal norm in our culture that people in the west began putting off the very idea of marriage until they were near middle-age.

Young couples used to marry young, start their lives together, share a lifetime of love and laughs and hardships, and come out the other side with a rock-solid marriage. They would emerge from their early experiences more in love than ever and with a strong family because they *learned* from the beginning of their adult lives to endure things as one, to do life *together* rather than as lone wolves, to get through problems as a unit instead of two separate individuals. Those are the marriages that lasted, and they still are.

Just ask my great-grandmother, who married my great-grandfather when she was 16 years old! Those two were crazy about one another and grew crazier about each other for well over five decades, up to the day my great grandfather went to be with God. Mema was still in love with him even fifteen years after he passed away, to the point, when she was battling brain cancer, she would look at me (a practical clone of my great grandfather) and be convinced that she was looking at her late husband. By the way that she would speak when she thought her late husband was in front of her, there was no doubt in anybody's mind that she greatly looked forward to seeing him again. She finally passed on and followed him to heaven when I was 17.

Statistically, those who marry young and grow their lives together have a microscopic fraction of the divorce rate compared to those who wait until they are "old and mature enough." You can be sure that those younger married couples tend to have far less extramarital history on average, contributing to those low divorce rates. History tells us that young married couples mature and develop in faster, healthier ways, and they have a slight tendency to stay together until death. These are the happy people whose marriages last for life, and yet somehow, I am the crazy one for pointing that out and endorsing the things that those people do. If you want to be physically fit, you study the habits of physically fit people; if you want good relationships and lasting marriage, you study the lives of people who have that. It's not complicated.

Some of the most frequent objections I hear from people, young and old, when I talk about marrying young, are on this issue of maturity. Not surprisingly, I hear things like: "I don't know who I am at 18! No one is mature *enough* to get married that young! How can I commit my life to someone when I'm not even fully grown up yet? Neither of us will be the same in 10 years!"

These objections to young marriage are so frustrating because it is obvious that those who voice them are repeating talking points that they have heard. They have never seriously, critically thought about their words and seem to have little idea of the implications. If you think about these talking points, they honestly make little sense.

Who says you can't be mature at the age of 18? Does anybody ever stop to consider what "maturity" is or what it even looks like? And what does it mean to be mature *enough*? When you add the term "enough" to the end of a statement, you immediately claim that statement is arbitrary and subjective. Saying that a young man does not have enough maturity carries about as much subjective weight as me not feeling like I have *enough* chips and queso at the dinner table.

If the man is willing to work a job, provide for himself and others' needs, and has outgrown picking his nose, he has some level of maturity, albeit he has not yet reached his pinnacle level, nor will he ever! That being said, if 18-year-olds are old and mature enough to join the military (generally speaking), they are probably also capable of making other major life decisions as well.

I know 28-year-old men today who are less mature than I was at 18! How is that? It probably has something to do with the fact that I was making conscious decisions to be responsible when I was 18. I was working hard and taking on more and more responsibilities. It's a simple equation: the more things you take responsibility for, the more mature you tend to grow as a result.

A 30-year-old man who has never worked a day in his life or had a lick of true responsibility thrust upon him because his wealthy parents pay for his lifestyle is going to be an immature, useless brat. An 18-year-old who works two jobs while putting his new bride through nursing school will have maturity and competence pouring out of every pore on his skin!

When a kid gets married at a young age, his level of responsibility skyrockets; by necessity, his maturity level must rise to the occasion. I am not saying that he has all the answers or reached his peak level of wisdom, but he has the chance to learn and grow quickly, and he does so in cooperation with his lovely young bride, who is growing together beside him. Two developing minds are stronger than one, are they not?

Of course, some do not take their responsibilities seriously and consciously refuse to grow. Those are the exception to the rule—the men and women who have no intention of growing up, detest hard work, and despise wisdom. These individuals usually do not take on more responsibility by choice but eventually, have it thrust upon them—such as when a guy makes an immature decision that results in a pregnant girlfriend. Too often, that guy will reject the responsibility being "imposed" on him (by his deeds) and choose to remain an unfortunate child, to the detriment of others—namely his child and the mother. Do not mistake anything I tell you as an endorsement of marrying a young man with poor character qualities. Still, those qualities often have virtually nothing to do with their age. Men and women who accept responsibility grow, those who reject it shrink and fade.

No, you will not be the same person at the age of 28 years that you were at 18! That is called *development*. You will grow and improve, or you will shy away from growth and devolve. Either way, you will change. I will not be the same at 35 as at 25, and I should hope not! If I don't grow or change in any way by then, I'm dead!

We never stop the need to grow, and we never cease changing. It can't be helped. It comes with being *alive*. You will never "know who you are" whether you are 18 or 50 because who you are is always changing, be it for better or worse.

We don't get to decide whether time goes on or whether we grow older. However, we *can* decide if we will grow and develop alone or do so alongside the one we love, growing and maturing alongside us.

Money and Education

The objection to marriage based on money or the lack of it is an excuse that has never quite made sense to me. Frankly, it makes even less sense the more you take the time to slow down and think about it.

I, along with countless others, grew up hearing the message that it is best to wait until you have enough money—until you are "financially secure"—before you even think about endeavoring to get married. The people who tell us this seem to be under the impression that poor people cannot have good marriages or that a couple's financial situation and struggles perpetually freeze when exposed to matrimony. I guess, if we are not financially stable when we commit our lives to another person, we are somehow doomed for all of eternity? But what does *financial stability* even look like? How will I know when I am "stable?" How will I know when I am ready to get married if no one ever tells me what the proper dollar amount to possess is? Finally, if being broke is the bane of all marriages, how is my marriage great even though my wife married me when I had next to nothing?

What were our elders smoking when they implied that having a lot of money results in marital success or makes things easy? And where did they learn that, once you get married, your career and prospects dry up, and you no longer have any chance at financial success?

It's all nonsense. I know many poor people with wonderful marriages, and I know rich people whose relationships seem always to crumble. Conversely, I also know poor people with unhealthy marriages and relationships and rich people with solid ones. Money is not a factor that impacts whether or not one is ready to marry. Although, one's marriage *might* be capable of determining whether or not someone is ready for money.

If you introduce a financial fortune to a couple with a solid marriage, that money can amplify the best attributes of their relationship. On the other hand, introduce the same fortune to a bad marriage, and all you have done is give that couple something big to fight over. Watch as each of the partners' worst traits, such as selfish greed, rise to the surface, and the money becomes the straw that breaks their marriage's back.

Waiting until you have money to get married is just an excuse for wasting your time and your life, nothing more. Do you know what statistics say you should do if you want to make more money? They say to get married! Married people, on average, make noticeably more money than single people do, and not just because they commonly have two incomes in the household!

That being said, I can promise you married couples who become financially successful are *not* the ones who prioritize career and money above marriage and family. People who put their money first are the ones who lose it all, including the marriage.

Not everybody's choice hang-up about marriage is purely financial, however. Some choose to wait for marriage in favor of going to school and receiving a higher education first. If you are under the impression, as so many people seem to be, that a college student cannot possibly have a marriage, I have one question for you: are you joking?

What do you think marriage is? It is not something that takes up 100% of your time and effort! It just means that you have someone to share the load with. That is how it currently is in my home, with Lauren still in nursing school. I carry the bulk of the financial responsibilities while she focuses on the challenges and the stresses of her education, and I try to lend some emotional support.

The education excuse for postponing marriage is the same as the money excuse, with a different combination of words. It is not something that can cause an inability to function within a marriage, but it *is* an endeavor that a marital relationship can bolster. Statistics tell us that married students in college are more successful than single students. Married people have better stress and time management, make better grades on average, and tend to have a wider net to cast when seeking post-education employment. I can tell you from experience that being single and alone in college is far more stressful than having a consistent supply of love and commitment, like what my wife has at home while in nursing school.

If you meet someone, fall in love, have sexual desires towards one another, then why the heck are you waiting? "Better to marry than to burn with passion," the Apostle Paul writes. Stop putting off marriage for something as silly as money or college. You can be poor and married, and you can be a married student! It's significantly more pressure being broke *and* single anyhow.

I wish to communicate that the longer you wait and intentionally put off getting married, the harder certain things can become. It is hard to remain sexually pure, it is hard to meet quality spousal prospects, it becomes harder to learn how to share your life with someone, and it eventually becomes harder to start a family. God warns us against these things, and He does command us to be fruitful and multiply, marry if we experience sexual desire, and put His ways ahead of the things of this world. I think it is about time that we, as Christians, started prioritizing the God of Creation over the god of money and material things (the created). "Put first the kingdom of God, and all other things shall be added to you" (Matthew 6:33).

Dating "Long Enough"

The last of the most common and, frankly, sometimes annoying reasons that people delay getting married is the pseudo-obsession with dating someone for a "long enough" period of time. The premise of this mindset seems to be that one cannot commit their life to a separate person until such a time as they know that person inside and out, everything about them, and are at least 80% certain in the depths of their soul that they will not fall out of love or want a divorce somewhere down the line. "I must make sure that I am marrying the 'right person,'" they will say, "and to know a person well enough to be sure that they are perfect for me, I must date them for no less than 5-10 years!" That is an actual statement that I have heard said by many a person in one form or another, which is ridiculous. Of course, no matter how long you live, 5-10 years is a massive chunk of your life that you cannot get back and represents years wasted if you do not marry the person—not to mention the emotional and mental torture you would be putting yourself through by breaking off relationships you invest that much of yourself in.

No doubt those who lived in the America of the 1940s would have laughed at this approach to dating and marriage. When World War II was going on, and men were being shipped out to war every day, men and women were very commonly getting married on a whim! A couple might know each other for a day or an evening and get hitched the very next morning, just before the man had to ship out to Okinawa! When that man came back from the war alive, God willing, that couple was still married and had the rest of their lives to get to know one another—to fall deeper in love every day!

That used to be the most common approach to marriage—marry first, fall in love, or learn to love more accurately. It's no surprise if that sounds off to you, but that is the order in which such things have almost always worked for most of human history.

Until the last century, there was no such thing as dating. "Dating" was a concept invented in the early 20th century, and, at the time, the term insinuated something very different from our modern connotation today. When the term first came about, to go on a "date" meant to rendezvous with a prostitute. It wasn't until later that the term was expanded upon and ultimately redefined to imply courtship with the intent to marry, and, even then, dating was not what we picture it as today. Mostly, it meant a man visiting the family home of a girl he was interested in, speaking to her and her father simultaneously about his intentions, and the father deciding whether or not the man was worthy of his little girl. Even that seems a far cry from how dating is approached in the 21st century.

Dating does not have a particularly long history. For most of human history, the primary method of people being unified in marriage has been one form or another of *arranged marriage*. Such would be the practice of your family finding a suitable mate *for* you and, depending on which culture you belong to, you might have about a day or two to meet this potential spouse and decide if you want to marry them. Very seldom did a culture deny either spouse an option of saying "no" to a union, but it is not unheard of in the vast history of civilization. For most human existence, a couple getting to know one another for a long time before marriage was extremely rare—much less so for them to be "in love" before the wedding ceremony.

Places like India still consist of cultural groups that practice arranged marriages today. Dating is nearly nonexistent in these societies, and couples who marry rarely know one another for more than a weekend before the wedding, and yet, guess who has the lowest divorce rate in the world?

I am not suggesting that everybody in western culture start getting married to people they have known for a total of 24 hours. However, I would like to point out why arranged marriages have such a stellar track record relative to those that result from extended periods of courtship: they necessitate that two people *learn how to love one another*. I don't even know which word to emphasize the most in that statement. There is no over-romanticized notion of falling in love with "the one" because the one is the one whom you happen to agree to marry. These people understand quite clearly that love is a verb. They do not rely on emotions for their love to blossom because they learn to love one another *intentionally* after they get married.

You may think that the suggestion sounds strange, but that is how marriages have been done for the bulk of human history, and the method is a tried and true one. Western culture's method of dating for years and then getting married is relatively new and does not reflect nearly the same success rate. The statistics do not lie. Again, I am not suggesting we all start practicing arranged marriage again as a society. I doubt it would work very well in our culture, considering how our minds are culturally trained to operate. The reasons that such relationships are successful concern me—the perception of intentional love or the refusal to accept the termination of marriage as a legitimate option.

Western culture doesn't understand how love works anymore, though many are trying to help fix that problem. Everybody wants a guarantee that they can stay *in* love with the person they marry—they want proof before commitment that he or she is the *right* person for them. They want to *feel* love, but they don't want to learn *how* to love. So, they date for 2-10 years, wasting their lives trying fruitlessly to get to know somebody well enough and feel confident they can hold onto that emotion for at least a few decades. That is not love; that is selfishly chasing a feeling.

These people put off commitment because they want some sort of assurance that "this is it, my perfect person, and everything is going to be okay." People with that approach to commitment have the highest chance of getting divorced someday because their motives and concerns are entirely self-serving and because divorce is always thought to be an open possibility/option from the very beginning. It becomes a self-fulfilling prophecy if you fear divorce enough and allow it to always be on your mind.

Do you know how you can guarantee that she is the one? You marry her! You commit to her and refuse to let her go or give up on her! When you do that, she is the only one, and you choose to love her through everything! You *learn* to love her rather than just feeling love for her.

Don't tell me that you just don't know each other well enough to get married. You will *never* stop getting to know someone—in the same way that you will never stop getting to know yourself. You are both always growing and developing. Just resolve to do so together.

Legitimate Reasons to Wait

Once you find somebody you like, somebody to love, somebody you can manage to live with and not kill, it's time to get married! Please, for the sake of all that is good, enough of this nonsensical waiting for five years because, "I'm not sure, yet." If you cannot tell inside of one year whether or not you want to marry the person you are dating, or if they just haven't seen fit to agree to marriage by that point, it is then time to dump them and move on! Stop wasting your life on a drawn-out relationship that is going nowhere! And, of course, don't even think about moving in with the person who hasn't married you yet. That is *not* a step in the right direction—just a sly attempt to stall the clock, postpone any real commitment, and get some of the perks of marriage without having to put a ring on it. And, when it ends, years will have been wasted, and hearts will have been devastated. Don't fall into that trap.

If there is no engagement ring within a year of the first date, it is time to break things off and look elsewhere.

There *are* a handful of legitimate reasons, in my estimation, to postpone getting married for a little while, but not forever: If the man or woman who has your heart is not a believer or is of a different religious affiliation than you are, it is not opportune to get married. I question why you would be in a romantic relationship with a nonbeliever in the first place—maybe you came to Christ while the two of you were dating, and they did not. Maybe you were hoping they would follow your example or have a change of heart. In any event, I have seen stranger things happen.

If you do find yourself in that unideal situation of being in a relationship with a nonbeliever, you have no business marrying them while they are still nonbelievers. If they come around and give their heart to God, go right ahead. However, there are some pitfalls you must avoid when in this unorthodox situation: if this nonbeliever wants to date you, but it is clear that Christianity is not in the cards for them, don't invest your heart in them.

I would seldom give my blessing for a Christian to date a non-Christian, with rare exceptions. If a seed has been planted in the non-Christian's heart and acceptance is in the cards for the near future, that's a maybe. Though, preferably, they would be followers of Christ *before* you invest your heart in them romantically. And you can't wait forever for it to happen.

If there are legitimate constraints on your actual capability to marry, such as one of the two potential spouses attending a military academy (i.e., West Point), which has restrictions and rules against its cadets marrying while enrolled, or one of them is away on military deployment, it is then perfectly forgivable to defer the marriage vows until such obstacles are removed—provided, of course, that both parties can manage to remain sexually chaste for that period until their wedding night finally arrives.

The third and final example of a circumstance that may demand deferment of any wedding would be in the case of pornography addiction. I, generally, do not recommend getting too romantically involved with an individual who is also involved with porn. If it ever happens or I just failed to talk you out of it, I must tell you that as long as said individual has pornography in their life, you have absolutely no business whatsoever marrying them.

You may think that I am overreacting on the pornography issue, but you would be mistaken. A porn habit on the part of either party is *not* an issue that you want to drag into your marriage or any relationship that you care about. It will not disappear after the wedding. It will follow you into the marriage, kicking and screaming, and it will tear up your relationship as long as it goes on. Unless the partner in question is free of pornography and self-gratification (or any other addiction, for that matter) *before* the wedding—implying that they have gone for up to a year without indulging in it—no marriage for the two of you!

There are very few legitimate reasons to put off getting married, and virtually none for doing so for an extended period of time. That is, of course, assuming that marriage is in the cards for you. What I mean by that is, according to the Apostle Paul, if you have no sexual drive to speak of, or if you have such desires as should never be acted upon in any context (single or married), you should remain single. If, on the other hand, sexual desire beckons, it is best to find a spouse and marry ASAP. I see no fault in this biblical author's reasoning.

If you wish to marry at any point, it is better and indeed biblical to do so as soon as you legally and reasonably can. I, personally, wanted to get married younger than I did, but I didn't find anyone crazy enough to marry me until I reached my mid-20's. Such is life, sometimes. Not everything is within your control. That does not excuse you from trying.

Also outside of your control is the will of your family. Your parents may not favor you marrying at a young age, as is often the case nowadays, for the very reasons that I spent this chapter dispelling. With that being said, while we are to honor our parents, it is an adult's right and responsibility to make his own decisions. If you and the one you love are both adults of legal, marrying age, then the choice is ultimately up to you, not to any member of your family.

Honoring one's parents does not mean submitting to their every wish and living your adult life by their rules. Had I done that, I would be an unmitigated disaster today! You can honor and respect your parents without obeying them at every turn. Do not be afraid to listen to the advice of your family, but do not think that you are obligated to conform to every piece of advice, much less that you have to obey your parents' demands as a grown adult living on your own.

If your parents or other family members warn you that your significant other and potential spouse shows hallmark signs of being a scumbag, then yes, perhaps you ought to take that input seriously and consider its validity carefully. Trustworthy outside eyes may see something that you are overlooking. On the other hand, if your critics are just worried about you getting married because of money, education, or because they think you should wait until you are a certain age, you might just be justified in politely rejecting that criticism.

The responsibility of utilizing wisdom is central to the freedom of adulthood, and indeed freedom of any kind. You possess a free-thinking mind, so you are responsible for using it rightly. As a mature and free individual, think through the advice you receive, but do not be afraid to turn it down if your conscience pulls you in another direction.

I would prefer to listen to the advice of my Father in heaven over that of the father I have down here on the ground if one ever contradicts the other. God's word says that it is better to marry than to be ablaze with passion for one another, so I think that it is safe to say that it is wise to get hitched if you and your loved one are itching for love. It is preferable to marry the one you love rather than wait to marry for some arbitrary reason and eventually fall into sexual sin while "waiting." Furthermore, Jesus claimed that we would sometimes be forced to choose between His way and our family's traditions (see Matthew 10:34-36). Presented with such a choice, we should choose His way. Your family may not be particularly happy about it at the moment, but you are obligated to make the proper and wisest possible choice as a moral being.

In summary, marriage is a good thing! If you are in love then, for the love of all that is good and holy in this world, have a wedding! If your parents do not want you to get married, but you are a grown adult who wants to do life right, then do not be afraid to elope! Live, love, and be *married*!

For Further Study:

Dennison, Renée Peltz. "Do Half of All Marriages Really End in Divorce?" *Psychology Today*, Sussex Publishers, 24 Apr. 2017, www.psychologytoday.com/us/blog/heart-the-matter/201704/do-half-all-marriages-really-end-in-divorce.

Lewis, Rhona. "How Many Eggs Are Women Born With? And Other Questions About Egg Supply." Edited by Amanda Kallen, *Healthline*, 26 June 2020, www.healthline.com/health/womens-health/how-many-eggs-does-a-woman-have.

Pullmann, Joy. "10 Top Reasons You Should Have Kids Before 30." *The Federalist*, 10 June 2016, thefederalist.com/2016/06/08/10-top-reasons-you-should-have-kids-before-30/.

Chapter 26

Practical Advice for Getting the Date

We have spent nearly the entire book talking about the moral, philosophical, and theological dimensions of single life and dating—the should and should not, the whys and why nots. I wrote this book in response to a loss of perspective in Christian circles. The culture has so confused our young people and penetrated their minds that it is understandably confusing to answer how a Christian is expected to behave, especially in this area of singlehood and courtship. I wanted to take us back to the basics and lay out the moral quandaries that face single Christians in everyday life and help them navigate this crazy world while searching for love and human connection. I pray that I have done so effectively. It is vital, of course, to have a moral compass and ethical awareness, but I have not spent much time laying out the "how" of dating.

"How do I get the date with somebody I am interested in?" you may indeed be asking. I realize that it may seem as though the moral side of dating might feel less significant if one cannot get a date, but rest assured that the moral side has set the foundation for your success. As I have implied before, getting any man or woman you want to date is not necessarily the goal here. Anybody can get a date, but you want to end up with a marriageable person, yes? Your goal is to find the right kind of person to marry, somebody who shares your faith, core values and who is compatible enough with you to spend your life with. That compatibility factor is why it is important to have your moral foundation firmly planted. Getting any girl you want to date is meaningless if none of those girls are marriageable. Your moral stances will help you filter out the people who are not and help you attract those who are.

It does matter, though, how you get the date. You want practical advice that you can use to go from single status to "in a relationship" and later to "married." Most of us will naturally gravitate towards somebody with similar values and desires to ours at one point or another, but I do not mind helping some folks along where I can with a few pieces of advice that can be acted on today. Be aware that I am not some dating coach or relational mastermind, nor do I proclaim to have all of the answers to "how" you can get a member of the opposite sex to like you. If I am being perfectly honest, some of them simply won't, no matter how hard you try. Trying too hard to get somebody to like you might make them like you less. Desperation is not altogether attractive, after all.

As much as I wish the contrary were true, I do not hold all the answers in the palm of my hand or the depths of my mind. There are, however, some practical tips and pieces of dating advice that I can offer that I did not dedicate a standalone chapter to but that I would be remiss to neglect—some pieces of advice for getting a date that I wish I had learned earlier than I did.

If you are just getting started in your search for love, or you are still single and unmarried after trying to find love for a while and want a couple of extra tools on your utility belt, allow me to offer what little help I can in a world full of terrible advice.

Don't Be a Phoney

Cell phones and other Internet-capable communication devices have become etched in our society as favored methods of human interaction, keeping in touch with people and communicating with one another. It is no surprise they have come to play an important role in modern dating and courtship. If you want to get a date or start a relationship with somebody in the 21st century, it is more important—dare I say fundamental—than ever to know and understand how to utilize, implement, and take full advantage of the communication devices to that end.

First and foremost, a long-standing myth says a man should not call or contact a girl for three days after he gets her phone number. Somehow, I get the impression that he who started that rumor was trying to keep his buddy from getting the girl they *both* liked by giving him stupid advice. This popular 3-day rule is frustrating, annoying, and counterproductive and yields very poor results.

Those who put this 3-day waiting period myth into practice can aptly expect up to three things to happen:

After three days, the girl he is finally calling has effectively forgotten about him and their interaction three days prior.

She remembers him, but any positive emotions he may have stirred up in her on their last meeting may have fizzled out by now. She is now indifferent to him, if not disinterested.

She assumes he is not interested because he never contacted her, so she moves on with her life before the three days have expired.

In none of those scenarios do we see any indication that implementing the 3-day rule was worth the patience or had any positive outcomes. In every outcome, the man finds that he waited too long and, even if he can somehow salvage the situation and still get a date with the girl, he feels like he is starting from scratch. It would have been better for him not to have waited for three stinking days, to begin with, especially after getting the girl to like him enough to get her phone number.

It would improve the man's chances of making a good impression was he to call the girl within the following 12 hours of getting her phone number. When I first got my wife's phone number upon our first meeting, I did not call her immediately, but I *did* text her within 15 minutes after she left the club where we met. It was nothing profound, just a message proclaiming that it was a pleasure to meet her and check that she made it home safely. While I may have tried a little bit too hard to be funny in that initial text message, there was no pressure to be smooth or sly. And thankfully, my clumsy attempt at humor was appreciated by this particular girl who still giggles at my corny sense of humor to this day—even when I perform my impression of a cheeseburger. Don't think too much about that last part; it's an inside thing between my wife and me. You wouldn't understand.

Anyway, all that I did in that first message after meeting this girl, who would one day be my wife, was express an interest in her well-being, as well as the joy of having made her acquaintance. The message was mostly short, sweet, and to the point. There was no flirtatious language or extravagant monologue, just interest in her and her safety.

On the topic of text messaging, there are a few traps that most people, man or woman, have fallen into at least once and are still in danger of getting snagged on. The first trap of this nature is responding to your text message. If you text somebody and they do not respond as quickly as you might like, it is usually a bad idea to send a follow-up message. Whether you feel indignant that you are being ignored or experiencing some other variety of emotions, it is best to avoid looking insecure by blowing up the other person's phone with more words. I have done this; I have regretted it. You do not know why they have yet to reply—what is accruing on the other end of that line—but I can assure you it will not be fixed by your making a fool of yourself or making the person uncomfortable by jumping to conclusions and sending a message loaded with negative emotions. When in doubt, just put down the phone.

Sometimes, you may indeed be *ghosted*—have your messages ignored, never to be answered. Such a thing happens to virtually everybody today, not just you, I assure you of that. The reasons and possibilities for such a thing happening can be just shy of infinite and may have absolutely nothing to do with anything you did or said. If it ever happens that you are the recipient of ghosting, best to let it go. If the person is still interested in you, they will reach out. If not, do not take it too personally, as you have no idea of their reasons. Assume you will probably not marry the person and move on.

Another common and often fatal trap for dating success is having all interactions with the person of interest be through the device and waiting too long to set up an actual date involving human interaction. A phone is a great tool for staying in contact, but you cannot have a relationship on it. Save for rare circumstances, such as living a world away from each other, I would advise against going more than 5-10 messages without setting up a date unless you want the relationship to live and die in cyberspace before it even truly begins in real life.

Personally, I find phone calls or even video chats preferable methods of communication, rather than purely communicating by text, but to each their own. If you want to connect, though, hearing the other person's voice rather than seeing words typed out on a screen is much better.

Be Confident

Everybody who has ever given dating advice, for better or worse, has uttered something to the effect of: "Be more confident, confidence is key, all you have to do is be sure of yourself!" That word, *confidence*, is thrown around so much that it gets annoying when we hear it. You just want to shout, "I know that already! Confidence is a good thing, obviously! I don't know *how* to be confident! If your advice is going to be so vague and unhelpful, then please stop giving it!"

It is always easy to say, "be confident," but nobody ever takes it a step further and explains how such a task can be achieved. The truth is that most people don't know how to help with that. It is not a simple matter to teach. I will do my best to assist with the dilemma. The simplest answer to the confidence question is *repetition*. If you do something that scares you, like talking to attractive members of the opposite sex, repeatedly and with practice, your confidence in that area will naturally rise. That is a long-term solution, though, arguably, the best and most straightforward approach. But what can you do *right now* that will give you a boost in confidence?

If you want to be a confident person, you must study and practice the habits of confident people. What do the self-assured people do? Why do they have that self-assurance? What do they do to develop it and maintain it? I will reveal the simplest of these not-so-secret secrets to you: confidence is not acted out, nor is it hereditary; it is earned via actions and habit—even in the short term. If you want confidence, you need confident personal habits.

Practice good stewardship. Self-assured people take care of the gifts and resources that God has entrusted to them, no matter how insignificant some of them may seem. Keep that car clean and drive it attentively; make sure it is well maintained. If you ride a bike, treat it well by keeping the tires full of air, the paint from chipping, the metal from rusting, and the dirt from gathering. If you walk everywhere, then hey, keep those shoes clean and boots polished!

A confident person never has to worry about visitors in their home or room because it is always kept clean—worthy of being seen by visitors. It is never embarrassing for a guest to see or smell the place. There is no sense of dread when a friend or family member stops by unexpectedly. A confident individual runs a tight ship, takes pride in their home, and always keeps that toilet of theirs bleach white! There is nothing worse than walking into a dirty bathroom, especially when visiting a place. Make that porcelain and ceramic shine!

Financial responsibility is just as important as being a good steward of one's belongings and home. It is appealing when a man or woman has their affairs in order, has a touch of self-control (doesn't spend everything they have on impulse), and controls their money rather than letting their money control them. Broken, shallow, and timid people are crushed beneath credit card debt, car loans, habitually poor decision-making, and no budget or plan. Confident people live intentionally and make wise decisions rather than excuses for always breaking them. If you blame other people or outside forces for all of your problems, I can probably guess your confidence is lacking because you have relinquished control of your own life.

As I write this chapter, the world is going crazy. The panic over the COVID-19 virus has the country in a fear frenzy. The American government is enforcing widespread quarantines and stay-at-home orders, and millions of people are out of work because the cogs of the economy have stopped turning. The majority of people who are being hit financially by the crisis are being crippled by anxiety and relying on government handouts to eat and pay their bills. On the other hand, some of us have made plans not to be completely reliant on unreliable outside forces to provide for us and took it upon ourselves to be prepared—taking responsibility for our own problems before they even arise. Some of us are not neck-deep in financial debt and do not spend our money without thinking.

I, for one, am not exactly wealthy. Still, I have a sizeable cash fund set aside for unforeseen emergencies such as this one, so when my boss told me that I was on leave and wouldn't be working or earning income for an unspecified period, my face was calm—my emotions barely felt a thing. While most of my coworkers were panicking because they essentially live paycheck-to-paycheck, I was confident because I had prepared for this without knowing what I was preparing for. Living intentionally and with a plan pays off. Being fiscally responsible, rather than greedy and overly consumptive, is a great way to feel confident yourself and put your loved ones' minds at ease because you can handle a storm when it comes. If you want confidence, that means you do not have to live in fear of every light rainy drizzle, much less a full-scale tempest, read a Dave Ramsey book or some such, and get your financial act together!

Speaking of books, it is a fact that successful and confident people read at least one non-fiction book every month. According to statistics from research done by Thomas Crowley, 85% of millionaires make a habit of reading two or more books in any given month. I like to aim for no less than one book per *week*, though I read a total of just over 200 books last year, which would mean I averaged approximately 4 per week, so don't think that there's anything wrong with surpassing your goals.

Knowledge and wisdom are the most powerful forces in the mortal world, and books are still the best way to grow in each of them. We become a product of the media we consume, the music we listen to, and the books we read, so make a habit of consuming the best of each category. Give reading more books a try, if you don't make a habit already—you are reading this book right now, so you're obviously capable. Develop new habits and interests, gain new knowledge, and foster skills. Always be looking for ways to improve. Confidence is earned, so earn some.

Be a steward of your own body as well as other things. Eat foods that provide your body with more energy than they leech from you! As somebody who has an addiction-level fondness for chips and queso, I understand that maintaining healthy habits can be a challenge. Still, the rewards for habitually living well are worth it both physically and mentally. Healthy foods and regular exercise will promote a steady influx of energy, endorphin rushes, and a positive outlook, so make an effort at least. You do not necessarily have to achieve a Greek god's bodybuilder physique, but going for a run or working out for 30-60 minutes a few times a week can make a significant difference in your physical and mental health.

Do not skip social life no matter how much of an introvert you may or may not be. I almost feel like a hypocrite in this area because I am naturally inclined to spend most of my time alone or at home with my spouse, but an effort must still be made, nonetheless. Social skills are like those muscles that I just told you to work out: you must use them and exercise them, or they will atrophy. You have to use it or lose it, and confident people are figuratively ripped in this capacity!

I do not expect everybody to be the life of the party everywhere they go, mind you. I am certainly not built that way, myself. However, it can only benefit you to make an effort to build and maintain some semblance of social life. If you are somewhat socially awkward, as I am, then do not be afraid to practice, at home, how you would respond to certain social situations. Do some adlibbing or even take an improv course—that's always fun.

When having conversations with people, avoid the common conversational ticks that folks commonly display. Avoid using the word "like" in every sentence, for example. We have all met somebody who sounds like Shaggy from Scooby-Doo: "What do you, like, think about that? Like, is this, like, totally annoying or what?" Do not do this. It is lazy use of the English language, and it is hard to take somebody seriously who talks like that. If you feel I am attacking you personally on this subject, I apologize. But, for your good, like, drop the habit.

It would also be to your benefit to avoid run-off sentences. For example: "Do you want to eat at that restaurant, or…" and, "should we meet at that place, or…." The word "or" was never intended to be the focus of any sentence or its ending. It is a segue word that implies there is more to come. If you want to end your sentence or question, end it properly. Runoff sentences make one appear insecure and unsure of themselves—a message which is sent both to the recipient of the conversation and ingrained into the mind of he who sounds insecure. Your habits and behavior will become etched into your outwardly expressed personality, so make a habit of expressing complete sentences and statements outwardly. You will sound far more competent and confident that way, and you will soon feel more confident as a result.

Get social. Get out of your comfort zone. Get involved in your community: do volunteer work, be an usher at your church, find any way to help out, and contribute to other people. This will help the condition of your heart as much as that of your confidence level. The most genuinely confident people I know have some of the biggest hearts, and they serve others with no expectation of reward. So, find a way to be generous with some of your time. Who knows? You may meet a wonderful potential spouse while volunteering with the church!

Be Genuine

You have heard the age-old advice one and a half million times before: "just be yourself." As with the vague advice for being confident, I am sure that you have asked, "what the heck does that mean, and how do I do it?" Being your genuine self *can* be one of the easiest things you can do, but it's also virtually impossible *if* you don't know yourself very well.

As I have said many times before, you will never be finished getting to know anyone, least of all yourself. On the other hand, you can have a basic understanding of who you are, what you've done in your life or aspire to do, and how you will respond to the world around you.

To be genuine with people, you must first have an honest outline of who you are: your personality, your likes and dislikes, beliefs, levels of confidence in different categories, life aspirations, etc. If you are the type, you should write a summary of yourself for reflection. Mind you; this is not meant to be a summary of who you *want* to be, but rather of who you *are*. If you are an outgoing person who loves to meet new people, write that down; if you are more of an introvert, write that. If you hate broccoli, fine, put that down under your dislikes; if you love to do something widely considered weird or dorky, then join the club and write that down in your likes! This is a summary of *you*, so shed off any inclination to paint an image of yourself that you think other people might like. Those people are irrelevant in this exercise.

Once you better know and understand yourself, it is significantly easier to act and portray your genuine self. You can be honest about your likes and disdains, truthful about your intentions and desires, and forthcoming with your values and beliefs.

An honest and genuine person is not a people-pleaser by any means. People-pleasing is for the "nice guys," who always finish last, not for the "good guys." And yes, there is indeed a difference between nice guys and good guys.

A *nice guy* can be defined as a sponge—he soaks up affirmation wherever and however he can get it. He is not always honest, but he is usually radically friendly at the expense of that honesty. He goes out of his way, not to be a good and noble person, but to be liked by the people he encounters. Nobody knows the real him any more than he knows himself because his personality is composed of putty—molded by whoever he is trying to please.

The *good guy*, on the other hand, is significantly different. His concern is not to appease people or con them into liking him but be genuine with them whether they appreciate his honesty or not. Feelings are not generally a priority worth sacrificing the truth for, and the truth can be courteously broken if it is a "bad news" kind of truth. The good guy is not a jerk, he treats people well, but he does not bend to their will or go out of his way to be liked. People know who he is because he shows them and tells them, within reason, whether he thinks they'll like who he is or not. As you may have surmised, the more genuine *good guy* is generally perceived as the more attractive of the two.

A genuine person knows who they are and what they stand for. They know when to walk away from a person or situation and move on. They have standards for moral values and how they ought to be treated. Suppose an individual whom the genuine person wants to date or pursue romantically does not meet those moral standards or is a threat to negatively influencing the genuine person's moral values; in that case, that individual is not pursued any further. It is vital to live equally yoked with a significant other—to pursue a partner who shares

beliefs and values. Absent that connection, a genuine person understands they would be forced to live a lie, to compromise their values
or beliefs, and to live inconsistently. One cannot live a genuine lie—an
oxymoronic concept.

Arguably, the largest, or most obvious, the separation between
the *nice guy* and the *good guy* is the Friend-Zone fiasco: when one person has romantic feelings for another person who does not reciprocate
and who considers the other person a "friend."

Nice people are masters of the friend zone. They are the most
prone to suffer in this platonic hell. Any time they get close to a member of the opposite sex and develop romantic feelings for them, they
find themselves trapped or stopped by the phrase, "just friends." Most
people have found themselves caught in this dilemma at least once in
their life, but only the *nice guys* of the population seem to endure this
problem chronically and repetitively.

How does one escape from the friend zone? Contrary to what movies and television shows might try to tell us, escaping the "just friends"
status is not a promising prospect. It happens, on rare occasions, but
only rarely, and when the other "friend" shares similar feelings beneath
the surface. Everybody wants a magical formula for getting their friend
to fall in love with them and move beyond mere amicable friendship,
but that friend is their own person with their own free will. There is no
formula to *make* them do anything willingly and without manipulation.
It is possible to see their friend-zoned victim in a different light, but it
won't be from any formula that you concoct or deception you stage, I
promise you that.

The predominating advice for the exit of the friend zone seems to
be: "tell the person how you feel." Freeze! Stop! Do not do this! I beg
you to stop and think before you do anything so brazen. Allow me to
suggest to you why this might be terrible advice.

Hypothetically, first, you formed a friendship with this individual
under the guise of platonic feelings. You let this friendship grow and
develop over time—the friendly bond getting stronger and romance
getting farther from the other person's mind and intentions. Now you
think that it is a good idea to reveal that you were lying to them about
the entirety of that friendship, hiding your true feelings? That can only
go poorly—though not as poorly if romantic feelings developed *during*
the life of the friendship, and then only recently. In that case, if you
nip those feelings in the bud and tell the recipient of those emotions
immediately that they are developing, I suppose you may receive some

grace. Still, simply word-vomiting your romantic feelings to somebody who sees you as only a friend seems a failing strategy.

As someone who has been on both ends of the "tell them how you feel" conversation at one point—both confessor and recipient—I can assure you from personal experience that such conversations only make people uncomfortable and put sudden and immense pressure on the individual receiving the revelation. It is virtually impossible for the conversation to progress well in that highly emotional, scared, and pseudo-panicked state of mind.

Let me break down such an interaction, piece by piece, as simply as I can: Boy meets girl, boy likes girl, girl doesn't like boy but enjoys his company, boy keeps his romantic feelings toward girl a secret to keep spending time with girl, boy and girl become great friends over a long time, boy confesses love for the girl, girl is surprised beyond words, boy is heartbroken beyond belief, girl loses her friend, boy loses the love of his life. In that hypothetical scenario, which many of us in the real world have lived a live-action version of, how worth it do you think it was for the boy to keep his feelings a secret? If this strategy only led to amplified heartbreak for both the boy and the girl involved, was the struggle with hidden love even worth it?

A while back, my brother (I won't specify which of the three) asked me for advice about approaching a particular situation with a girl that he liked. He found himself interested in a seemingly great woman but, when summoned the courage to ask her out on a date, she revealed to him that she was already dating another man. She then told my brother that, while she was presently spoken for, she would not mind going out with him "just as friends." Of course, my brother has more character and moral fiber than trying to come between this girl and her current boyfriend. However, he wanted to know if he should still go out with her as a friend; in case things were to change in his favor, and she was to become single and available and end up being interested in him.

My advice to my brother was as follows:

"Of course, if she is dating someone, you do not have the best shot with this girl. A general rule to follow is that you never enter a platonic relationship *expecting* to escape the friend zone. You can make it clear to this girl that you would be interested in dating her, if she is ever single, and risk scaring her off (which would probably be the case if her relationship isn't brand new), but in that case, I would also advise that you *do not* spend time alone with her. Spending time alone with any member of the opposite sex who has a significant other is a question-able proposition, period.

"Your second option would be; you need to be content to remain in the friendship camp with this girl. If you agree to friendship, with the secret intention of moving beyond friendship some time down the road, you are not only deceiving her but also setting yourself and prob-ably her up to get hurt. You need to be genuine about your feelings and intentions from the beginning, and you will save yourself a world of heartache, no matter if things go the way you like or not."

How do the genuine *good guys* handle the "just friends" dilemma? They do not get into that friend zone, to begin with!

Being genuine means, you are not dishonest about your feelings for someone. If she says, "I just want to be friends," you do not pretend to be alright with that so that you can silently suffer. You tell her, in your words, "I don't feel that way." As a genuine person, you can be honest enough to say that just being friends with someone you have romantic feelings for might kill you inside. If the relationship ends right there, it may still be better than the intense heartache that would follow had you lied about wanting to be friends. On the off chance that that is not the end for you two, then feel free to play things by ear; good luck and God bless you both.

Conclusion

The idea for this book entered my mind when I saw how degraded our culture was becoming in the sense of all things good and moral. I always knew that we lived in a broken world, but I found it impossible to deny that God's children were wandering further and further from Him in this great nation of the United States of America. We have been gradually convincing ourselves that the institutions that He put in place no longer matter—that virtue, traditional marriage, the family, even distinctions between male and female must somehow be irradicated— that somehow the infinite and omnipotent God has an expiration date, and that we can somehow progress beyond Him.

That is effectively the idea behind the *progressive Christian movement*—that God, the very essence of what is good, is not good enough for us and that we must "invent" our own morality, separate from the true moral law. I am sure that Satan is shaking with laughter at such clear efforts being made toward self-destruction, not dissimilar to his fall by similar displays of pride and arrogance.

The atheists and materialists of our culture have similar goals in mind: the erasure of the nuclear family, the collapse of Judeo-Christian traditions, and the total eradication of the values that we hold dear, that make life beautiful. I say none of this out of anger or to spite anybody, but to point out that, to the purely materialistic mind, God doesn't seem to exist, and thus nothing can have value, not even our moral values. They do not see that this attempt to purge virtue from the culture cannot result in anything good because there is no good remaining with which to build something new.

If there is no God, then nothing has meaning. If nothing has meaning, then nothing can matter—nothing can matter to us, nor can anything have significance in general. If you deny the existence of God and ascribe to a meaningless universe, then to be consistent, you do not have the privilege of believing in the concept of anything good or moral. You cannot truly appreciate beautiful, wonderful, often majestic things because there is nothing beyond them to grant them such grandeur and dignity.

On the other hand, if God is true, then there is nothing more significant or good. Nothing then matters more than the good, and He is the sole standard for what is good.

It matters what you believe about God, and it matters just as much how what you believe is acted out. Suppose you say that you believe in Jesus, but you habitually live contrary to His teachings and His ways. In that case, you are essentially sending a message to the world that Jesus is a liar and that following Him makes no difference. If you call Jesus a liar, how can you believe in Him?

As the scripture says, "not all who say to me 'Lord, Lord' will inherit the kingdom of heaven" (Matthew 7:21), and "faith without works is dead" (James 2:17). As far as I can tell, if you do not live out faith in any way—if your faith does not affect your lifestyle or your moral decisions at all—you are effectively displaying a message to God and the world which sees you that you do not genuinely believe you are born again. In that event, your faith is dead, and thus it does not exist because you are proving that you do not trust in or follow Christ.

I do not care if you may not be a missionary or a minister. We are *all* ambassadors of Christ. That is part of the deal when one accepts Christ as their Lord and savior. One cannot simultaneously be a born-again Christian and live like a heathen. When one accepts Jesus, one commits to following Him, and eyes are watching to see what that looks like. Your lifestyle *is* your ministry, and countless souls are at stake.

If we follow the relational rules laid out for us in scripture, our lives are better for it. Our relationships, our marriages, and our entire culture eventually feel the effects of that betterment when it happens on a wide scale. As of late, however, and unfortunately, the Christian community has largely been conforming to the whims and trends of the secular world and the ideals brought to the forefront of the western mind by movements like the Sexual Revolution, among many others. When enough of us started behaving like heathens, we gave credence to all of the wrong things and told the secular world that even followers of God grant legitimacy and preference of their ways over those of God. We loudly decided that God was somehow steering us wrong and chose to go our own way, to our own detriment.

When we do that, large swaths of God's blessings are removed from our lives, and we discover too late that our lives are worse off for our rebellion. God's ways work just as much and as consistently today as they did at the beginning of mankind's existence. His rules were instituted with purpose. I understand that if we were to live His way, our personal lives, families, and communities would be better off, and the rest of the world would notice. When people see that Christians are happier, have better marriages, and live more fulfilling lives *because* they adhere to God's word and not in spite of it, they are more receptive to the possibility that maybe, just maybe, there is merit behind God's word.

How we choose to live absolutely matters in the grand scheme of things. How we choose to pursue or ignore God's ways has a definite impact and influence on those around us who may be skeptical. We do God a great disservice when we do not lead people to Him by example.

I have been there. I have indeed been worse than a nonbeliever in that I said to God, "Lord, Lord," and professed to believe in Him, but lived as though His name held no weight or meaning for me. Before I got right with God, in many ways, I would describe myself as having been a rather terrible person, leading a predominately immoral life while claiming that God was at the center of that life. I succumbed to FOMO, "the fear of missing out," on more than a few occasions, particularly when I entered the university atmosphere, and I did many things that I know I never should have done all because those things looked fun from a distance when other people did them.

By the witness of God's word, I was worse than a pagan. I was a deceiver and a hypocrite. I professed to know the truth of God and His ways, but I chose to ignore Him almost completely and live by my own asinine and ever-fluid rules.

By the grace of God, I have since changed my ways and repented for the mistakes I have made. I wish that I could claim to be some great exemplar of virtue even today after having committed my life to God fully, but I am still a fallen creature. I often still find myself speaking as Simon Peter did before Christ for the first time: "Stay back from me, Lord, for I am a sinful man. I am not worthy of your time or presence."

Like most young men, I wanted not only to have found a great spouse, but I wanted to *be* a great spouse. I want to be the kind of husband that my wife can cherish and that my future children can admire. First, though, I have to deal with my greatest obstacle between me and my goal of loving my spouse well: myself.

My love, by itself, is toxic and harmful. My love is inwardly focused and self-serving. My love comes with baggage; it has been calcified and ossified with past abuses, porn addiction, alcohol abuse, and a host of other past sins. Without God's example and guidance, my attempt at loving people will not end well. I would dare say that there is a history of my "love" harming people. I needed a frame of reference—a foundation from which to grow upon. I needed to know what true, genuine love looks like. I needed to learn real, life-giving love from the master.

I had to look no further than God, who was always right there, and who had already shown His love when He sent His son to die for me—I had to look no further than Jesus, who was willing to die the most agonizing of deaths for me. That is what true love looks like—sacrificial love which gives of itself.

Without God, I had what can be described as a heart of stone. Ezekiel 36:26 says, "I will give you a new heart and put a new spirit in you; I will remove from you your heart of stone and give you a heart of flesh." My heart of stone, the selfish heart which served only to feed its cravings, could only damage my family. My heart of flesh gives life to them and is nourished by witnessing joy in them. That is God's doing. I could not have done that all by my egocentric self. I am still far from perfect, but I know that I can love my family far better when I know where the source of that very concept of love springs from and remember to drink from that spring regularly.

I wrote this book for you in hopes that you do things the right way when seeking love and companionship in this crazy world we inhabit. I know that I am getting very preachy and deep here at the end, but I want to make sure that the central message of this book stands clear: how we choose to live our lives, how we choose to represent the love and grace of our Heavenly Father, matters more than I am even capable of putting into words. I am not a good enough writer to even try, much less succeed at expressing that with due importance and emphasis. Jim Rohn made the point, as well as anyone. He wrote: "Don't let your learning lead to knowledge; let your learning lead to action."

Nothing that you learn from me, from this book, from the Bible, or God Himself will make a difference if you keep the fruits of that learning hidden away in the vaults of your mind and never apply the information. No knowledge of scripture, or even of right and wrong more generally, will ever mean a thing to anybody if you live as though the Bible is foreign to you and as though the Lord is a stranger. In order to matter, what we learn must be lived out. So, go out into the world and live out the good things that you have learned, and hopefully will continue to learn. Do life well, do life right. Let's live in love and live for what is good. Let's get *back to the basics*.

www.ingramcontent.com/pod-product-compliance
Lightning Source LLC
Chambersburg PA
CBHW052033090426
42739CB00010B/1885